LAUNCH OUT!

A Theology of Dynamic Sanctification

LAUNCH OUT!

A Theology of Dynamic Sanctification

Gerald E. McGraw

CHRISTIAN PUBLICATIONS
CAMP HILL, PENNSYLVANIA

Christian Publications, Inc.
3825 Hartzdale Drive
Camp Hill, Pennsylvania
www.cpi-horizon.com

Launch Out
ISBN: 0-87509-879-7

00 01 02 03 04   5 4 3 2 1

*An unedited academic version particularly suited
for classroom, research or pastoral use.
Also available in a shorter version for laymen
under the title* Empowered.

*The need for this book and its theology was affirmed by
General Council, 1996, and its concept was endorsed by
the Board of Managers of
The Christian and Missionary Alliance.*

Dedication

to

MARTHA HOPE SWAUGER McGRAW

Practical as the biblical Martha,
yet a dreamer of exciting dreams
Always *sincere,* always *genial,* always *loyal*
True to her middle name—always full of *hope*
Always ready to venture
Never a disappointment
My greatest earthly joy
Charming model of what sanctification means

Contents

Preface

W hen selfishness snags a marriage, replacing a fragrant self-less love, the couple should renew and improve their relationship without delay. Even as a business or a local church can lose its spark of vitality, so a Christian life can seem stale, dull, self-filled, and lacking in victorious power. In other words, an unsanctified Christian desperately needs the empowering that Christ urged his followers to receive (Acts 1:8). Sanctification can rescue one from a purposeless, merry-go-round existence that gets the rider no nearer home.

This book examines sanctification's many facets, including Christ's purchase of sanctification, our positional sanctification received at conversion, and the possibilities of final sanctification in heaven. The book focuses, however, on the believer's *entry* into and *walk* within experiential sanctification—sanctification in practical experience. That walk is progressive sanctification.

This book refers to the entry, the vital point of full surrender in a believer's life, as *dynamic sanctification*. Our English word "dynamic" comes from the Greek word δυναμις, *dunamis*, power, which in turn derives from "to be able." Dynamic sanctification, then, involves divine empowering making us able for holiness and service.

Dictionaries note that our English adjective "dynamic" relates to physical force, energy or effective action. We should see dynamic sanctification as God's energizing, especially in the spiritual arena. God designed it to make the ineffective Christian effective. Even as the English "dynamic" normally relates to productive activity and change, so dynamic sanctification produces action in serving Christ. It changes lives from self-centeredness to the Christ-centeredness that is the essence of spiritual love.

As "dynamic" suggests forceful energy and vigorous activity, so the Holy Spirit brings to God's child God's power for life and for service. God impels believers to vigorous activity in spiritual fruit production and serving.

Why are you reading a Preface—of all things? Have you joined the wonderful ranks of the dissatisfied already? Many dissatisfied believers today and throughout the ages opted to forsake Christian mediocrity by plunging into the depths of God's ocean of holiness. Don't sit on the sand. Don't read this book as a seascape onlooker. Launch out into the deep (Luke 5:4). *You* will be glad you did—as will lost sinners who await a dynamic witness to tell—*and show*—them the meaning of the gospel.

Part 1

Down to the Foundations: The Basis of Sanctification

The foundations of the thresholds (Isa. 6:4).

As the cluster of church leaders crossed the threshold of the white frame house, they wondered whether this home, so near the stone extension church at the community's main corner, might prove a serviceable parsonage for me. The pastor of the congregation that had previously worshipped in the stone church had lived here.

Passing through the front door, the ladies surveyed the room arrangements while the men headed immediately for the basement to examine the foundation. Regardless of floor plan or color schemes, the men knew that a structurally sound house depends on a solid foundation.

Foundational elements underlie the doctrine of sanctification. Although our task in this book will involve studying all major theological and practical aspects of sanctification, we should start by looking beneath it at the foundations.

As a lad I learned much about sanctification through reading an article. Dropping to my knees, I requested that God grant me sanctification, but instantly I popped up on my feet again, feeling that I had surely asked amiss. Perhaps I felt overwhelmed by the complexity of what I had sought, if not by the very size of the five-syllable term.

If I had resisted the enemy's scare tactics, I might have escaped several years of spiritual unrest. I hope no one will close this volume in fright when I admit that it explores the doctrine of sanctification.

Focusing on everyday Christian behavior, sanctification enables a believer to demonstrate a more Christ-centered life. We can define sanctification as the Holy Spirit's gracious activity in releasing a Christian from enslavement to a warped nature and empowering him or her to conform daily conduct to God's will.

Since the Holy Spirit serves as agent, sanctification centers in divine activity rather than human. In the above definition, "gracious" provides a reminder that human beings always appropriate God's redemptive work by grace through faith.

As Chapter Two shows, sanctification does include a positional aspect, but this involves only the term's preparatory feature. The true thrust of sanctification keeps it among experiential, behavioral, moral terms rather than judicial, theoretical, positional ones. In other words, it fixes on human experience: how does a Christian behave in right and wrong situations? Thus, sanctification feels more at home in the kitchen, family room, business office, and shop than in the library or the debate hall. Sanctification refers to an internal spiritual dynamic which enables the sanctified to evidence transformed behavior.

By contrast, justification—a judicial, theoretical, positional term—connotes the fact that when one places personal trust in the Lord Jesus Christ, God declares that sinner not guilty on account of Jesus Christ's bearing his punishment. Calling up illustrations of the court room and a person's position before God as judge, justification relates to how a person is believing, not how he is behaving. Of course, the usual evangelical position correctly holds that regeneration, which involves a life-transforming experience, occurs simultaneously with justification.

If God insists that Christians become holy, the initial step of our journey should seek a grasp of the meaning of holiness. Furthermore, since a holy God requires holiness in his people, understanding God's attribute of holiness should profit us immensely. Chapter 1, "God's Awesome Holiness," scrutinizes and appreciates God's holiness. Chapter 2, "Can I Serve a Holy God?" shows the scriptural and logical necessity of holiness. A Christian must necessarily become a sharer in God's own holiness (Heb. 12:10, 14).

Like every feature in God's redemptive plan, sanctification begins at the cross. Before we later investigate the meaning and time of God's sanctifying work, we should glimpse God's provision at Calvary.

An oft-recurring inquiry concerns how sanctification relates to conversion. God does not produce a holy life apart from regeneration. Among the many terms we meet to describe an enriched Christian lifestyle, which ones best denote God's sanctifying activity? Thus, chapters on "Buying Land" and "Signing the Papers," and "Can We Talk about It?" look at these three foundations—provision for sanctification at Calvary, positional sanctification at conversion, and proper terms for adequate communication.

1

God's Awesome Holiness

*Holy, Holy, Holy
(Isa. 6:3).*

Spectacular sights rarely astound churchgoers. When they attend church today, many expect to see their friends, the minister, or at best some new truth. Contemporary humanity has lost a sense of wonder. A generation that learns world news instantly, stores volumes on tiny chips, and sends spaceships among the planets has lost interest in spiritual marvels.

Also living in a period of unbelief (Isa. 7:10-13), Isaiah likely expected no overwhelming revelation in God's house. Imagine his shock in visiting the temple to behold the Lord himself!

As the prophet peered at that high throne, God's trailing royal robes seemed to fill the entire temple more grandly than a bride's train seems to fill the center aisle. The room began trembling. Smoke appeared.

Isaiah heard six-winged seraphim who stood above the Lord calling out, "Holy, Holy, Holy, is the Lord of hosts, the whole earth is full of His glory" (Isa. 6:3). In that disheartening year when death claimed King Uzziah,[1] on whom Judah had pinned her hopes, Isaiah suddenly realized:

"God lives." Judah's true monarch was still reigning—the Holy One.

Although contemporaries spend the word "awesome" thoughtlessly, its true distinctiveness reminds us that Jehovah is absolutely unique. Not one "holy," but three, can begin to describe him to a generation with jaded spiritual sensitivities—Isaiah's or ours.

Even as Isaiah's life vibrated with new challenge when he gazed upon a holy God in the vision, so can believers now. Today's Christian can find new meaning by discovering the same Holy One. Although our confrontation will seldom involve a vision, the sense of God's holiness should, nevertheless, absorb our full attention.

One cannot properly encounter the holy God of the universe without admiring wonder. As A.W. Tozer once declared in a camp meeting sermon, "Great saints can never be made with a small conception of God." God is awesome in holiness.

No creature has holiness in and of itself. Holiness characterizes Deity. Even as our lone gleaming white natural satellite provides the sole source of earth's moonbeams, so only God makes us holy. The only holiness that can describe or transform a person, place, or object has come from God, its sole source.

No angel exhibits inherent holiness apart from the Holy One. Holiness comes through contact with God. God is the fountainhead of holiness. Only as God fills the life can a Christian manifest true holiness.

Its Permanence

In a changeless God

Calling holiness one of God's attributes, the theologian intends us to understand it as a characteristic of God. An attribute is something that is true about God.

Since God the Father is invisible, one wonders how we can know his character. We know it from what we learn of him in the inerrant Scriptures. We know much about him through observing his holy activities in his universe and in our lives, even though we observe as fallible mortals who lack his comprehensive perspective.

We also know of God's holiness through the character of Christ. "In the person and life of the incarnate Son of God we see the full development and realization of the biblical idea of holiness. . . ." Jesus lived in human flesh and blood a holy life with a single aim.[2]

When circumstances shift, our human characteristics may alter radically. Picture a meek housewife gently patting her baby's back. She may at another time, however, appear as a wild, forceful, unrelenting defender of her sobbing infant when an intruder threatens. A trusted local businessman hastily absconds with a large sum when confronted with too tempting an opportunity.

Although human beings often change considerably, God never does: "I, the Lord, do not change" (Mal. 3:6). Hence, we correctly understand all God's attributes as permanent. In philosophy of religion, one would call them necessary rather than contingent—that is, they cannot be otherwise. God will always remain a holy God. By definition, for God to remain God, all his attributes must remain.

In a perfect God

When I was a child, with a gleam in his eye my father used to inform me, "There's only one thing wrong with you." When I'd inquire, "What?" he would respond, "Your faults!"

If God had flaws, he would possess defective, deficient attributes. Since we serve a perfect God, he exhibits perfect attributes.

Under certain circumstances, things and people will improve. God will never improve because he is perfect. He never will worsen because he is holy. He never will worsen, moreover, because as changeless he will ever continue perfect.

In a limitless God

A selfless love for her husband may characterize a woman, but conceivably her love may have limits. When he persists in infidelity, she may choose to hate instead of love.

A brawny football player may appear absolutely invincible, yet he stands only one heartbeat from death. A rugged physique can conceal a fatal heart defect. One must, after all, describe that player's astounding stamina as finite.

Whereas humans exist as finite in every way, yet God is finite in no way. God possesses no limitations. Thus, only infinite attributes portray him. Consequently, God's attributes markedly differ from human characteristics. When we affirm God's holiness, we imply that he is totally, fully, perfectly holy forever.

Its Prominence

Scriptural importance

Past thinkers have disputed about which attribute shines supreme. Does love, for example, excel others? Since every divine attribute comprises a necessary, eternal, and perfect characteristic of God, however, such debates dwell on merely theoretical issues. Of more practical relevance stands the fact that holiness receives enormous emphasis in Scripture. Through the centuries theologians have described holiness as an especially noteworthy divine attribute.

A recurring Old Testament refrain proclaims God's lovingkindness as everlasting. In Isaiah's vision, however, the seraphim were not crying out, "Love, Love, Love, is the Lord of Hosts." Although Jesus fully appreciated his Father's love, he did not teach his disciples to begin their prayer with "May your name be considered love" (Matt. 6:9).

Sometimes children struggle to master math or English grammar. Omniscience means that God knows all things instantly, completely, accurately, effortlessly, without needing to learn. Although such a cry would accurately express an important truth, Isaiah did not hear the seraphim antiphonally calling "All-knowing, all-knowing, all-knowing is the Lord." More than 30 times Isaiah names God "The Holy One" or "The Holy One of Israel."

In Jesus' longest recorded prayer, he addressed God the Father not as "Loving Father," but as "Holy Father" (John 17:11). When John observed the six-winged living creatures at heaven's supreme throne, he listened to their cry, "Holy, holy, holy, is the Lord God, the Almighty" (Rev. 4:8). The Word of God depicts him as "ma-

jestic in holiness" as early as the redemption of Israel from Egypt
(Exod. 15:11).[3] Throughout the Bible writers evidence special regard for God's holiness.

Logical necessity

We show eagerness to employ reason and taste in the selection
of a new car, a new suit, or even a vacation site. Since Scripture so
significantly and so often proclaims God's holiness, do we not owe
some mental attention to the views of scholars on its logical necessity? While A. H. Strong terms holiness "the fundamental attribute in God,"[4] and J. Oliver Buswell identifies it as his "central
moral attribute,"[5] Millard J. Erickson ranks it "at least a very important attribute of God."[6] Likewise, William Bates designates it
as "most venerable,"[7] and John Miley remarks that "the Scriptures
witness to the holiness of God with the deepest intensities of expression."[8]

"Holiness belongs to the essential nature of God in a deeper and
more profound sense than merely as one attribute among others,"
declares H. Orton Wiley.[9] Following writers like Norman H.
Snaith,[10] several recent theologians unwisely consider holiness so
important that they refuse to call it an attribute. Thus, Albert
Truesdale claims: "Together holiness and love constitute the essential being of God. They are not attributes of God, but his essence. . . ." Since he regards as a significant error the notion that an
attribute of holiness exists, Truesdale rejoices that great theologians have rescued us.[11]

Such opinions harmonize too well with the thought categories
of the New Age movement, eastern mysticism, Christian Science,
and other pantheistic systems. If a person finds any love or holiness in the universe, that very love or holiness does not constitute
God or an aspect or "part" of God, does it?

When Paul writes, "Let love be without hypocrisy" (Rom.
12:9), surely he is not commanding, "Let God be without hypocrisy"! Similarly, can God grow cold although most people's love
will do so (Matt. 24:12)? Does God need perfecting as our love
does (1 John 4:17)?

Since the writer of Hebrews describes his readers as holy (Heb.
3:1), should we call them God? If a kiss can be holy (Rom. 16:16; 1

Cor. 16:20), does kissing a person impart God to him or her? Shunning imprecision as well as false ideologies, we must never forget that the exquisitely holy divine Sovereign remains a personal God. God is love (1 John 4:16), but love is not God. God is holy (Ps. 99:9), but holy is not God. Eternally existing as divine attributes, holiness and love must not attain the status of Deity itself.

Although the persuasive salesman insists, shall we spend without careful forethought? Shall we imbibe scholars' words without viewing their consequences? Snaith argues dangerously when he contends that in Amos 4:2 Jehovah's swearing by his holiness simply means swearing "by his deity, by himself as God."[12] At least if it were true that one can consistently use "holy" and "deity" as interchangeable terms, then God's command, "Be holy; for I am holy" (Lev. 11:44), could read, "Be deity; for I am deity."

Unfortunately, a variety of growing religions like Mormonism, Spiritualism, and at least the original teachings of Herbert W. Armstrong's Worldwide Church of God join the New Age movement in falling into the utmost deception. Proclaiming the human race's ultimate deification, such sects actually teach that they and/or all humanity will eventually become gods. Do such tidings sound familiar to Christians who have read in their Bibles of Lucifer's initial rebellion in heaven and of his temptation of Eve?

Instead of renouncing, without clear reason, the time-honored idea that holiness constitutes an attribute, we should logically see it as an extraordinary attribute both in Scripture and theology. H. Ray Dunning reasons that holiness is "the background for all the attributes,"[13] even as Strong counts it "the supreme good"[14] and Donald S. Metz as "the focal point of redemptive history."[15]

Presupposition for God to be God. Even unsaved neighbors resent residing near a scoundrel. When a rapist and drug dealer, known for shouting obscenities, moves into a community, who volunteers to live next door? The gods and goddesses of classical mythology engaged in a variety of moral evil even as human beings do. How the notion of an immoral god horrifies Christians! Scripture and reason teach that a God worthy of worship must be holy.

Do you desire to spend eternity with a dishonest, vulgar, unjust "god"? In Christian thinking, such a "god" should be considered a Satan. Could you ever fully trust a "god" who was supremely powerful but only "almost holy"? How could you be certain he would treat you fairly? If God is God, he must be totally holy.

Born some eight years after the Pilgrims arrived at Plymouth Rock, an English Puritan, Stephen Charnock, penned an extensive famous work on God's attributes. Expounding holiness, he maintains, "The nature of God cannot rationally be conceived without it. . . ." He judges a denial of divine holiness a greater insult to God than atheism. Whereas a creature derives his or her holiness from God, God independently, necessarily, freely chooses holiness.[16] One cannot properly conceive of God as unholy.

Partnership with other attributes. Since, in fact, God cannot be otherwise than he is, the conservative theologian lists not just holiness but all his attributes as necessary. Thus, we see the fascinating truth that all divine attributes harmoniously interact. Even as the human digestive system includes a whole cluster of properly functioning organs, each doing its part, so God—although he has no parts—possesses attributes which work together.

Without mercy, human righteousness struts with insensitive arrogance. Without righteousness, mercy doles out permissively. As justice without love can resound with harshness, human love without justice can degenerate into sentimentality. In our perfect God every attribute complements every other one.

Pillar for a moral universe. God's holiness forms the basis for a universe where morality matters. It embodies the standard by which people can assess the comparative uprightness of all actions.

Imagine living in a world where everyone considered all possible actions equally good. Robbing a kind hungry widow would be no worse than treating her to a sumptuous feast. By his own whim a medical doctor could cure or murder a patient without rationale or accountability. Although people in our present world disagree on various ethical issues, yet on such fundamental cases as the widow and the doctor, remarkable unanimity holds sway. Without a holy God, however, society would lack an adequate foundation for ethics. When everyone does what is right in his or her own eyes, as in the Israelite era of the judges, ethical chaos prevails (Judges 21:25).

Prerequisite for divine laws. God has not only supplied a standard for holiness, but he himself lives that standard. No law exists above him to which he must conform. He originates all proper law.

If the choice were yours, would you prefer that a group of legislators who all hate justice, peace, and honesty should devise every law that will govern you in the next decade? Would you trust Satan to make all the laws that govern the universe? Fortunately, a holy Creator inspired Moses to write proper laws. In the spiritual realm, we suffer if we disregard God's laws in Scripture. Moreover, he built right laws into the universe he formed. If I disregard God's law of gravity, accidentally stepping into the air from a third story ledge, disaster occurs. Misuse of my body by disregarding health rules or by taking harmful substances into it will induce bad natural consequences. If, contrary to Scripture and to principles God built into his universe, I habitually indulge in improper emotional reactions, my own emotional ill health can make life most uncomfortable, even spilling over into physical and spiritual problems.

Miley correctly regards God's own holiness as "intensely active . . . in his moral government."[17] Underlying his ability to provide right laws for humanity and other rational creatures, God's holy character also supplies enforcement for those laws.

Pattern for proper human living. How do we know the best way to live? Seeking "freedom," a society that discards moral restraint and biblical norms finds itself enchained in the slavery of suffering consequences of constant wrong choices. Playing God is no easy game for a fallen race. It requires superhuman wisdom to determine long-range results of proposed actions.

When a lady prepares to make a dress, she may find that a pattern saves time and material. God's holy character constitutes the only ideal pattern for human behavior. Thus, Strong calls God both "the source and standard of the right."[18] The seventeenth-century Puritan, Thomas Watson, explained, "As God's nature is the pattern of holiness, so his will is the rule of holiness."[19]

Despite human preferences

Divine love forms the basis underlying redemption. In proclaiming the gospel, witnesses speak most of divine love which provided redemption. Because we stumble so easily, humans enjoy God's mercy more than his sterner attributes. When someone mentions God's justice, we recall that our sins deserve divine wrath. Although Scripture so frequently alludes to God's holiness, people prefer to dwell on God's grace, because holiness suggests a standard from which we fall short. Despite human preferences for certain attributes, every divine attribute essentially and harmoniously works with every other. Strong cleverly illustrates that "holiness is the track on which the engine of love must run. The track cannot be the engine."[20] Obviously, the engine cannot be the track either.

2

Can I Serve a Holy God?

Holy, Holy, Holy, is the Lord of Hosts (Isa. 6:3).

Testifying at the sunset of his life, Joshua issued Israel a challenge: "Choose for yourselves today whom you will serve . . . but as for me and my house, we will serve the Lord" (Josh. 24:15). They insisted, "Far be it from us that we should forsake the Lord to serve other gods; . . . We also will serve the Lord, for he is our God."

Instead of the jubilant response we would anticipate, Joshua retorted, "You will not be able to serve the Lord, for He is a holy God" (Josh. 24:16-18). What a startling reply! God demands holiness of his worshipers. Having resided many years with the Israelites in the wilderness and in Canaan, Joshua perceived their idolatrous temptations and carnal inclinations. As this chapter probes into our Creator's perfection in holiness, readers today must inquire, "*Can* I serve a holy God?"

Unfortunately, most contemporary Christians cannot spare the time to read or meditate about God or even to spend extra minutes in God's house. If Isaiah had been so remiss, he would have basked in no transforming vision.

People of this age miss the bliss of basking in God's holiness because they

15

remain reluctant to depart from evil. They miss the richness of contemplation because God is not important enough to them to devote serious thought to him. Instead, they dutifully indulge in instant devotions. Too intellectually lazy about their own spiritual health, they want spiritual food predigested and packaged in convenient capsule form.

Its Definitions

When the word "holiness" seems so unmistakable in English, one wonders how anyone could find the term difficult. Usually pointing out that the derivation affords a puzzle, scholars often see two or more major meanings in holiness. Separation stands as a very central concept of holiness in both testaments.

Radiance

Writers commonly comprehend this separation as an "absolute otherness,"[21] a "uniqueness"[22] perhaps in the sense of radiance, greatness, or "majesty-holiness,"[23] infinitude—almost a sense of divinity as over against the limitations of a human creature.

When distinguished guests visit, some host families adorn the table with genuine silverware and fine china. They count such utensils special—reserved for company. Similarly, God in Old Testament times asked his people to keep certain objects reserved, sacred—for his honor alone. Beyond question, the Old Testament constantly deals with ceremonial holiness. To teach moral holiness God told Israelites to regard as holy those objects he wanted set apart and dedicated for worship.

The problem comes when writers ignore other meanings of holiness. Pointing to holiness as *only* a "religious" ritualistic idea of ceremonially separate objects, places, and people, some scholars unfortunately deem the term as including no moral connotation whatever. Later, they theorize, people began to attach a holiness idea to God as the one who supremely represented otherness.[24]

The doctrine of holiness, however, far exceeded a belief in sanctified items. Furthermore, the heart of Israel's theology did not gradually evolve by chance or human effort. Having supernaturally revealed his own moral holiness, God required moral holiness in his people.

Purity/moral excellence

Surely purity constitutes the most important element in God's holiness.[25] Purity stands in striking contrast to humanity's iniquity. God's purification of a human being's sinfulness results in the restoration of moral excellence in that person. Moral content constitutes the vital central core in holiness—never totally missing nor marginal. Ceremonial holiness always pointed beyond itself to moral realities. In Isaiah's temple vision, when the seraphim called out "Holy, Holy, Holy," neither his own creatureliness nor his dullness smote the prophet with conviction, but his impurity. Hence, holiness involved purity far more than radiance or "Godness"—the differentiation between humanness and deity.

When God told Moses at Sinai to charge the Israelites: "You shall be holy, for I the Lord your God am holy" (Lev. 19:2), he added a cluster of commands about moral issues. Hence, on the basis of the immediate context, we know that God was not here raising the point of whether the people should keep ritualistically clean (ceremonialism). Nor did the Lord order the people to become God (creatureliness vs. divinity)! Through the centuries rabbinical and Christian commentators have noticed the close connection of this context to the Ten Commandments, the essence of moral instruction.[26]

The classic Old Testament theologian, Gustav Oehler, reliably holds that divine holiness "mainly" consists of *separation from the impurity and sinfulness of the creature,* or, expressed positively, the clearness and purity of the divine nature, which excludes all communion with what is wicked."[27]

Its Distinctives

Incomparable

Several distinctives can refine our grasp of God's holiness. Nothing compares with God's holiness. In a category all its own, it stands absolutely unique. We sometimes assert of our beloved spouse or advertisers of their product, "There's no comparison in the world." As John Gill expresses it, "The holiness of creatures is but a shadow of holiness, in comparison of the holiness of God."[28] Can we seriously compare the light of a firefly with that of the sun? Holy creatures have derived all their holiness from the thrice-holy Lord of hosts.

After winning their final triumph over the beast, in Rev. 15:4 the redeemed sang to God, "Thou alone art holy." Charnock explains, "No creature can be essentially holy, because [it is] mutable. . . . God is infinitely holy, creatures finitely holy. He is holy from himself, creatures are holy by derivation from him."[29] Only God is absolutely holy.

Even when we describe anything human as "perfect," we employ the word only with qualifications. In contrast with our constant human imperfections, God has flawless character and exhibits the utmost moral excellence. No blemish whatsoever exists in the Holy One.

Even as water and oil do not mix, God uncompromisingly loathes evil. Permanently tolerating no moral evil, he detests it universally—without favoritism, intensely—without compromise, and perpetually—without end (Hab. 1:13). As Erickson remarks, God is "allergic" to it.[30]

"It is this intolerance of all evil," Richard S. Taylor articulates, "that is the ultimate ground for the necessity of atonement on the one hand, and the requirement of real holiness in created moral beings on the other."[31] Despite our inability to understand it, yet for his greater glory, he chooses to allow evil to persist in the present age—within certain limitations. Scripture, however, assures us that a future reckoning will obliterate sinning and forever banish all creatures who have persisted in evil.

Incomprehensible

Even as the mysteries of nature puzzle us, who can fathom the infinite depths of God's holiness? Overwhelmed by the greatness of the God of creation, Job admitted the justice of God's charge against him (Job 38:2), submissively, repentantly crying, "Therefore I have declared that which I did not understand, things too wonderful for me, which I did not know" (Job 42:3). His ways surpass fathoming (Romans 11:33). Mortals can only understand a realm of limitations and boundaries. Outclassing angels (Job 15:15; 4:18) and the Gentiles' gods (Exod. 15:11), God's holiness is incomprehensible.

Intrinsic

Whereas the holiness of righteous angels and redeemed human beings comes from God alone, his holiness inheres in his own person. It springs from no external source. We call it intrinsic. "Who has first given to him that it might be paid back to him again? For from him . . . are all things" (Romans 11:35-36).

Immutable

No divine attribute can change, as noted earlier. Although Satan and his allies stood in the host of holy angels, they chose to fall, relinquishing their holiness.

Even though God created Adam and Eve holy, Eve chose to heed the serpent and Adam to follow his wife's example and counsel. Since all holiness derives from contact with God, they forfeited holiness by choosing a wisdom apart from God's and deciding to displace God as the center of their lives.

God himself is immutable. God alone has always lived in total holiness. Since his attributes are intrinsic, his holiness can never change. God will continue throughout eternity to manifest a spotlessly holy character and utterly holy actions.

Irrefutable

Scripture affirms the fact of God's holiness. God's words and actions proclaim it. Since all creatures share unholiness in the present evil age, who can possibly refute the truth of divine holiness? Even heretics and wicked people have frequently confessed it. Rational arguments tend to support rather than to upset the doctrine.

Its Demand

How casually and smugly people now dare to flit into God's
throne room with a long shopping list but without self-examination!

Does a holy God not insist on holiness in his creatures? Only a holy person can fellowship with the Holy One.

When Isaiah sensed God's infinite holiness, an awareness struck him of his impure speech and that of his people. Convicted, he cried, "Woe is me, for I am ruined!" (Isa. 6:5). Can we assume that previously he had been unaware of a serious problem?

If I know that God has justified me from all sins because of Christ's sacrifice, am I not fully prepared for fellowship with God? The disturbing reply of Charnock, that insightful seventeenth-century Puritan, haunts the frivolous:

> None are partakers of the divine blessedness that are not partakers of the divine nature; there must be a renewing of his image before there be a vision of his face, Heb. 12:14. He will not have men brought only into a relative state of happiness by justification, without a real state of grace by sanctification. And so resolved he is in it, that there is no admittance into heaven of a starting, but a persevering, holiness. . . . [32]

The holiness of God requires holiness in his people. Packer insists that ". . . holiness is every Christian's calling. It is not an option, but a requirement."[33]

Proper present fellowship with God necessitates holiness. Eternal fellowship with the Holy One in a holy city where he is adored by holy angels likewise compels us to be holy people.

J. Paul Taylor contends that "there must be a holy God, with one heaven of holiness and one hell of unholiness, or an unholy God with two hells and no heaven."[34] The book in your hand delves into Scripture to learn how a Christian can find the holiness which the Holy One demands as a prerequisite to fellowship with himself.

3

Panorama of Provision: Christ Prepared for Our Need

Whom shall I send, and who will go for us (Isa. 6:8)?

My eyes have seen (Isa. 6:5).

I well remember standing in the parsonage dining room holding the phone receiver. "How do you plan to pay for this hospital expense your wife will incur?" asked an unknown female voice from the hospital in the nearby city. Although it was not the first time a question stumped me, this time I felt clueless.

My wife and I were expecting our first baby in some eight months. We had confirmed this fact quite recently at the physician's office.

Our meager better-than-nothing hospitalization policy barely paid for anticipated doctors' charges. We had no savings. Our pay was shockingly low and never sure, since we lived on a "free-will offering" system rather than a salary. In weaker moments, I have quipped that such a system works well if a congregation is both free and willing. Perhaps our handful of worshipers, however, could scarcely give better than they did.

Yet God had constantly provided for every need. Surely it would sound presumptuous or pious to tell the nameless voice on the phone that the Lord would *provide* (Gen. 22:8, 14). Yet God did exactly that.

God enabled us to pay our hospital bills for *both* of our children's births and all other bills as well. When we left town in three years to pastor another congregation, we had never gone hungry and we left no unpaid bills behind—thanks to the Lord's marvelous provision.

Understanding Provision in Scripture

"Provision" literally means to see the needs beforehand and prepare whatever is necessary to supply them. As he made provision for my wife and unborn infant, so Christ made supreme provision for the sanctification of his people. Although Chapter 4 will focus on Christ's death as the price of our sanctification, the present chapter will more broadly survey provision. Like a panoramic view from a mountain peak, it will attempt to glimpse the immense breadth of Christ's provision for sanctification.

Humiliation: Cost of sanctification that Christ paid

An anonymous collector paid $850,000 for an extremely rare one-cent British Guiana postage stamp on April 5, 1980 in New York City. When its original owner had placed that black stamp on an envelope on April 4, 1856, he surely never dreamed how radically his one-cent investment would eventually appreciate if he had retained it.

Much more precious than any monetary investment stands Jesus' investment of his own life, that provided a full salvation for all humanity from the guilt and power of sin (1 Pet. 1:18-19; Isa. 53:10-11). What did it cost Jesus to offer dynamic sanctification to his Church?

Borrowing Erich Sauer's book title, we could say that the full cost for full provision stretches *From Eternity to Eternity*! It extends from before Jesus' stepping out of heaven to his present ministry in heaven for us! In a comprehensive sense, the cost reaches back before creation when Christ submitted to the Father. There he agreed to come into the world to rescue people from sin's grip. The cost reaches to a blood-stained cross and into the tomb of death where Jesus' release makes ours possible.

On the other hand, Christ's provision includes also his resurrection, ascension, outpouring of the Holy Spirit, and present ministry. *What did it cost* Jesus to offer dynamic sanctification to his C? *Picture an invoice listing five items.*

Incarnation. The initial item encompasses the incarnation itself. Relinquishing the glories of a holy heaven where God's will consistently prevailed (Matt. 6:10), Jesus entered this planet. The fall had marred this world, which was dominated by a rebel called the god of this age (Rom. 8:20-23; 2 Cor. 4:4).

"For both He who sanctifies and those who are sanctified are all from one Father; for which reason He is not ashamed to call them brethren. . . . Since then the children share in flesh and blood, He Himself likewise also partook of the same. . ." (Heb. 2:11, 14).

If you wished to communicate fully with ladybugs, surely you would need to become one. In order to provide rescue and sanctification for humankind, Jesus joined our race. He needed a body with blood to live among humanity—with the ultimate purpose of dying representatively.

Suffering and shame. The second and third lines on the invoice specify suffering and shame. Illustrating that priests burned Old Covenant sin-offering animals outside the camp, Scripture concludes: "Therefore Jesus also, that He might sanctify the people, . . . *suffered* outside the gate. Hence, let us go out to Him outside the camp, bearing His *reproach*" (Heb. 13:11-13, emphasis mine).

Body. Human bodies vary immensely, from the Mexican-born dwarf, Lucia Zarate, who at age 17 weighed 4.7 pounds with a height of 26½ inches to Jon Brower Minnoch of Bainbridge Island, WA, a 6-foot, 1-inch former taxi driver, whom a consultant at Seattle's University Hospital scientifically estimated at over 1400 pounds in 1978.

The heaviest lady with whom I have been personally acquainted, a former parishioner, by strange coincidences bore the family name, Weight, and resided at 123 Broad Street. Stating that she could find no scale on which to ascertain her true weight, she promised to attend church if we would move one rear pew back some distance to accommodate her. Although neither the weight, height, beauty, nor color of the body scores extra points with God, he esteems a human body totally yielded to himself in life and death. Jesus alone fully pleased the Father in every detail. Jesus gave his body.

When Jesus paid to sanctify the Church, the demanding invoice included this fourth item, his very body. Under the Old Covenant, as noted above, worshipers had offered beasts' bodies to God as the law directed, but God most prized not such bodies but the body he would prepare for his Son, the unique body that would fully obey every directive of his will. The Father had prepared for Christ a body through which to carry out the divine purpose—the body offered to sanctify us: "Therefore, when He comes into the world, He says,

SACRIFICE AND OFFERING THOU HAST NOT DESIRED,
BUT A BODY THOU HAST PREPARED FOR ME;
IN WHOLE BURNT OFFERINGS AND *SACRIFICES* FOR SIN
THOU HAST TAKEN NO PLEASURE.
THEN I SAID, "BEHOLD I HAVE COME . . .
TO DO THY WILL, O GOD." . . .

By this will we have been sanctified through the offering of the body of Jesus Christ once for all" (Heb. 10:5-7, 10; cf. Rom. 7:4). Similarly, in dynamic sanctification the Lord requests our yielded bodies (Rom. 6:12-13, 19; 12:1).

Blood. In the fifth place, when Jesus shed his blood, he purchased our sanctification. Jesus suffered "that He might sanctify the people with His own blood" (Heb. 13:12). Since God informed Moses that life resides in the blood (Lev. 17:11), Jesus' blood represents the surrender of his life to grant the believer abundant life.

A familiar verse exhibits how the blood cleanses the nature of one who already practices walking in the light, i.e., an obedient believer: "But if we walk in the light as He Himself is in the light, we have fellowship with one another, and the blood of Jesus His Son cleanses us from all sin" (1 John 1:7).

Commentators often observe that the singular word "sin" here, corresponding to the word "unrighteousness" in verse 9, denotes the inner nature rather than a deed. Glenn W. Barker, e.g., remarks that "the use of the singular 'sin' reminds us that the emphasis is not on sinful acts but on the work of God in Christ that meets and deals with the sin principle itself."[35] Also elaborating on verse 7, W.M. Clow of Edinburgh writes that

> Salvation by Christ, speaking broadly, is a twofold experience. It is, to use the language of Paul, justification and sanctification; to use the words of Peter, pardon and holiness; to use the speech of John, forgiveness and cleansing. . . . The second need is that cleansing which shall renew us in the whole man after the image of God.[36]

John R.W. Stott argues that the verb "cleanse" in this verse "suggests that God does more than forgive; He erases the stain of sin. Alford . . . insists that here and in verse 9, cleansing indicates 'sanctification distinct from justification.'"[37] Whereas "forgiveness" relates to the pardon of an act, "cleansing" deals with a stain, a spot—pollution itself.

When your young son spills grape juice on the table cloth, you can choose to forgive his act, but the spot remains. Now you must remember which advertisement for a "miracle" spot remover was making the most fantastic claims.

Ed "Spike" Howard of Philadelphia achieved the apparent world record for donating 1056 pints of blood throughout his lifetime. Although many people probably benefitted with longer physical life through his generosity, yet he obviously did not give all of his blood at one time. In Jesus' case, the entire human race benefited in the availability of spiritual life.

Jesus' blood sacrifice contrasts with the Old Covenant's temporary covering provided in oft-repeated daily, situational, festive, and annual Levitical sacrifices. It constitutes "one offering" presented "once for all" (Heb. 10:14, 10). Simply pointing forward to what Jesus would actually accomplish, such rituals teach that human works and ceremonies now can add nothing to the eternally sufficient divine provision. Within dynamic sanctification, the

blood intimates cleansing from iniquity, the breaking of slavery to
a twisted nature.

Exaltation: Resurrection from the tomb and ascension to the throne

Not only does sanctification's provision involve Jesus' redemption on the cross, but also his resurrection from the tomb and ascension to the throne.

Arose to sanctify his brothers. Although Scripture calls Jesus the
Sanctifier, a Jesus who remained in the grave could offer no help.
The same passage that so emphasizes Jesus as Sanctifier shows
how he overcame death's grip on human emotions—the Sanctifier
who conquered the one who had the power of death now calls the
sanctified his brothers (Heb. 2:11-15; cf. Eph. 5:25-27). Hebrews
13:20-21 identifies the God who raised Christ from the dead as the
God who equips believers to do his will, working in them what
pleases him, perhaps implying the interrelationship between Jesus' resurrection and our sanctification.

Sometimes a widower or widow who had enjoyed a delightful
marriage finds himself or herself ready to plunge again even at an
advanced age. I do not know whether the Avramovichs fit this category or whether as childhood sweethearts they simply had trouble making decisions. In either case, at Belgrade, Yugoslavia, in
November 1963 at age 101 Dyura married Yula, who admitted to
only 95 birthdays. When a believer died to the law, he became
joined to Christ, a new husband, Paul signifies. Released from the
law's obligations, a believer should realize the benefits of this new
union "to Him who was raised from the dead, that we might bear
fruit for God" (Rom. 7:4). Paul here proclaims the production of
spiritual fruit, a part of sanctification, as one reason for Jesus' resurrection.

Ascended to fill his people with the Spirit. Included as a second stage
in Jesus Christ's exaltation, the ascension also relates to Christ's
provision of sanctification, for "we have been sanctified through
the offering of the body of Jesus Christ once for all . . . but He, having offered one sacrifice for sins for all time, sat down at the right

hand of God" (Heb. 10:10, 12). When he ascended, Jesus sat down as Lord of all, making provision for our crowning him as Sovereign in our lives.

Only when God had *glorified* Jesus would the Holy Spirit dispensationally come to fill and flow through the thirsty believer (John 7:37-39). Although theologians sometimes differ on the time of Jesus' glorification, it apparently centers in the acquisition of a glorified body at his resurrection.

Paul Enns, however, comments that "his glory was no longer veiled following the ascension (John 17:5; Acts 9:3, 5)."[38] This seems a perceptive comment since (1) Mary could suppose the risen Christ to be the gardener (John 20:15) and (2) Cleopas and his companion walking toward Emmaus could surmise him simply a stranger visiting the area (Luke 20:13-18), (3) yet, his transformed body had strange properties such as ability to pass through locked doors and to disappear suddenly, demonstrating its glorification. Charles B. Williams translates John 17:5, "So now, Father, glorify me up there in your presence just as you did before the world existed."

On the day of Pentecost Peter preached,

> This Jesus God raised up again, to which we are all witnesses. Therefore having been exalted to the right hand of God, and having received from the Father the promise of the Holy Spirit, He has poured forth this which you both see and hear (Acts 2:33).

Hence, Jesus Christ's perfect provision for sanctification included both his resurrection and ascension as well as his crucifixion. Noting Jesus' death for original sin and all sins, the historic Augsburg Confession, which dates from 1530, asserts that "the same Christ also descended into hell, truly rose from the dead on the third day, ascended into heaven, and sits on the right hand of God, that he may eternally rule and have dominion over all creatures, that through the Holy Spirit he may sanctify, purify, strengthen, and comfort all who believe in him. . . ."[39]

Appealing to the Father for his people. Even as the ascension denotes the removal of Christ's bodily presence from the earthly sphere and his arrival in the heavenly one, his session identifies his present sitting at the Father's right hand, the central place of authority in the universe. Obviously the ascension and session bear a close relationship as event and resultant process.

While they rightly disdain the Roman Catholic custom of praying to deceased interceding saints, Protestants neglect to profit from biblical passages portraying Jesus as our present intercessor. Jesus' present priesthood constitutes a constantly recurring theme throughout much of the Epistle to the Hebrews, which demonstrates him as the best possible mediator. Seated with the Father, Jesus prays for believers.

Since his detailed intercessory prayer prior to his death and glorification requested believers' sanctification (John 17:17, 19), can we imagine that he now supposes such petitions unnecessary? Do believers still need to be sanctified, so as to be unified, preserved from the evil one, and powerfully sent forth with a message for the world?

Although it might mean "for ever," several better lexical scholars favor such meanings as "completely," "to the uttermost," or "wholly" for a rare Greek word, $\pi\alpha\nu\tau\epsilon\lambda\epsilon\varsigma$, describing Christ's saving ministry: "Therefore he is able to save *completely* those who come to God through him, because he always lives to intercede for them" (Heb. 7:25, NIV, emphasis mine). Supporting this word "completely," Leon Morris notices also that in the verse "the verb 'to save' ($\sigma\omega\zeta\omega$) is used absolutely, which means that Christ will save in the most comprehensive sense; he saves from all that humanity needs saving from."[40] Often including more than a conversion point, salvation represents a rescue from the power of sin, not just its penalty. Apparently then, Christ's session affords an intercessory basis for our sanctification.

In a famous hymn, Charles Wesley traced sanctification to Christ's intercession:

> I know that my Redeemer lives
>   And ever prays for me;
> A token of His love He gives,
>   A pledge of liberty.
>
> He wills that I should holy be:
>   What can withstand His will?

The counsel of His grace in me
He surely shall fulfill.

Experiencing Provision through Identification

The New Testament's key deeper life motif revolves around the cross and the empty tomb. Dynamic sanctification stems from our identification with Christ in his death and resurrection. No one should evaluate this pattern as simply an interesting but empty figure of speech. Even as turbines provide electric power for an immense city, Jesus' redemptive activity fills this paradigm with might.

Crucifixion

Highlighting the historical or provisional aspect of sanctification in verses like Galatians 2:20, Paul testified, "I have been crucified with Christ; and it is no longer I who live, but Christ Jesus lives in me." Even as a simple marriage ceremony should change a person's status for life, the verb tense in "crucified" indicates an action in the past which brings lasting results into the present. "When Jesus died, I died," Paul was observing.

As a married status never automatically frees a bride from loneliness, so our status of union with Christ in his death does not in itself guarantee release from wrong ways of thinking and reacting. Although this past transaction at the cross provided to today's Christian no automatic release from bondage, it laid the tracks and generated the steam by which a believer can travel into the deeper life.

Resurrection

Although Paul claimed to have died, in Galatians 2:20 God had also resurrected him, for beyond the crucifixion the apostle identified "the *life* which I now live." Only because Jesus arose can the transformed life displace the life of carnal bondage.

When colonists had found a lack of representation in government intolerable, on July 4, 1776, their delegates adopted a Declaration of Independence, separating the thirteen colonies from Great Britain to form the United States of America. If you live as a native United States citizen, in a certain historical sense you gained the freedom you enjoy today on July 4, 1776.

On the day of your birth, you were born free. You could flaunt that freedom, disobeying your country's laws and consequently living all your days behind bars, stripped of certain of your "inalienable rights," but historically, potentially, and theoretically, you have freedom.

If you have experienced the new birth, then in a historical sense, when Jesus arose, you arose—though Jesus left the tomb many centuries before you learned to breathe. When you trusted Christ for salvation, you were newborn free—risen to a new life.

Many Christians never actualize this freedom, ignoring God's laws and his revealed principles. Thinking that their eternal life furnishes fire insurance against hell, they by default behave under the control of the old nature. Yet, historically, potentially, and theoretically alive with Christ, they need to accept Scripture's remedy and live up to their rights.

4

Buying Land: The Price of Our Sanctification

Your sin is atoned for (Isa. 6:7, NASB mg.; cf. NIV).

Visualize moving into your new home—with 250 rooms. Which weekday will you devote to cleaning house? If you misplaced some item, in which room will you start searching? Boasting as the world's largest private house, the 250-room Biltmore House in Asheville, NC, cost George Vanderbilt $4,100,000 to erect between 1890 and 1895 on a 119-thousand-acre estate.

Although one might discover some way to survive on less acreage than the Vanderbilts, an obvious initial step in building any home will involve the purchase of land. Next, employing a contractor, selecting a house plan, and securing a loan immerse many young families in a totally new realm of responsibilities. In this process they must sign many papers. Only then can construction begin. Preparations precede construction.

Similarly, dynamic sanctification does not begin in a human life without significant prior preparations. Corresponding to land acquisition stands God's purchase of the lost person two thousand years ago. Because redemption occurred when the Lord Jesus Christ died for the sinner, the convicted transgressor can trust the Savior to enter his or her heart, producing a new birth. This step necessitates a transaction so revolutionary that its gravity far exceeds the signing of those many papers that commit the homebuilder to contracts for house construction.

As this chapter shows, dynamic sanctification can logically happen only after the divine work involving the death of Jesus Christ. Apart from the atonement, sanctification would entail merely meager human striving for self-reformation.

Infinitely more significant for human welfare than the battles of Carchemish and Waterloo, the Calvary event marked the supreme clash between the forces of good and evil. Embracing Jesus' crucifixion, resurrection, and ascension, the Calvary event forms an inseparable cluster of episodes that scored the decisive blow against the satanic kingdom. That blow will ultimately banish forever the devil and all who insist on aligning with him.

When the Lord Jesus Christ suffered crucifixion, he thereby purchased us sinners from the just penalty of our evil deeds, releasing us from the authority of the prince of darkness. To exhibit God's continuing love for wayward Israel, Hosea, with churning emotions traveled into a seamier part of town to buy his wife back (Hos. 3:1-2). This incident vividly depicts Jesus' venturing into a sordid world to purchase the transgressor to be his own treasure, a part of his bride.

Even as Boaz redeemed Ruth from poverty and widowhood to become his bride (Ruth 4:3-12), so Jesus purchased the Church as his bride. In so doing both Boaz and Jesus took responsibility to provide for the bride's needs.

Incentives

When she tenderly cares for her newborn infant, a young mother displays at least three motives for devoting herself so diligently to her demanding task—love, voluntary choice, and a sense of duty. Did similar motives impel Jesus' stooping to buy back strayed human beings? Three important motives include undeserved love, voluntary choice, and obedience to the Father's will.

Undeserved love

In Peru in 1532-33, the Incas paid history's most extravagant ransom—a hall half-filled with silver and gold, valued by modern standards at $170 million. This enormous sum bought only one man—the Incas' chief, Atahualpa.

Yet in a far greater transaction, the Son of God paid his life's blood for the redemption of the entire human race. Since he was Deity, his sacrifice had infinite worth and could pay for both the sinfulness and each individual act of sin of every human being.

Undeserved love brought him to redeem the ungodly from sin's penalty, for John notes that he merits all the glory "who loves us and released us from our sins by His blood" (Rev. 1:5). Indeed, when as lawbreakers we remained under God's just curse, "Christ redeemed us from the curse of the Law" (Gal. 3:10, 13).

Even as a prime gospel passage attributes our justification to this redemption (Rom. 3:24), another vital benefit accrues to the believer from the very same redemptive act. Paul affirms that "Christ also loved the church and gave Himself up for her; that He might sanctify her . . ." (Eph. 5:25-26).

Lovingly dying to justify the sinner, Christ, with the same love motive, was also dying to sanctify the Church. When a person procures a field, normally he or she acquires rights to the mineral wealth in that field (Matt. 13:44) and rights to build a house on it. Similarly, by the same purchase, Jesus affords justification and sanctification.

Voluntary choice

When under the law animal victims perished, they did not choose to die. In contrast with this type, Jesus made it clear, however, that he would die voluntarily: "I lay down my life that I may take it again. No one has taken it away from Me, but I lay it down on My own initiative" (John 10:17-18).

Uttering these words, Jesus was attesting his volitional choice. This voluntary death produced the basis for our sanctification, for "Christ also *gave Himself* up for" the Church "that He might sanctify her" (Eph. 5:25-26, emphasis added).

Obedience to the Father's will

In every matter involved in acquiring redemption, Jesus submitted himself willingly to execute his Father's orders. When the promised Messiah came into the world, in keeping with Old Testament prophecy his very life was proclaiming, " 'BEHOLD, I HAVE COME (IN THE ROLL OF THE BOOK IT IS WRITTEN OF ME) TO DO THY WILL, O GOD. . . . BEHOLD, I HAVE COME TO DO THY WILL,' " and the writer to the Hebrews added, "By this will we have been sanctified. . ." (Heb. 10:7-10). The basis for a believer's ability to lead a life obedient to God includes Jesus' total compliance with his Father's will.

Intent

Perfect position

When Jesus died to produce our sanctification, the Word emphasizes three objectives that believers should enjoy—a perfect position, present purification, and a prospective presentation. Despite many Christian imperfections observable in conduct, from conversion onward the believer has a perfect position, "for by one offering he has perfected for all time those who are sanctified." Positional sanctification will receive more attention in chapter 5.

Present purification

Dynamic sanctification mainly focuses on present behavioral issues. We can be certain that Jesus died to alter the child of God's current inner nature. Paul reports this metamorphosis by informing us that Christ died for the *Church* "that he might sanctify her . . ." (Eph. 5:26).

Cleansing from sins. Divulging the Holy Spirit's dispensational coming at Pentecost, which issues in results throughout the present age, Jesus mystified his disciples by identifying the Spirit of Truth as the one "whom the world cannot receive." Jesus added that in the coming of the Spirit, he himself would disclose himself to the believer but not to the world (John 14:17, 21-23).

As John later employs the identical title, Spirit of Truth, he expands the dichotomy he had learned from Jesus' lips in the upper room discourse. Greater is the Holy Spirit who makes his permanent residence in believers than the antagonist, the spirit of error and of the antichrist, who rules over and abides in the world system. While the world heeds those speaking from the world, believers have positionally overcome those powers of darkness that speak through false prophets (1 John 4:1-6).

If you had been born blind, your physical eyes would fail to perform as God intended when he designed a human eye. Every person born into Adam's fallen race possesses spiritual eyes incapable of functioning. Devoid of life, in fact, in his human spirit until a new birth ensues (John 1:12, 13; 3:3-6; Eph. 2:1-6), an unsaved person lacks the spiritual organs to perceive the Spirit (John 14:17). No wonder Paul exclaimed: "But the unregenerate man of the highest intellectual attainments does not grant access to the things of the Spirit of God, for to him they are folly, and he is not able to come to know them because they are investigated in a spiritual realm." (1 Cor. 2:14, Wuest's *Expanded Translation*). James Moffatt picturesquely translates the latter part of this verse, "He cannot understand them. And the reason is, that they must be read with the spiritual eye."[41]

When a sinner repents and trusts the Lord Jesus Christ, God then and there both forgives each sinful act, cleansing it away, and imparts spiritual life. This marvelous impartation supplies a perception to communicate in the spiritual realm. Even as I cannot converse with a Swede in his native tongue without learning his language, so I remain helpless to perceive the language of God's kingdom apart from the faculty the Holy Spirit imparts.

God's Word serves as the agent for this "washing of regeneration" as Titus 3:5 describes it (1 Pet. 1:22-23; James 1:21; John 15:3). Although the worldling cannot receive the Holy Spirit's filling, the regenerate person can.

Cleansing of sin. Other passages, however, reveal that a deeper cleansing awaits the believer—not a cleansing of sins but of sin. The twisted nature requires purification. Paul reminds us that

Christ Jesus "gave Himself for us that He might . . . purify for Himself a people for His own possession, zealous for good deeds" (Titus 2:14).

Once again, God's Word itself furnishes the purging agent. Interceding not for the world but for believers belonging to the Father and to himself, Jesus prayed that God would sanctify them through the Word (John 17:9, 14, 17). The Father apparently fulfilled this petition at Pentecost, for Peter later recalled that God had at that point cleansed their hearts by faith—when the Holy Spirit came in power (Acts 15:9). Even as Jesus' high priestly prayer for dynamic sanctification had included "those also who believe in Me through their word," Peter rejoices sometime after Pentecost over the heart cleansing of new believers at Caesarea who had heard the Word from his mouth (John 17:17-20; Acts 15:9).

When Paul penned a letter to recent converts at Thessalonica, interceding and urging them toward dynamic sanctification, he taught them how God's Word "performs its work" in them, now that they had become believers (1 Thess. 2:13). Later, commending trusted Ephesian church elders to God, he reminded them that the Word can both edify and grant them an inheritance among the sanctified (Acts 20:32).

Instructing converts in provincial Asia, he elucidates that Christ's intention to sanctify the Church centers in cleansing. Christ gave himself that "He might sanctify her, having cleansed her by the washing of water with the word" (Eph. 5:26).

Although some commentators valiantly argue for differentiating cleansing as separate from and earlier than sanctification in this verse, the cleansing concept simply delineates what occurs in this sanctification. Thus, viewing sanctification here as "inward ethical purification," Wuest correctly observes that "`cleanse' is a modal participle, showing how or in what manner the sanctification takes place."[42] As several aforementioned passages show, the entrance of God's proclaimed Word into a believer's heart produces a powerful purifying effect. The psalmist confirms this truth:

> How can a young man keep his way pure?
> By keeping it according to Thy word. . . .

Thy word I have treasured in my heart,
That I may not sin against Thee (Ps. 119:9, 11).

Although the Holy Spirit, who fills yielded believers (Eph. 5:18), performs inward cleansing, and although water sometimes stands as a symbol of the Spirit, yet it appears a bit strained to import the idea of the Spirit into Eph. 5:26 when the text simply states that Christ cleansed the Church "by the washing of water with the word."

A host of commentators imagine that water here represents baptism, and some even think the word pertains to the recitation of the Matt. 28:19 formula by a baptizer. Still others relate it to a candidate's testimony at water baptism. Paul, however, likely simply desired his readers to see the purifying agency of proclaimed Scripture. God's Word cleanses.

Prospective presentation

When Jesus died for the Church's sanctification, he provided for her future as well as her present purification. With vivid touches, Paul writes of her prospective presentation for marriage to the King of kings.

Since my father-in-law had passed away the year prior to our wedding, my bride asked her uncle to "give her away." Leaving his ministry in the Kentucky mountains, he traveled to Syracuse to accompany the bride down the aisle to the altar, where he stood and stood and stood. Eventually he quietly sat down; the minister had forgotten to inquire, "Who giveth this woman to be married to this man?"

In New Testament times, the groom's special friend, perhaps corresponding to the best man, instead of her father, gave the bride away (2 Cor. 11:2; John 3:29). At the marriage supper of the Lamb, Jesus will both give the bride away and marry her, for Scripture affirms that he will "present to Himself the church in all her glory, having no spot or wrinkle or any such thing" (Eph. 5:27).

Some commentators see an allusion in the "washing of water" to the bridal bath traditional before a wedding in ancient Greek times. If so, the passage metaphorically uses a bath and a spotless wrinkle-free wedding dress to demonstrate that at Christ's return, he will look for both actual purity of the inner self and a spotless, attractive outward moral testimony.

Even as justification imputes Christ's holiness to our *account* as new Christians, so dynamic sanctification imparts Christ's holiness to our *lives* so we will appear holy and unblemished when we constitute a bride who will delight the Groom. In addition to a perfect position and present purification, sanctification concerns the prospective presentation of the bride to Christ.

5

Signing the Papers: Conversion— Site of Positional Sanctification

My eyes have seen the King (Isa. 6:5).

Commitment to Positional Sanctification

Peter, a prospective employee delightedly accepts the offer of a new position. The pay sounds best. It is nearly double what he has been earning. Since the store where he will work stands in the same block as Peter's home, he considers the location ideal.

After the first week, his high expectations have evaporated. No one told him that demanding customers might treat him rudely. He found it exasperating that his employer insisted that he arrive on time *every* morning. Peter soon grew weary of taking orders from his boss all the time when he knew how he could accomplish the work more easily.

To accept employment means to commit oneself to certain responsibilities and to accept someone's authority over us. The new birth— like employment—makes demands upon us as well as providing enormous benefits. Conversion places us under the authority of one called Lord—the supreme Lord of the universe. Too many convicted sinners pray to receive Christ as Savior without accepting the responsibility of beginning a holy life.

At the point of a true conversion, God begins to treat us as saints, holy ones. To receive the forgiveness of all our sins obligates us to begin a walk of initial or positional sanctification.

At conversion a sinner turns in repentance from his or her sins and trusts the Lord Jesus Christ to enter the life. Figuratively speaking, already Christ purchased the land—long ago in the Calvary event. Here and now one commits to the task of house-building by signing the papers. Conversion involves this definite commitment.

Since God has agreed to exchange any repenting sinner's wicked record with Jesus' perfect record, God instantly declares that sinner righteous. In addition, God imparts divine life to the human spirit when a new birth happens.

This new believer has been born into the historical possibility of immense freedom. The problem to unravel now deals with whether or not that new Christian has automatically found a sanctified life by accepting from Jesus the gift of eternal life.

Aspects of Positional Sanctification

Difficult inconsistency

At report card time, I once joyously asked my father if he knew my grade in deportment. Sufficiently deflating me, he inquired, "At home or at school?" The Apostle Paul disdained inconsistency. When he penned his first inspired letter to the Corinthian church, he addressed an assembly comprised of individuals manifesting substandard Christian behavior. Examining their spiritual health chart, he found a mixed record. While signs of new life heartened him, remnants of the old life abounded.

State. Addressing them as God's church at Corinth (1 Cor. 1:2) and reminding them that God had extended them his grace and fellowship (1 Cor. 1:4, 9), Paul betrayed no doubt of their salvation. Yet he admonished them about quarrels between divisive segments of the congregation (1 Cor. 1:11-13), about complacency at flagrant immorality by a member of the assembly (1 Cor. 5), and about lawsuits against believers (1 Cor. 6:1-8).

Responding to perturbing questions in their letter (1 Cor. 7-14), Paul expressed concern about their marital mores, arrogant attitudes on ethical standards, and unsuitable worship practices including abuses at the Lord's table and misuse of spiritual gifts. Some of them were even denying that the dead will experience any resurrection (1 Cor. 15:12).

In short, Paul bewailed their spiritual immaturity and the demeanor so inappropriate for a Christian. Although he confronted them as a church, obviously carnal individuals compose a carnal congregation.

Standing. Diagnosing the Corinthians' unspiritual state, Paul still does not shrink from labeling them as "those who have been sanctified in Christ Jesus." After he details some ten kinds of sinners whom God will exclude from the kingdom of God, Paul adds, "and such were some of you; but you were washed, but you were sanctified, but you were justified in the name of the Lord Jesus Christ, and in the Spirit of our God" (1 Cor. 6:9-11). Thus despite unholy past actions, God still sees the Corinthians as washed and sanctified.

Paul wrote, "But thanks to Him you are in Christ Jesus: He has become our wisdom from God, which is righteousness and sanctification and redemption" (1 Cor. 1:30, Weymouth). Although the King James Version considers wisdom in 1 Cor. 1:30 as the first of four equal elements, the biblical evidence convinces a number of contemporary translators and commentators otherwise. In the light of (1) the construction of the verse in the original language, and (2) the ongoing discussion of the world's wisdom vs. God's in the context, the most likely interpretation of the verse, like Weymouth's above, understands righteousness, sanctification, and redemption as the content of divine wisdom—the vital message God desires humanity to understand.

Pressing his original readers to avoid lawsuits "before the unrighteous," Paul shows in 1 Cor. 6:1 that "the saints" should settle such disputes. That he identifies the saints with the Corinthian believers becomes clear from the following verse: "Or do you not know that the saints will judge the world? And if the world is judged by you, are you not competent *to constitute* the smallest law courts?" Thus, Paul names them saints, a word for holy ones.

He addresses the Corinthian letter to "saints by calling" (1 Cor. 1:2). Perhaps this verse contributes a clue to assist in solving the apparent dilemma in which we find ourselves mired. Because God's call to them requires holiness, Paul can call the unsaintly Corinthians saints, for he can behold what they shall become through his grace. Having received the holy Lord Jesus Christ, they have ventured a first giant step.

Again, God calls the unholy Corinthians sanctified, because he has granted them a sanctified position from the moment of conversion. God's plan includes their allowing Christ to become their sanctification in daily practice (1 Cor. 1:30).

Although he probably did not classify it as positional sanctification, John Wesley taught that sanctification commences at conversion. About ten o'clock on Friday, August 2, 1745, in Bristol, as some associates conversed with him, one queried, "When does inward sanctification begin?" He replied,

> In the moment we are justified. The seed of every virtue is then sown in the soul. From that time the believer gradually dies to sin, and grows in grace. Yet sin remains in him; yea, the seed of all sin, till he is sanctified throughout in spirit, soul, and body.[43]

Wesleyan holiness theologians often abhor a doctrine of positional sanctification, complaining that it excuses vile wickedness under a cloak of deception. J. A. Wood insists that "Christ *imparts* and never *imputes* holiness. . . . Many who are living in sin are cherishing the delusion that they 'are complete in Christ,' through an imaginary imputed holiness. . . ."[44]

A recent writer challenges "some kind of 'positional relationship' that would allow a sinful heart condition to remain while covered by an atonement that places one in a 'position' of holiness," adding, "That sounded like a game of pretense, as if God were using the atonement merely as a blindfolding apparatus."[45]

In justification, however, God pronounces a guilty sinner righteous from a past lifetime of crimes. Why does positional sanctification appear more objectionable than positional righteousness? Without doubt, if he contents himself with pursuing sin instead of holiness, the justified, positionally holy man deserves censure. He has earned reproach if he ignores divine provisions for imparted righteousness.

Throughout the Old Testament a sort of positional sanctification appears constantly. Since no intrinsic nor imparted holiness resides in utensils, tabernacle furniture, or in the priesthood per se, God positionally separated such items for his own service.

Similarly, in the first epistle to the Corinthians, so often noticed in this chapter, an unmistakable instance of a form of positional sanctification occurs. When, in 1 Corinthians 7:14, an unbelieving husband is sanctified by living with his believing wife, the hallowing does not automatically regenerate him, nor does it drastically deal with his defiled fallen nature. He experiences no immediate moral transformation. Instead, he profits from a positional setting apart with the result that positive beneficial spiritual influences surround his life and children.

If no positional sanctification exists, how can one account for the evidence of 1 Corinthians? How else can one honestly explain passages throughout Scripture that seem to demand such a premise? On the other hand, if no sanctification but a positional one exists, how can one honestly explain passages throughout Scripture which implore Christians to experience sanctification?

Logically prior to the believer's surrender in dynamic sanctification comes the commitment of the sinner to Jesus Christ in regeneration. Apart from regeneration the sinner usually finds no concern and no ability to live a holy life.

Definite improvement

Awarding the new believer a perfect record (justification), God at that same moment has imparted a new nature (regeneration). Not from Adam but from Christ has that new nature come. Moreover, in addition to receiving the tag of saint (positional sanctification), at conversion one surely begins the climb of holy living (progressive sanctification). Paul explains that Christ

> died for all, that they who live should no longer live for themselves, but for Him who died and rose again on their behalf. . . . Therefore if any man is in Christ, *he is* a new creature; the old things passed away; behold, new things

have come. Now all *these* things are from God. . . (2 Cor. 5:15-18).

Hence, true conversion definitely transforms a human being's character and behavior.

Disappointing insufficiency

When, however, a new Christian regularly displays behavior inconsistent with a sanctified heart, he or she betrays the need for further divine work. Spiritual immaturity at this stage should surprise no one. Your baby cries, eats, and communicates like an infant, not like a businessman. Hearing of Corinthians' party spirit, Paul chided: "And I, brethren, could not speak to you as to spiritual men, but to men of flesh, as to babes in Christ. I gave you milk to drink, not solid food. . ." (1 Cor. 3:1-2).

Fitzwater reminds us that positional sanctification represents "God's side of sanctification"—not our human viewpoint.[46] In other words God, who declares us righteous because of Christ's sacrifice, also chooses to view us as completely sanctified. Even as a mother's high expectations for her son's moral uprightness can inspire him to integrity, positional sanctification can goad us. We must live a holy life because God, who sees all, expects it of us. He treats us as the holiest of people.

If, however, a believer banks on a tag of positional sanctification without allowing God to make the inner life holy, he or she seriously errs in doctrine or life quest or both. By contrast, Paul exhorts positionally sanctified new creatures at Corinth to pursue inward cleansing and to perfect holiness (2 Cor. 7:1).

Similarly, the writer to the Hebrews prodded them to pursue sanctification (Heb. 12:14). Although God initiates sanctification at conversion, one must never confuse initiation with graduation. Attending the first day of classes falls short of preparing a freshman for a career.

6

Can We Talk about It? Proper Terminology

Go and tell (Isa. 6:9).

I f you try on a new suit, its actual fit merits more attention than the size professed on the tag. In Christian experience as well, the reality outweighs the label. Yet, clear communication demands a mutual understanding of terms.

Various terms identify God's activity in making people holy in life and effective in his service. Since different individuals prefer or abhor certain terms, semantics sometimes separates sincere saints.

A native Portuguese speaker may not necessarily understand Mandarin. Thus, we readily sense that two people must be familiar with the same language for effective communication. Similarly, a grasp of sanctification terminology assists in communication. Although it will not list every possible term, this chapter will delve into some key names for dynamic sanctification.

Various Terms

Sanctification/holiness

In its moral use, the common theological term, sanctification, denotes the

divine activity in effecting holiness within a human life. Following
the language in Paul's prayer in 1 Thessalonians 5:23, writers
sometimes distinguish entire sanctification as a point of full surrender in contrast to sanctification, the more general term including initial and progressive elements.[47] Although in its simplest
definition, holiness identifies the quality of being holy, some ministers employ it interchangeably with entire sanctification.

Deeper life

For more than a century, nontechnical phrases like deeper life,
higher life, and victorious life have appeared. Showing that sanctification embraces a pattern of behavior, not simply a traumatic beginning, such phrases sometimes substitute for more controversial
theological formulas. Those who utilize them imply that converted people should discover a richer quality of Christian lifestyle
than the uncommitted mediocre variety often practiced.

Consecration

Suggesting a fully surrendered life rather than a halfhearted
one, the nomenclature, consecration, pleases many churchmen
who view it as a personally demanding but theologically inoffen-
sive word. Although critics see it as one-sided, involving only humanity's part, the expression does demand total dedication of
oneself to God.

The word does not show what, if anything, God does with or
within a completely devoted life. Logically, however, consecration
may presuppose some point of surrender followed by a continuous
attitude of surrender.

Fullness of the Holy Spirit

Since the Holy Spirit applies the results of redemption within
human lives in the present age, his work strongly relates to dynamic sanctification. Writers frequently note that fullness connotes control by the Holy Spirit after a believer has voluntarily
surrendered the reins to him.

Rarely a contemporary Christian will state that since the Holy
Spirit lives in all born-again believers, every saved individual re-

ceived the fullness of the Spirit at conversion. A careful study of
biblical passages on the Spirit's fullness fails to support such a notion. Used occasionally by Old Testament writers and by Paul in
Ephesians 5:18, fullness terminology principally occurs in Luke's
writings. Although sincere exegetes differ on the interpretation of
a few passages, Scripture consistently shows that the Spirit's fullness comes only to members of the believing community. Many
Christians at or near the moment of conversion sense no need for
the Holy Spirit's special superintendence. Unfortunately, some
Christians never arrive at a point of full surrender. Moreover, not
every Christian remains under the Holy Spirit's control.

Second blessing

Those who cherish the term, second blessing, hold that even as
conversion marks a blessed monument of spiritual beginning, so
entire sanctification later does. It constitutes a second definite
work of grace. Springing from divine grace, without question dynamic sanctification enriches a believer's entire life—to the extent
that a child of God sees its implications and applies its benefits.

Why should anyone object to such a term? Complaints abound.
While some charge that sanctification stands in such a close relationship with conversion that no one should call it second, others
inquire why anyone should limit God's benefits to two when life's
innumerable problems supply opportunities for myriads of future
blessings. Of course, second-blessing advocates do not restrict
God's blessings, aiming rather to convey that theologically two
major provisions care for two major human needs.

Perhaps one should contest the term "blessing" more readily
than "second." Even though the Bible frequently alludes to blessings, yet in popular thinking the word either broadly suggests anything beneficial or narrowly focuses on happiness. In either case, it
poorly describes an entrance into the Christ-life; sanctification
neither denotes unspecified goodness nor floods of sparkling emotions.

A.W. Tozer teaches the folly of seeking exhilarating emotions as
an end in itself: "There is an ignoble pursuit of irresponsible happiness among us. . . . I do not believe that it is the will of God that
we should seek to be happy, but rather that we should seek to be

holy and useful."[48] Earlier, Andrew Bonar had warned that "the fulness of the Spirit does not manifest itself in mere feeling. It always shows itself in some grace."[49]

Of course, great joy can accompany the realization that sanctification has occurred. Moreover, the Holy Spirit yearns to provide the continuing fruit of joy.

If misdirected hatred for her father prevents a woman from spending her inheritance, she may die in misery and squalor. Similarly, after one has trusted God for dynamic sanctification, he or she may allow Satan to steal rightful joy through focusing on feelings rather than fact. Majoring on deception, the devil accuses and confuses Christians. The fact that one possesses a sanctified heart, therefore, can be vastly different from enjoying clear assurance of a sanctified heart. Since a host of Christians gear their religious profession to the ebb and flow of emotions, we perform a disservice in suggesting that one must feel a blessing or else he or she positively lacks a holy heart.

Christian perfection

In a baseball game against Milwaukee on May 26, 1959, Harvey Haddix, Jr., of the Pittsburgh Pirates pitched a perfect game for twelve innings. Allowing a hit in the thirteenth inning, however, he and his team lost the tight game. How elusive do humans find perfection! "No one can be perfect," states a common maxim by which we justify our faults. A noted minister wrote, "To seek perfection is the way to great achievement, but to believe that one has attained it is death to creative work."[50]

Wesleyan Arminian writers have frequently referred to what I have called dynamic sanctification as "Christian perfection" or "perfect love." Teaching that God regards heart attitude as more pivotal than actions, they insist that dynamic sanctification frees and fills a believer to love God supremely and one's neighbor as himself or herself. Christian perfection involves a perfect *attitude.*

A half dozen years before John Wesley's conversion on Aldersgate Street, an Anglican minister, William Law, wrote in his book, *Christian Perfection:*

> As this is the highest standard for the Christian to emulate, it is also the lowest degree of holiness which the gospel al-

lows. . . . If this be perfection, who can exceed it? Yet what
state or circumstance of life can allow anyone to fall short of
it?

   To illustrate this, Christians are to love God with all
their heart and all their strength. Can any Christian exceed
this? Yet who may be allowed to be defective in it?[51]

Highly praised by Samuel Johnson, Aldous Huxley, and John
Wesley, Law's work influenced Wesley although Law and Wesley
differed at points.

Most opponents attacking the Christian-perfection doctrine
produce Scripture or logic to demonstrate that no one can live
without sinning. Hence, instead of carefully reading or wanting to
understand Wesleyans on Christian perfection, its enemies have
constantly assaulted a "straw man." Rejecting the despised label,
sinless perfection himself, John Wesley also contrasts his doctrine
with absolute perfection, an attribute limited to God.[52] Thus,
Donald S. Metz cleverly defends the doctrine as "imperfect perfection."[53] In fact, the Wesleyans' doctrine of what constitutes a
sinful act, although distasteful to many evangelicals, relates more
to the new birth than to Christian perfection.[54]

In a notably helpful 1990 volume on dynamic sanctification,
Murphree explains its focal point in *"a special love relationship with
God"* which constitutes "the highest scriptural ideal."[55] Discussing
perfect love which casts out fear, the Apostle John differentiates
some who *have* been made perfect in love from people who have
not (1 John 4:17-18). In both of these verses as well as in 1 John 2:5
and 4:12, John uses the Greek perfect tense for the verb "perfect,"
indicating a present state which results from specific activity in the
past.

In Greek, a verse like 1 John 2:5 is affirming that love became
perfected at a point in the past with resulting perfection continuing to the present. In his Expanded Translation, Kenneth S.
Wuest, cumbersomely but keenly brings out shades of meaning
lost in most versions: "But whoever habitually with a solicitous
care is keeping His word, truly, in this one the love of God has
been brought to its completion with the present result that it is in
that state of completion" (1 John 2:5).

Although some Scriptures mentioning perfection in human beings concern other issues, yet a number of verses certainly seem to
relate to entire sanctification. Hebrews 10:14 connects perfection
with the sanctified.

Likewise in the context of Jesus' petition to sanctify the followers whom the Father had given him *out of* the world (John 17:17,
19), Jesus prayed that as a result of his indwelling them "they may
be perfected in unity" (John 17:23). Again John employs a perfect
tense in the Greek participle expressing the perfected state that
should result from the divine sanctifying and indwelling.

The major New Testament word for "perfect" derives from the
word "end," indicating whatever has reached its end or is "finished, complete, perfect." When it describes persons, it depicts (1)
physical development or spiritual maturity or else (2) someone
complete in goodness, whether or not mature.[56] In his helpful
chapter on "The Concept of Perfection in the New Testament,"
George Allen Turner finds 20 total uses of various words with the
$\tau\varepsilon\lambda$ = perfection root relating to moral qualities in human beings.[57]

After he had commanded unselfish love toward one's neighbor,
Jesus charged his audience on the mount, "Therefore you are to be
perfect, as your heavenly Father is perfect" (Matt. 5:48). Soon after Paul had disavowed reaching perfection himself, he dared to
face the Philippians with the exhortation: "Let us therefore, as
many as are perfect, have this attitude" (Phil. 3:12, 15). Unless he
was employing irony, Paul includes himself and his readers as in
some sense perfect although he had not reached life's final goal.

Despite its strong biblical roots, the term "Christian perfection"
has some obvious drawbacks that deter common use today. One
problem springs from the fact that it remains open to such easy
misunderstandings. Another difficulty relates to our contemporary society's disgust at a demand for any kind of perfection and
for anyone who would dare to profess any kind.

A more forceful argument against the term is the logical assumption that if anyone could reach perfection, that Christian
would need no further growth. By contrast, Scripture shows ongoing Christian growth to be essential.

Baptism with the Holy Spirit

Contrasting the water baptism he was administering with a spiritual baptism Jesus Christ would perform (John 1:26-34), John the Baptist introduced this term. He announced: "I baptized you with water; but He will baptize you with the Holy Spirit" (Mark 1:8). Reporting the same declaration, both Matthew and Luke add that the element into which Jesus would baptize hearers would also include fire (Matt. 3:11; Luke 3:16).

Both Jesus himself and Peter repeated the prediction that the former would baptize with the Holy Spirit, relating the start of the fulfillment to Pentecost (Acts 1:4-5; 11:15-17). Using similar phraseology in 1 Corinthians 12:13, Paul elsewhere uses "baptism" metaphorically in various contexts.

Although John Wesley did not select the "baptism with the Holy Spirit" to describe sanctification, his esteemed theologian John Fletcher did.[58] Various individuals and groups have rallied around the term, especially during the past two centuries.[59] Charles G. Finney and later the American Wesleyan Holiness movement have prized it.[60]

Like Oberlin theology and Wesleyanism, varied renewal movements have interpreted this baptism experientially to identify a crucial point of divine visitation within a Christian's life. Advocates include various deeper-life champions, some pre-Keswick and Keswick speakers,[61] Pentecostalism,[62] and the charismatic movement.[63] Such pioneering evangelists as Asa Mahan,[64] W. E. Boardman,[65] R. A. Torrey,[66] and A. B. Simpson[67] concur. Some contemporary respected non-Wesleyan, non-Pentecostal professors and ministers like Harold Lindsell,[68] Martyn Lloyd-Jones[69], John R. Rice,[70] Tony Campolo,[71] Keith M. Bailey[72] and Armin R. Gesswein[73] agree.

Many revivalists who employ the term would interchange it with sanctification. Exceptions include charismatics and Pentecostals. In the latter camp, the Assemblies of God, like Charismatics, see the baptism as gifts-oriented rather than holiness-oriented. Agreeing, the various Pentecostal holiness denominations have viewed the baptism as a third encounter with God, following both conversion and sanctification.

Slight variations occur, with some writers choosing "baptism of" and both Pentecostals and Charismatics preferring "baptism in." Through the persuasive influence of dispensationalists, the term's popularity has plummeted considerably among mainstream evangelicals for about a century.

Others who have fought it have done so to oppose what they perceive to be abuses by Pentecostals and Charismatics. Thus charisphobia controls exegesis and terminology. Some critics assume that use of the term capitulates to the entire Pentecostal/Charismatic agenda.

In other words, the complaints include the idea that embracing "baptism" terminology would open the door to the evidence doctrine or to the ignoring of biblical guidelines on tongues use. Still other opponents see the baptism of the Holy Spirit as only a positional rather than an experiential term, citing 1 Corinthians 12:13 as support.

If, however, this Pauline verse refers to a different spiritual baptism from the Gospels/Acts references, the latter objection falters. If we judge by most translators, Paul speaks of a baptism *the Spirit* performs, wherein the implied pool represents *the Church*. This differs markedly from John the Baptist, who instead emphasizes that *Jesus* will baptize, with his baptismal pool symbolizing *the Holy Spirit and fire*. Thus the two concepts are contrasting rather than identical. Jesus' and Peter's mentions of the baptism in Acts appear to echo John the Baptist's concept—as fulfillment follows prediction.

Certainly the figure John chose roots in experience rather than the Holy Spirit's relationship with the Church as a whole. In other words, water baptism happens individually to individuals—not corporately to all believers of all ages.

Luke equates the "promise of the Father" (KJV and NASB mg., following the Greek) with the baptism with the Holy Spirit, the power source for Christian workers (Acts 1:4-5; Luke 24:49). Inch cautions that although "Paul urges his readers to be *filled* with the Spirit (Eph. 5:18), there is no comparable injunction to be *baptized* by the Spirit. . . ."[74]

The Savior himself does identify this Holy Spirit baptism with the promise of the Father. Moreover, Christ does command his followers to receive it (Acts 1:4-5; Luke 24:49). The vast majority of Bible readers see the Great Commission verses as applying to the entire Church living throughout the entire age. (The Lukan form of it is in Acts 1:8b; Luke 24:47-48.)

Does it not seem inconsistent that many deny the continuing relevance of the empowering to fulfill that commission (Acts 1:4-5, 8a)? Mentioning it in the immediate context, Jesus and Luke considered this empowering baptism with the Holy Spirit absolutely essential.

Evaluation of Terms

Fullness of the Holy Spirit

Unless they confuse fullness and the Spirit's residence in every Christian, most see that God intends the fullness for believers. A careful reading of Scripture shows that God bestows the fullness of the Spirit on his people.

One of today's most acceptable terms, the fullness of, or infilling with, the Holy Spirit emphasizes the Spirit's empowering ministry. In virtually every branch of Christian theology, people realize that believers need to live in submission to the Spirit. He performs so vital a ministry in this age.

Certainly, we must not unduly elevate the Holy Spirit above the other two Members of the Trinity. When the Holy Spirit fills a Christian, however, he will certainly seek to honor, glorify, and bear witness to the Lord Jesus Christ through that believer (John 16:14; 15:26).

Deeper life

The deeper life and certain variations of this phrase stand out also as comparatively innocuous. Accenting an ongoing life rather than a point in time, such titles find less favor with Wesleyans than with other groups, however.

Consecration

Even though everyone values "consecration," yet traditional reformed and baptistic groups utilize it oftener than other denominations for deeper-life experience. Sometimes "consecration"

connotes an ongoing life of commitment. Since sanctification entails such elements, for example, as separation and filling in addition to consecration, we should prefer the broader word if we were
limited to one term.

Second blessing

One of the less valuable terms, "the second blessing," accentu-
ates an emotional connotation which many believe should not occupy center stage. Many dispensational writers see in Scripture
and experience an entrance point into the deeper life. John F.
Walvoord, for example, holds that "Wesley is right that, subsequent to the initial act of being born again and receiving salvation
in Christ, there is normally a later act of the will in which individuals surrender their life to the will of God."[75]

Dispensationalists, however, along with most non-Wesleyan
evangelicals, normally find distasteful an expression like "the second blessing." The term's opponents argue that the word "second"
(1) seems to place that point on an equal footing with conversion,
(2) too distinctly separates dynamic sanctification from regeneration, or (3) places too much emphasis on a single point to the neglect of growth and additional experiences.

Christian perfection

Outside the Wesleyan Holiness movement, a major reason for
widespread rejection of the term "Christian perfection" for sanctification lies in its susceptibility to misunderstanding. One can easily jump to the conclusion that perfection must arrive by
self-effort or that any sort of perfection must, by definition, be absolute. Shunning dependence on a static perfect state, A. B.
Simpson championed a vibrant relationship with an indwelling
perfect Christ as the core of a believer's sanctification.

Baptism with the Holy Spirit

Revivalists, as well as Wesleyans, have heralded the baptism
with the Holy Spirit as a vital post-conversion experience coincid-
ing with the initial filling with the Spirit and with entry into sanctification. Agreeing that the baptism in the Holy Spirit occurs at a

point after conversion, Pentecostals and Charismatics differ with Wesleyans and earlier revivalists in that the baptism does not sanctify but climaxes in speaking in tongues as a necessary evidence.

To most dispensationalists and reformed traditionalists, on the other hand, the baptism of the Spirit happened as an unrepeatable event at Pentecost. For dispensationalists, it centers in the creation of the Church but has nothing to do with individual experience.

Although traditional reformed theologians had generally ignored the term, yet in response to the Charismatic renewal they have addressed it. They have written ably in recent decades, alleging that since Pentecost "Spirit-baptism is . . . identical with regeneration."[76] Such writers apparently mean that throughout the present age new converts automatically become included in the body of Christ.

Earlier in this chapter, I have defended the term as a biblically appropriate one to refer to dynamic sanctification. Since my coverage here has affirmed that much diversity persists on Holy Spirit baptism, anyone who employs the term should exercise care to define it and prepare to defend his or her position. Otherwise confusion will prevail.

As this chapter has shown, several terms sufficiently convey the concept of dynamic sanctification. Since Scripture itself uses such a variety of terms, it seems unreasonable to insist that everyone limit himself/herself to one term. On the other hand, the need for clear communication and instruction favors focusing on a few better terms if not one optimal term.

Sanctification/holiness

Since "holiness" refers to the quality of *being* holy, it does not fit as precisely into our present search as a word meaning to *make* holy. Indicating the act and process of making holy, the word "sanctification" includes elements of separation, dedication, and filling. Its unfamiliarity in common speech constitutes one of its few disadvantages.

Forms of the word "sanctification" appear to describe divine provision, positional holiness, a point of entry, a life of growth, and possibly a final consummation. This *breadth* of biblical usage signals both a drawback and an advantage. It signals an advantage because of its scripturalness but a hindrance unless a communicator keeps explaining how he employs the term.

Theologians, regardless of their doctrinal heritage, tend to use forms of "sanctify." After eliminating the words "sanctify" and "sanctification" from their 1946 New Testament, translators of the Revised Standard Version restored them in their 1952 whole Bible—after strong complaints.[77] Surely this scriptural word comprises one of the best terms to describe God's deeper work in energizing Christians to live victoriously.

In referring to the Christian's entry point into sanctification, Wesleyan Arminians have often used "entire sanctification." This expression seems to have biblical support in 1 Thessalonians 5:23. The term annoys many contemporary evangelicals, however, since they suppose it implies that nobody can become more holy beyond this marvelous point. For reasons cited in the Preface, I have chosen the phrase "dynamic sanctification" to denote the believer's entrance point into sanctification.

Part 2

Drowsy or Desperate?
The Need for Sanctification

Woe is me (Isa. 6:5)!

I magine being isolated on gigantic flat rocks in midstream with nothing to drink. Carolyn, Martha, Roberta, Hattie, and Ruth, five Pennsylvania girls, had gone for an all-day outing. A family member had taken them to their planned destination in a car and would pick them up at sundown.

The hot dog roast and the picnic were each tasty, but the ever-gurgling, polluted creek rushing by reminded the crew of their thirst. No one had remembered to bring sodas or ice water. As the sweltering hot sun beat down upon them, they kept quoting to each other those familiar lines:

Water, water everywhere,
But not a drop to drink.

At dawn daily during the Feast of Tabernacles, priests formed a procession to the pool of Siloam from the temple. One priest filled a golden pitcher that he carried to the temple to pour out at the appointed moment. The ceremony reminded Jews of God's provision of water from the smitten rock at Horeb for the thirsty wilderness generation.[78]

As the culmination of this water ceremony, Jesus stood on that final climactic day of the feast,[79] crying out: "If any man is thirsty, let him come to me and drink." John adds the inspired interpretation: "But this He spoke of the Spirit, whom those who believed in Him were to receive; for the Spirit was not yet given, because Jesus was not yet glorified" (John 7:37, 39).

At Pentecost, the glorified Jesus poured out the Holy Spirit, so that believers there assembled could receive his baptism and fullness (Acts 2:33). Freligh accurately notes that

> in the Scriptures the Holy Spirit uses these three terms, baptize, fill, receive, interchangeably (e.g., John 7:39 and Acts 2:38; cf. Acts 1:5, Acts 2:4). It is well, therefore to keep this in mind and not quibble over terms that have the divine sanction of Scriptural usage.[80]

The prerequisite to drinking is thirst (Isa. 44:3). Jesus gives the fullness of his Spirit to the desperate, not to the drowsy, the lackadaisical, the time-server, the self-sufficient.

Alas, many believers sense no need because they imagine they can fulfill their Christian duties sufficiently by their own efforts. Only the desperate need apply.

Only the open, empty-handed can receive—neither those whose hands clutch self-holiness nor the hands filled with self-efforts. Paradoxically, only the unable are able to receive. Barth affirms that "sanctification is entirely God's grace. It is not man's affair, but God's—the affair of the God who works for man in Jesus Christ."[81]

Only those who cannot overcome the bondage of carnality, only those who know their inadequacy to serve Christ effectively can meet the requirement. Only the poor in spirit inherit the kingdom. Only those who hunger and thirst for righteousness shall be filled (Matt. 5:3, 6). Only those who moan, "Woe is me!" ever hear the "Lo" assurance of cleansing and the "Go" command for anointed service (Isa. 6:5, 7 KJV, 9).

No one should seek the infilling as an add-on spiritual vitamin for greater pickup, zest, or endurance. Our sanctification cost Christ his very life, and we cannot apply for it without surrendering to him literally everything. With such high stakes, genuine desire is essential—the intensity that impelled young George Fox. Kelly explains that "the insatiable God-hunger in him drove him from such mediocrity into a passionate quest for the real whole-wheat Bread of Life."[82] "The infilling is for those who are conscious of a dryness of soul that is intolerable," notes Campolo.[83]

Ought we to see our need of sanctification? Yes, a holy God calls us to holiness as proper preparation for living a holy life here and for living eternally in a holy heaven. Bloesch prods us to see that "the call to holiness resounds throughout the Scriptures, and in every church and theology rooted in the Scriptures."[84]

7

Who Broke Johnny? Inner Distortion Discovered

I am ruined!
(Isa. 6:5).

If the microwave fails to function properly or the computer keeps inserting nonsense syllables into your document, you need a technician to repair the damage. What happens if Johnny fails to do the right thing? Can I find a repairman for Johnny in the yellow pages? Something is wrong within the microwave and the computer. Is something wrong within Johnny?

Tragedy of Inner Distortion

Jesus explained to his disciples that

> that which proceeds out of the man, that is what defiles the man. For from within, out of the heart of men, proceed the evil thoughts and fornications, thefts, murders, adulteries, deeds of coveting and wickedness, as well as deceit, sensuality, envy, slander, pride and foolishness. All these evil things proceed from within and defile the man (Mark 7:20-23).

Jesus traced evil actions to an evil heart.

Why do his parents never need to teach Johnny to lie, disobey, or steal? Why must they teach him to tell the truth, obey, and respect property rights? Theologians from varied backgrounds agree that wrong actions spring from a basic wrongness of a person's very nature. They identify it as a depravity, inward corruption, an inborn or inbred bias, a nature, or sin as distinguished from sins.

Buswell, a Presbyterian, notes: "One of the most difficult lessons for us to learn is that sin is not only what we do, but also what we are. Sin, in the form of corruption, is in our very nature."[85] John Gill, the great eighteenth century Baptist, calls it "the corruption of human nature" derived from Adam.[86]

Richard S. Taylor, a contemporary theologian from the Church of the Nazarene, observes that "the defect is both negative (a weakness), and positive (a dynamic proneness to evil)." What disgusts you more than food that has spoiled? Negatively the food fails to satisfy your hunger and lacks the ability to cure itself. Positively, it creates a positive nuisance, emitting a disgusting odor and capable of poisoning anyone who would dare to eat it. Similarly, the carnal nature involves an inability both to lead a holy life and to cure itself. Positively, springing from rebellion against God, it produces wicked deeds and leads toward divine judgment.

Looking into Romans 7, Taylor comments that "there is now an enemy, an inner abnormality, which can appropriately be called 'a law, that, when I would do good, evil is present with me' (v. 21, KJV)—a law not in the sense of a commandment but a principle of action." Is it natural or unnatural? He explains that "it is not endemic to human nature as created, but now normal to human nature as fallen."[87] For example, although he possessed a complete human nature, Jesus Christ had no carnal self, even as unfallen Adam and Eve had none. All other humans inherit a perverse nature, however, from fallen Adam.

Metz correctly perceives this blighted nature as "a quality, predisposition, bias, twist, or state of the human personality from which arise all actual transgressions and all unchristian attitudes such as pride, selfishness, self-will, and enmity against God."[88] Although the new birth imparts a new nature, proof seems abundant that this internal wrongness continues to trouble Christians.

Charles Hodge, the famous Princeton theologian, confirms this fact:

> But according to the Scriptures, the universal experience of Christians, and the undeniable evidence of history, regeneration does not remove all sin. The Bible is filled with the record of the inward conflicts of the most eminent of the servants of God. . . .[89]

At justification, God wipes the sinner's record clean from *all sinful acts*. On the other hand, *sinfulness*—the inner nature—remains.

Terms for Inner Distortion

Carnality

Scripture uses a variety of terms to portray this inner distortion. The Apostle Paul refers to immature divisive believers as not spiritual but "carnal" (KJV), "men of flesh," "fleshly" (1 Cor. 3:1-3). Even as all New Testament epistles consistently address believers, so the Corinthian church comprised "babes in Christ" rather than unregenerate individuals. What did Paul mean when describing true Christians as dominated by the *flesh*? What is *carnality*?

In English, the word "host" may mean—among other things—a large company of soldiers. Also, a host invites someone to a fellowship evening in his or her home. Roman Catholics call the communion bread a host. The context helps a reader see how an author intends it. Occurring some 150 times in the New Testament, the Greek word σαρξ, *sarx*, usually translated "flesh," likewise has several meanings. Similarly, context throws light on how a writer intends it.

Some 27 times in the epistles, the word "flesh" concerns not the physical body but our inner distortion (e.g., Col. 5:24; Rom. 8:8-9, 12-13).[90] Thayer explains this word's ethical sense as denoting *"mere human nature, the earthly nature of man apart from divine influence, and therefore prone to sin and opposed to God;* accordingly it includes whatever in the soul is weak, low, debased, tending to ungodliness and vice."[91]

A fleshly person allows the attitudes, mind-set, and cravings of the distorted self to maintain control. As Swindoll charges, "I cannot be filled with the Spirit while at the same time conducting my life in the energy of the flesh. I cannot be filled with the Spirit while I am walking against God's will and depending upon myself."[92]

Double-mindedness

Cars equipped for driver's education often have a brake pedal on the right side as well as on the left. Imagine a car with two separate independently-operating steering wheels as well. How would the car know whose hand to obey?

Paul's warning in Rom. 8:5-7 against "the mind set on the flesh" or "the carnal mind" (KJV), seems comparable to the dilemma of *double-mindedness*, for whose cure James urges heart purification (James 4:8; 1:8). Unfortunately some contemporary believers are fighting an uphill battle against double-mindedness.

Since the mind directs the body to act, a person with two opposing minds would have no single controlling center. What an apt illustration of the believer's struggle against inner distortion! When a double-minded person prays, one mind doubts as the other seeks to believe God.

While my inner wrongness tells me to punch an obnoxious man in the nose, my renewed mind urges my hand to refrain from violence. When my inner wrongness impels my mouth to pour bitter angry words on him, God's Spirit suggests some kind ones. Working through my renewed mind, the Spirit leads me to show him Christ's love.

Have you ever fought this battle? Do you live in daily conflict of this sort? A double-minded person is no more stable than a car with two steering wheels.

Sin

Referring to this inner wrongness as *sin*, Paul warns, "do not let sin reign ... for sin shall not be master over you" (Rom. 6:12, 14). Paul treats sin like an active being that almost has a personality: "sin, ... produced in me coveting of every kind, ... deceived me, ... killed me. ... No longer am I the one doing it, but sin which indwells me. ... I am no longer the one doing it, but sin which dwells in me" (Rom 7:8, 11, 17, 20).[93] One can identify the inner wrongness as a sin nature, sin principle, or simply *sin*—as distinguished from *a sin*. "To let sin alone in our lives is to permit sin to grow until it chokes and blinds the conscience. Not to conquer sin is to be conquered by sin."[94]

Former person

Paul actually calls this sin principle our "old man" (KJV) or "old person," since the word Paul uses with "old" is the common term for a human being, not for maleness (Rom. 6:6; Eph. 4:22; Col. 3:9). This original word "old" tends to connote something superseded—like strawberries from the year before last in your freezer after you have stowed away this year's fresh crop. Hence, Charles B. Williams' translation, "former self" (Rom. 6:6) has considerable value.

Thus, Paul's expression, while not castigating old age, denotes the continued existence within the saved person of inner wrongness. Hence he is pointing out the *former person* within that too often determines a Christian's present actions. Elucidating the term, Godet insightfully but a bit loquaciously calls it

> human nature such as it has been made by the sin of him in whom originally it was wholly concentrated, fallen Adam reappearing in every human *ego* that comes into the world under the sway of the preponderance of self-love, which was determined by the primitive transgression. This corrupted nature bears the name of *old* only from the viewpoint of the believer who already possesses a renewed nature.[95]

Self-life

The mention of self both in Williams' translation and Godet's comment suggests another common term, the *self-life*. Centering life on self rather than on Christ, the unsanctified believer suffers from an improper focus. An array of hyphenated self sins dominates one's experience—like self-conceit, self-will, self-righteousness, and self-pity.

Adamic nature

Who broke Johnny? Apparently Johnny became broken in Adam. Because the distortion originated with Adam's original transgression in Eden, theologians sometimes refer to it as the *Adamic nature*.

In original sin, God counts us as in Adam when he fell, even as Scripture regards Levi as paying tithes to Melchizedek because his ancestor, Abraham, had done so (Heb. 7:9-10). As the New England Primer expressed it, "In Adam's fall, we sinned all."

In natural depravity, however, we actually inherit Adam's nature since we descended from him. This Adamic nature comprises our inner wrongness, for "through the one man's disobedience the many were made sinners" (Rom. 5:19).

Inbred sin

Who broke Johnny? Since he was born broken, one might assert that he, like every human being, suffers from the worst possible birth defect—a defect incurable by natural means. Since his Adamic nature arrived as soon as he arrived on planet earth, theologians sometimes designate it *inbred sin*—sinfulness that is inborn. John Owen states that ". . . because it is inbred, it is strongly compelling."[96]

This idea overwhelmed King David when he confessed a lack of truth in his innermost being:

> Behold, I was brought forth in iniquity,
> And in sin my mother conceived me (Ps. 51:5).

That Adamic nature makes it seem natural for human beings to sin. After we experience divine rebirth, however, we detest sin. So, opposite forces are pulling us in two directions at once—like the girl who yearns to eat chocolate to which she is allergic.

"I"

When Godet mentions the fallen Adam in human *ego*, we recall that the inner wrongness is *our* former person still residing, even though rightfully succeeded by the new regenerate person. It is like a retired pastor who continues to occupy the parsonage and wants full use of the church study. The Christian's problem converges upon the "*I*."

Bible students spot the frequency of first personal pronouns in Romans 7:14-25. Similarly, in Galatians 2:20 the "I" has experienced crucifixion with Christ so that the indwelling Christ can reign.

Although holiness has not resulted from human effort, both passages verify that Christ desires to transform, not to obliterate or dehumanize the believer. While the believer must count the carnal I crucified with Christ, the resurrected I lives, and Christ indwells me.

As A. B. Simpson viewed it, inner distortion is not something apart from me, but me! He wrote:

> There is a foe whose hidden power
> The Christian well may fear;
> More subtle far than inbred sin
> And to the heart more dear.
> It is the power of selfishness,
> The proud and wilful I,
> And ere my Lord can live in me
> My very self must die.[97]

A variety of terms has depicted inner wrongness, such as carnality, double-mindedness, sin, former person, self-life, Adamic nature, inbred sin, and the I. Both Scripture and theology have used analogical language to characterize it.

Hence, it is no wonder that some nineteenth and early twentieth century holiness teaching has imagined the wrongness as an entity—a removable thing. They taught *eradication*, which literally means the act or process of pulling something up by the roots. The "something" was to be the inner distortion.

Can a gardener uproot it like a weed? Can a surgeon remove it like a tumor? Can a mechanic remove it like a faulty machine part?

Since the wrongness is I, myself, evidencing immaturity and "twistedness" within, centering on myself, and relating to others improperly, the illustrations of the gardener, surgeon, and mechanic fall far short. Calvinists, Baptists, and moderate deeper-life advocates have consistently shunned an eradicationist analogy as inadequate—for grasping both the problem and the remedy.

In addition, most of today's Wesleyan theologians have discarded an earlier earmark. Mildred Wynkoop, for example, spurns the tendency to see original sin as "a 'something.' . . . Man's problem is not a substructure of some alien substance clinging to his soul but his own alienation from God."[98]

Similarly, Ray Dunning explains "what Wesley meant when he used metaphorical language such as 'inbred sin,' 'the seed of sin,' or 'the root of sin.' These are to be taken, not as referring to something within one, but one's condition of disordered love, focused incompletely on God."[99]

Showing that Wesley, Calvin, Luther, and Augustine alike rejected the notion of sin as a substance, United Methodist theologian Laurence W. Wood agrees. He affirms that "it is a confusion of categories to think that Wesley believed that sin was a physical-like substance which was extracted through the circumcision of the heart (entire sanctification)."[100]

8

Does Johnny Act Inconsistently? Inner Distortion's Deeds and Downfall

A man of unclean lips (Isa. 6:5).

How many jewels have you found in your garden lately? If yours resembles mine, lots of stones keep appearing, but never jewels. A maxim calls consistency a jewel. This saying implies the rareness of consistency.

As noted in chapter 7, carnality affects all humans. Although one can find carnal behavior rather consistently evil in the unsaved, yet even their behavior proves inconsistent with aspirations and resolutions. For the Christian, however, the inconsistency of carnal behavior becomes glaring.

The Christian has chosen to forsake Satan's kingdom to serve the Righteous One. Reborn with a divine nature, the new believer yet finds deep within a rebel that belongs to the past life. That rebel brings along evil desires, stubbornness, and a mind-set of wrong.

Consequently conflict often occurs, resulting in a sense of bondage (Gal. 5:17)—especially until one learns about dynamic sanctification. After examining the traits of inner distortion, this chapter will briefly preview the way of triumph over it.

Traits of Inner Distortion

Does Johnny know he is broken? In introducing Part Two, we noted the importance of knowing about the brokenness. In fact, people will not hurry to seek a remedy unless they discern an urgent need. The deadliness of the inner corruption shared by the entire race emerges from a study of the scriptural evidence.

The New Testament epistles likewise divulge the traits of this inner distortion. There one can infer carnality's several deportment patterns.

Deportment patterns

Immaturity. First, as hinted earlier, Christians dominated by a carnal heart evidence *immaturity*. Illustrating that he had sensed the necessity to feed them with milk, not solid food, Paul addressed his Corinthian readers as "babes in Christ." Paul found no way to use the language that "spiritual men" could understand, for these people lacked the expected surrender to the Holy Spirit's control (1 Cor. 3:1-2). Fixing attention on one's own life and hindering interpersonal relationships, carnality stunts growth.

Instability. Carnality produces *instability*. When David, the shepherd boy, had courageously volunteered to withstand Goliath, he never vacillated. Christians should serve as brave soldiers of Jesus Christ.

Although the spiritual person resolutely stands for the right regardless of public opinion, the carnal Christian seesaws between conquest and compromise. After destroying hindrances to spiritual growth, he or she rebuilds those very obstacles (Gal. 2:18). Faith soon gives way to wavering (James 1:8).

Inability. Loathing his misery, the struggling victim described in Romans 7 is discovering that carnality results in *inability*. Desiring the right, the sufferer has become a prisoner to the self-life. Despite his wishes to do good and avoid evil, he does just the opposite because the freedom-destroying sin nature at home in him keeps him impotent toward righteousness (Rom. 7:19-20).

Such a person hates what he is doing (Rom. 7:15). It is no wonder that God also hates behavior that compromises with evil. He declares that "the people who live on the plane of the lower nature cannot please God" (Rom. 8:8, Williams).

Many expositors see Paul as relating his own testimony. One can easily understand, however, how he could use first person singular pronouns to make the argument vivid, as teachers today often do. This seems best to fit the setting.

Some would call Paul a representative person here. Even if he is relating his own pilgrimage, though, likely all will agree that he narrates the experience for its applicability. It benefits readers by affording some understanding of why the human struggle against evil becomes so intense.

Although people at various stages of spiritual development identify with the passage, biblical scholars have long disputed about whether Romans 7 depicts a regenerate or unregenerate struggler. Some Arminians think its frank admissions of defeat cannot refer to a currently regenerate individual. Some other theologians find inadequate evidence that the writer has ever experienced saving grace. Such writers include very able biblical scholars.

Several considerations, however, urge the conclusion that Paul writes of a saved person at least in verses 14-25, if not in the entire passage. (1) The outline of Romans argues for this conclusion. Having discussed justification in Romans 3:23-5:21, Paul deals with aspects of sanctification in Romans 6:1-8:17. Even as works of the law fail to justify, chapter 7 affirms the law powerless to sanctify. Wilbur T. Dayton cleverly targets us: "The law did not keep you from sinning. It only kept you from enjoying it more."[101]

(2) Chapter 6 throughout has dealt with the most basic issues in positional and experiential sanctification. Within chapter 7, Paul switches from past to present tense verbs at verse 14. If he had digressed to discuss pre-conversion issues first, he has returned to the need for sanctification by verse 14.

(3) Without the new nature, an unsaved person remains totally depraved and hence unable to "delight in" (KJV) or "joyfully concur with the law of God in the inner man" (Rom. 7:22). Scripture depicts the unregenerate as *dead* in trespasses and sins without any operative inner man or "better inner nature" (Williams). Horatius Bonar argues that the words of 7:22

are the words, not of an inquirer, or doubter, or
semi-regenerate man, but of one who had learned to say,
with saints of other days, "Oh, how love I thy law" (Ps.
119:97). . . . I do not see how any one, with a right insight
into the apostle's argument, without a theory to prop up, or
with any personal consciousness of spiritual conflict, could
have thought of referring this chapter to a believer's unregenerate condition. . . .[102]

(4) Although carnality dominates the unregenerate person, yet
without the advent of the new nature, obviously no conflict rages
between new and old natures. Some of the lost aspire to a nobler
life that seems unattainable. They remain unaware, however, of
the overwhelming combat against persistent indwelling sin—the
topic of Romans 7.

(5) Some of the most noted and finest Christian scholars consider the passage as describing Christian experience. One of the
Greek church fathers, the whole group of Latin fathers, Augustine, Jerome, Thomas Aquinas, Luther, and Calvin agree. Finding
in this passage the Christian's struggle against the old nature,
many contemporary expositors concur with the aforementioned
ancient and medieval worthies.[103]

Inadequacy. Carnality in many ways tortures its victim with a sense
of *inadequacy* (Rom. 7:8). For example, indwelling sin, using the law,
awakened in its victim all kinds of coveting. Carnality kept saying,
"You don't have enough. God doesn't even allow you to want more."

Although covetousness can work havoc in the poor of any age as
well, it dominates the mind-set in today's prosperous world. People
in affluent western nations seek to outdo each other in accumulating
material luxuries. People in grasping third world countries yearn for
their share of the world's wealth. Are Christians immune?

God furnished an ideal environment for our first parents. He
provided productive tasks, a variety of trees bearing wholesome
fruit, and each other for company, help, love, sexual fulfillment,
and procreation. At Satan's instigation, Eve allowed wrong desire
to lodge within her to the point of reaching out, taking, and eating
forbidden fruit. Adam followed suit. God's good command

against eating that fruit had aroused their wicked desire. Covetousness for something God had withheld had led to indulgence.

Paul explains that those under the Adamic nature's control allow sinful passions to work. God's good Law had indirectly aroused those passions. Active in one's bodily members, the passions will produce deadly results (Rom. 7:5).

Our contemporaries spend their lives fulfilling personal desires, powerful emotions, impulses, lusts—all elements connoted by the original word "passions" here. "If it feels good, do it," cries the "me generation." As God's people, do we dwell on the same low plane, driven by carnal urges and drives?

Although covetous, lust-driven living supposedly brings satisfaction, Scripture unveils the truth. Using a graphic figure of a criminal chained to a dead man as punishment, Paul depicts our struggle with inner distortion. We, too, remain fastened to "the body of this death," or as Williams translates it, "this deadly lower nature" (Rom. 7:24). In other words, without a remedy, deadly carnality offers hopelessness and misery (Rom. 8:13).

Living by inner wrongness leads only to hopeless frustration, misery, and despair: "Wretched man that I am!" (Rom. 7:24). Carnality indeed concerns inadequacy—not only evoking covetousness and sinful passions, but spawning wretchedness as well.

Insubordination. Another deportment pattern of inner wrongness is *insubordination*. Carnality wages war against the proper behavior that reason calculates we should practice: "But I see another power operating in my lower nature in conflict with the power operated by my reason, which makes me a prisoner to the power of sin which is operating in my lower nature" (Rom. 7:23, Williams).

Even as Saddam Hussein boasted that he would stand against the whole world to secure his ends, so our twisted nature shows dogged insubordination. No one can tell us what to do. Especially rebellious, carnality "is hostile toward God; for it does not subject itself to the Law of God, for it is not even able to do so. . ." (Rom. 8:7). A Christian cannot reform his inner distortion—this twisted nature.

Scripture exploration has unearthed some deportment patterns that carnality develops and perpetuates—even in people who have exercised saving faith. It is a negative list: immaturity, instability, inability, inadequacy, and insubordination. Are there more specific sinful acts for which carnality is responsible?

Deeds produced

What deeds does inner distortion produce? Even as the Holy Spirit produces marvelous varieties of fruit (Gal. 5:22-24), Scripture lists fifteen specific deeds that the flesh exhibits (Gal. 5:19-21). Possibly representing samples of a much longer list, these fifteen items themselves prove highly significant.

We do not see electricity, but its multitudinous uses are apparent in every room of the average house. Although the flesh—in the sense of inner distortion—remains invisible, its works are anything but. The deeds of the flesh constitute Satan's counterfeit provision for humanity's deepest needs.

When God created Adam and Eve, he integrated into their natures drives for food, drink, sex, worship, and ambition. It is natural to desire and strive to find satisfaction for these drives. God himself intends to supply what human beings need in these areas. For Adam and Eve, Scripture records God's making the best possible provision for proper fulfillment of the various drives he had created.

As food God *gave* them the fruit of every plant and tree—except the tree of the knowledge of good and evil (Gen. 1:29; 2:16-17). The inspired record mentioned the river flowing out of Eden—as yet unpolluted water of God's provision (Gen. 2:10).

To fulfill their sexual needs, God gave Adam and Eve each other. After God stated, "I will make him a helper," he "fashioned into a woman the rib which He had taken from the man, and brought her to the man." Although they were naked, they "were not ashamed" (Gen. 2:18, 22, 25). God directed them to "be fruitful and multiply" (Gen. 1:28).

God created humanity with great capacities for work. Although after the fall work became arduous toil (Gen. 3:17-19), yet work itself constitutes a blessing.

Before the fall, as fulfillment for Adam's ambition drive, God assigned him important and varied work. His vast job description included cultivating and tending the garden, naming the animals and birds, subduing the earth, and ruling over the entire animal kingdom (Gen 2:15,19-20; 1:28). When the long-awaited summer vacation has arrived, in a week or so, children often complain, "What is there to do?" It seems that Adam would never have suffered from that problem.

Deadly peril

When we understand several biblical facts about inner wrongness, its horribleness hits us in the face like an unexpected splash of cold water. For example, who deserves the blame for carnality? Of course, Adam chose to sin.

Instigator. Ultimately, the *instigator* is Satan, the virulent, implacable foe of God and therefore of God's prime creation, the human race. Since the devil initiated his rebellion, he determined to dethrone and displace God. Although he could not touch God directly, he decided to wreak havoc on earth, where he apparently already had important authority. He sought to gain the allegiance of humanity.

To accomplish this, he himself appealed to Eve in the form of a talking serpent. Throughout the ages he has continued to use evil supernaturalism to allure, persuade, frighten, and trick human beings. He uses demonic spirits in this process—often stealthily flashing messages to the mind or toying with human emotions. Sometimes these evil spirits gain access within a person where they can maintain a beachhead for further conquest. At all cost, the enemy seeks to keep the unsaved in darkness. He attempts to ruin the lives and testimonies of the saved.

Functioning as an integral part of Satan's kingdom, the world system includes fallen humanity (1 John 5:19). It encompasses the nations headed by seen and unseen powers intent on maintaining a godless society (1 Cor. 2:6; John 7:7; 14:30). Scripture employs such phrases as the world (age), this world (age), the present age (world), this present evil age (world). Vine aptly explains it as "the present condition of human affairs, in alienation from and opposition to God."[104] Bearing the title, "the god of this world" (2 Cor. 4:4), Satan wishes to conform believers to this world (Rom. 12:2).

By deceiving Eve and arranging the scenario so that Adam would make a free wicked choice, Satan injected inner wrongness into our first parents. All their descendants (except the miraculously conceived Jesus Christ) now would inherit a similar Adamic nature.

Playing a major role in Satan's campaign to win his war, the flesh thus will never lay down its arms to submit to God. The flesh seems even more horrendous when we discover that it is not a correctable weakness in human nature. The flesh forms part of a threefold cunning scheme for human ruin, the defeat of the Almighty, and Satan's own enthronement.

Even as military strategy includes simultaneous use of air, sea, and land attacks, so Satan employs the flesh as well as the world system and evil supernaturalism. Whereas the world remains external, the flesh provides an internal attack. Evil supernaturalism, however, can include either external attacks or a combination of internal and external attacks. Generally, Satan uses all three forces for his most devastating victories.

Internality. One also views the deadly peril inherent in inner distortion simply because of its *internality*. Bemoaning "a different law in the members of my body, waging war," Paul got the picture. He explained: "I find then the principle that evil is present in me, the one who wishes to do good" (Rom. 7:21, 23).

A pizza delivery man was attempting to make a delivery in an urban district known for robberies. Receiving a sudden blow from an assailant he never saw, he rapidly ran away. Without injury, he eluded his unknown enemy. With flowing adrenalin, heroic effort, and divine protection, one can sometimes withstand or dodge an external foe.

A fifth columnist masquerading as a loyalist affords more peril than many warriors wearing enemy uniforms. Defeating a British fleet on Lake Erie in the War of 1812, Oliver Hazard Perry sent a now-famous message. Triumphantly he proclaimed to Commander William Henry Harrison: "We have met the enemy, and they are ours." Instead, we must admit, "We have met the enemy and they are *us*!"

Imposture. The twisted nature's use of *imposture* unnerves us. Paul objects, "Sin . . . deceived me" (Rom. 7:11). Always the major tool in Satan's box, deception works over and over.

In his chapter, "The Nature of Indwelling Sin," John Owen writes, "We do not even know the secret intrigues and schemes, twists and turns, actions and tendencies of our own hearts."[105] Scripture urges watchfulness, for deception misleads in the least expected ways.

Imprisoning. Paul finds carnality guilty of *imprisoning* believers. Year after year, Christians have suffered incarceration from persecutors for proclaiming Christ from New Testament times until the present. But internal wrongness makes a person a prisoner spiritually—"sold into bondage to sin, . . . making me a prisoner. . . . Who will set me free. . . ?" (Rom. 7:14).

Owen explains that

> this captivity is to "the law of sin"—not to this or that particular sin, but to the basic principle of sinning. . . . *Captivity is a miserable and wretched condition . . . particular to Christians.* Unregenerate men are never held captive by the law of sin.[106]

The self-life's deadly peril reminds us that this question finds no answer ever—apart from Jesus Christ our Sanctifier.

Incurable injury. The terror of the carnal self lies in the *incurable injury* it etches in human personality. Living by the dictates of the flesh leads to constant dangers. "For when we were living in accordance with our lower nature, the sinful passions that were aroused by the law were operating in the parts of our bodies to make us bear fruit that leads to death" (Rom. 7:5, Williams).

Sin kills, "effecting my death." (Rom. 7:11,13). Paul warns his believing readers of the possibility of slavery to inbred "sin, resulting in death, . . . for the wages of sin is death," and "the mind set on the flesh is death" (Rom. 6:16, 23; 8:6). It is no wonder that the Apostle Paul dubbed carnality "this body of death" (Rom. 7:24)!

Triumph over Inner Distortion

Does humanity's cry remain unanswered: "Who shall deliver me?" No, Scripture refuses to leave us in suspense. A later book chapter deals systematically with the heart of the sanctification doctrine. Here, however, a glimpse of the context of the Romans carnality passages provides a "vision of victory."[107] God provides *triumph* over inward distortion.

Prescribed

He *prescribed* a remedy at the outset of the sanctification section: "Are we to continue in sin that grace might increase? May it never be!" (Rom. 6:1-2, Beck). The definitive response leaves no doubt. God does not purpose that a believer should live under the dominion of the sin principle. "Perish the thought!" is the force of the unambiguous inspired reply. "Certainly not!" Beck translates it.

Promised

"Sin shall not be master over you," the passage continues as God *promises* triumph (Rom. 6:14). God keeps his word. As a believer claims the promise, victory emerges.

Preferred

The anguished cry, "Wretched man that I am! Who will set me free . . . ?" (Rom. 7:24) shows well that a believer prefers triumph *rather* than carnal bondage.

Practiced

Several verses illuminate triumph *practiced*. A useless theory brings a bleeding heart no comfort. Can no one deliver me?

"Thank God! It has been done by Jesus Christ our Lord. He has set me free" (Rom. 7:25, TLB). Christ's lordship provides the divine answer for a bound believer. Paul had earlier celebrated that his readers had "been freed from sin" (Rom. 6:18).

Showing more fully the remedy, Romans 8:2 joyously announces freedom. "For the law of the Spirit of life in Christ Jesus has set you free from the law of sin and death." Despite much theology that leaves no hope for consistently victorious living, Romans, the New Testament's fullest doctrinal treatise, offers abounding hope for liberation from inner wrongness' iron grip.

9

Massive Task/ Unlimited Resources: Power for Christian Service

Behold, this has touched your lips (Isa. 6:7).

Then I said, . . . "Send me!" (Isa. 6:8).

And He said, "Go, and tell this people" (Isa. 6:9).

Returning to Africa for his second term, missionary Joe Nicholson, Sr., sadly discovered that most of his converts had fallen away. During his furlough in America, however, he had sought and found the fullness of the Holy Spirit. Not only was he winning more people to Christ as a result, but even after the next furlough he was finding that the converts remained true. Enjoying the anointing of God's Spirit in his own life, he now had a full gospel to share with repenting nationals, which doubtless made a difference in the depth of their commitment.

Christians often detect that their words fall flat when they witness to acquaintances about the need of a Savior. Others make attempts to sing or teach for the Lord but despite manifest ability, find only scanty spiritual results. The fullness of the Holy Spirit relates much to power for service.

The massive assignment that God gives a Christian overwhelms the imagination. He asks us to do God's own work. He requires us to speak and serve in such a way that sinners will understand the divine message, become convicted,[108] repent, and experience conversion and Christian growth. How can a mortal man or woman do what only God can do?

We cannot, but he can. He can do it through us. This can only happen when we have allowed the Holy Spirit to fully occupy our lives, our lips, our hands, our talents. Then the Holy Spirit can enable our testimony, our preaching, our teaching, our acts of mercy. Then the Holy Spirit through His Word can do what we can never do—He can convict and convert a lost soul.

Is it a coincidence that the generation that has rejected the need for a point of sanctification is the generation so often experiencing burnout? As long as people in Christian service fail to see this truth, we become more and more crushed by a massive, impossible task.

We must admit the inevitable. The task is overwhelming. It is too big for us. We lack the wisdom, the endurance, the words, to do what only God can do. Nothing but the unlimited resources in the fullness of the Holy Spirit can make us sufficient for the massive task of ministry.

Addressing a Christian worker, Paul wrote, "Let every one who names the name of the Lord abstain from wickedness." He added that only a worker cleansed and removing himself/herself from evils[109] can serve as "a vessel for honor, sanctified, useful to the Master, prepared for every good work" (2 Tim. 2:19, 21).

To our deep loss, we have forgotten what writers like Turner and Rice have shown us about the need of the fullness for service. Turner explains, "The world-wide gospel work of this era is accomplished *only* through the operation of the Spirit. . . . Inasmuch as the Spirit works only in and through men, everything depends on men being filled with the Spirit."[110]

"Always in the Bible," Rice insists, "Spirit-filled Christians were empowered for service and testimony, particularly prepared for soul winning."[111] In virtually every case where the New Testament specifically tells of people becoming filled with the Spirit, as soon as possible they engaged in uplifting Christ in some form of effective witness.

God admitted to Isaiah, however, the fact of that prophet's impossible assignment—apparently the minute he answered the divine call to service (Isa. 6:10-13). Isaiah's audience would adamantly reject the message. Yet in God's sight his ministry was effective since he ably delivered God's message with the Spirit's anointing. God's Word accomplished its effect.

Who? The Master Seeks Zealous Workers.

Purpose

Secular employment for some people represents a complex exercise in escaping as much effort as possible as comfortably as possible for as much pay and benefits as possible. Can any of this attitude infect work for the Lord?

Concerning Christian service, Scripture reveals some principles worth pondering. The term "service" obviously suggests that we are serving. Thus, we must exceed the minimums of putting in time and avoiding trouble. Even as love must have an object, so must service, logically. Whom do we serve in Christian service?

Some in Christian leadership cause dissensions and hindrances. Calling such people "slaves not of our Lord Christ but of their own appetites," Scripture cautions that we keep our eye on them and "turn away from them" because "by their smooth and flattering speech they deceive the hearts of the unsuspecting" (Rom. 16:17-18).

Too often we wink at such problems, hoping the offender will improve. The Holy Spirit, on the other hand, divulges that such people are serving themselves, not shepherding the Lord's flock. If the Spirit discloses that we show unworthy motivation, we need to search our hearts, repent of the wrong, and seek for the sanctifying of our motives. Henceforth we can help others rather than feeding our own lust and pride.

Although preaching sometimes focuses on the speaker, Paul testified, "We do not preach ourselves but Christ Jesus as Lord, and ourselves as your bond-servants for Jesus' sake" (2 Cor. 4:5). Refusing to provide "an opportunity for the flesh," "through love serve one another" (Gal. 5:13).

While negatively we refuse serving ourselves but positively serve others, supremely we should serve God. If our employer is the King of Kings, how carefully we should seek to please him! "Let us show gratitude, by which we may offer to God an acceptable service with reverence and awe" (Heb. 12:28).

Whether we serve in a paid or unpaid Christian or secular position today, Paul reminded first-century slaves, "Whatever you do, do your work heartily, as for the Lord rather than for men; knowing that from the Lord you will receive the reward of the inheritance. It is the Lord Christ whom you serve" (Col. 3:24). Having revealed believers' high calling in Scripture, the Holy Spirit waits to empower them—to serve.

Passivity

Too often contemporary Christians wish sparkling emotions and the free ride to heaven but remain content to sit back and let others engage in the service expected of believers. Passivity plagues the church.

Sometimes Bible students call sanctification the promised rest. Andrew Bonar mentions an intriguing paradox: "It is a peculiarity of the Divine rest that it gives us intense rest, and at the same time intense restlessness for the souls of others."[112] Jesus' invitation similarly alternates between activity and repose: "I will give you rest. Take My yoke upon you; and YOU SHALL FIND REST FOR YOUR SOULS. For My yoke is easy, and My load is light" (Matt. 11:28-30).

The writer of Hebrews likewise interlaces rest and activity. "For he who has once entered into [God's] rest also has ceased from [the weariness and pain] of human labors.... Let us therefore be zealous *and* exert ourselves *and* strive diligently to enter into that rest [of God]—to know and experience it for ourselves . . ." (4:10-11, Amp.).

Even as the rest of the deeper life consists not in total inactivity, so the heavenly rest itself will include delightful service. Although sanctified living here does not depend on works for acceptance with God, it shows restlessness to serve. Through us God brings the lost into the fold and leads God's flock to completeness in Christ (Col. 1:28-29).

Finney bemoans the lack of believers who can lead an anxious *Christian* to the sanctifying Christ. Sadly, in an age of abundant resources, this problem persists today.[113]

When a Christian surrenders all—even the use of his or her own time and body—the Holy Spirit kindles the flame which both purges away the dross and provides zeal for selfless service. Christ gave himself not only to provide redemption for justifying us, but also to "PURIFY FOR HIMSELF A PEOPLE FOR HIS OWN POSSESSION, zealous for good deeds" (Tit. 2:14). Not an end in itself, purification destroys passivity, engendering zeal for kind and worthwhile service.

The chapter that opens with the most frequently-quoted call to consecration proceeds to discuss both some gifts and graces of the Spirit. It includes a charge linking watchfulness, zeal, and service: "not lagging behind in diligence, fervent in spirit, serving the Lord" (Rom. 12:11). "Fervent" translates the Greek present participle, "keep on boiling."

In Bible study, sometimes it is difficult to determine whether the original language intends the human spirit or the Holy Spirit. Commentators differ. Often the definite article "the," which Paul *did* use here, indicates the Holy Spirit. Several versions, including RSV, Goodspeed, Beck, and Williams understand it of him: "always on fire with the Spirit, always serving the Lord" (Williams). The Holy Spirit keeps the yielded human spirit fired up to keep serving Christ.

How? Self-Effort vs. Divine Dynamic

Pride

"I can do it," shouts the preschooler who shuns parental help. Similarly, when a new Christian awakens to the responsibility of serving the Lord, the assumption often follows: "If God wants me to do it, I can do it." Plop. Someone should have told him that a divinely-appointed task requires divine enabling. God expects him to serve by use of divine power.

Discard humanism. Humanism, so pervasive in modern thought, looks to human accomplishment as the key to progress while shoving God out of his universe. Unfortunately, Christianity is not immune to the humanistic mind-set.

Paul's message derived, not from human wisdom, but from the Spirit (1 Cor. 2:4). He accepted no glory whatsoever for his ministry. Paul specifies that the Holy Spirit alone was providing him adequacy for Christian work: "Not that we are adequate in our-

selves to consider anything as coming from ourselves, but our adequacy is from God, who also made us adequate as servants of a
new covenant, not of the letter, but of the Spirit; for the letter kills,
but the Spirit gives life." In myself, I cannot; but by God's Spirit, I
can.

Avoid a works-mentality. Instructors have taught the new believer well that God's grace—not works—provided salvation. Yet,
immediately they urge him, "Get to work for the Lord."

Too often no one explains to the new convert the fullness of the
Holy Spirit or God's expectations. Supplying both the message
and the strength, God deserves all the glory from human service:
"Whoever speaks, let him speak, as it were, the utterances of God;
whoever serves, let him do so as by the strength which God supplies; so that in all things God may be glorified through Jesus
Christ. . . (1 Peter 4:11).

Follow the biblical pattern. The biblical pattern, modeled in Paul's
missionary service, entails Christ working through a yielded vessel: "For I will not presume to speak of anything except what
Christ has accomplished through me, resulting in the obedience of
the Gentiles by word and deed, in the power of signs and wonders,
in the power of the Spirit, so that . . . I have fully preached the gospel of Christ" (Rom. 15:18-19). Kelly remarks that "too many
well-intentioned people are so preoccupied with the clatter of effort to do something *for* God that they don't hear Him asking that
He might do something *through* them."

Powerlessness

Enduement—the Gift. God's cure for powerlessness involves his
own gift to believers, the Holy Spirit—filling the submitted
Christian. Paul prayed that his Christian readers might become
decisively strengthened with power by His Spirit in the inner person (Eph. 3:16).

Urging the apostles *not* to depart yet from Jerusalem to begin
serving, the risen Christ promised preparatory power. Not many
days from the day Jesus spoke, they would be ready to receive the
enduement: "You shall receive power when the Holy Spirit has

come upon you; and you shall be My witnesses . . . to the remotest part of the earth (Acts 1:4-8). Witnessing would follow empowering.

Did that one empowering on the day of Pentecost automatically fill all who have become Christians from that day until the present? Though that one outpouring completed the divine provision, Acts and the history of the intervening centuries confirm that others on many, many later occasions did enter into the fullness.

Thousands converted after the outpouring at Pentecost apparently entered into the fullness at that stirring prayer meeting in Acts 4:31. In Acts 8:14-17, Peter and John prayed for the new converts at Samaria, who had already trusted Christ and received baptism at the hands of Philip.

Various other individuals and groups in the Acts record deserve mention. Later in this book in your hand, considerable attention will focus on the various Acts cases, including the investigation of various interpretations of them.

Commentators seem vainly to concoct clever explanations for the various historical accounts. They seek to show why these groups and individuals might need to receive the fullness at a distinct point when we supposedly do not have that need. Would it not be easier to take the accounts at face value and appropriate today what we need in a similar fashion as those biblical characters did?

Opponents often raise two contrary arguments that require brief attention here and more detail later. (1) Can we properly treat a descriptive passage as prescriptive? In other words, since Acts contains a historical record, can we safely require people to practice something that Scripture does not command?

No, we should not automatically make every descriptive passage prescriptive. For example, Scripture asserts that Demas, an early Christian worker, forsook the missionary he was helping. He departed from the missionary because he loved this present world (2 Tim. 4:10). We, however, must not go and do likewise.

If, however, Ephesians 5:18, does command believers to be filled with the Spirit, it is not sensible to ignore passages in the Gospels and Acts that show how people experienced this fullness.

(2) Should we not build our doctrine totally from the epistles rather than from other Scripture? In reply, the epistles contain

much vital doctrinal instruction, which believers must heed. It is improper to limit doctrinal formulation, however, to any one part of Scripture as some dispensationalists do. After all, Paul wrote in an epistle, "*All* Scripture is . . . profitable for doctrine" (2 Tim. 3:16, KJV, emphasis mine). If a passage contains something involving doctrine, it is profitable for theologizing and instruction.

Endowments—the gifts. As the enduement with the Holy Spirit himself equips believers for service, so the gifts, or endowments, that the Spirit distributes provide valuable assistance in service. God intended gifts as service aids.

At the very dawn of the twentieth century, Pentecostalism elevated tongues, calling it the unique necessary evidence that every Spirit-baptized Christian will manifest. Consequently, this "evidence doctrine" spawned an unscriptural overemphasis that in some circles has never been rectified.

Counterfeits abound—even as the originator of the evidence doctrine, Charles F. Parham, boldly admitted. Ten years after the January 1, 1901 outburst of tongues at Parham's Bethel Bible School in Topeka, KS, he penned the following lines.

> Hear this: Three-fourths of the so-called Pentecosts in the world are counterfeits, the devil's imitation to deceive the poor earnest souls. . . . Many hundreds, in seeking Pentecost, were taught to yield to any force, as God would not permit them to be misled; under those conditions they were ripe for hypnotic influence. . . . Two-thirds of the people professing Pentecost are either hypnotized or spook-driven, being seized in the first place with a false spirit or coming under the control of one afterward. We cannot be too careful to try or test the spirits, and any person unwilling to have their [*sic*] experience tested by going to God for themselves or with the brethren, reveal [*sic*] the fact that they are demon-controlled. . . . They plead the blood, and claim to be Jesus, giving messages, and imitate every gift of the Holy Spirit and Pentecostal tongues. . . . [114]

Throughout the same century, Christendom developed much fear of gifts because of abuses in some circles. Traditionalists had long been teaching that at least the spectacular gifts terminated with the end of the apostolic age. Most Dispensationalists concurred.

Despite controversy, counterfeits, misunderstanding, and neglect, God still delights to endow believers with true gifts—especially those he describes as the greater gifts (1 Cor. 12:31). Rightly interpreted, Scripture never states that God will withdraw the gifts during the present age. Gifts are gifts for the body. The entire Church comprises that body—not just the Church in an early transitional period.

God's direction still stands: "As each one has received a special gift, employ it in serving one another, as good stewards of the manifold grace of God" (1 Pet. 4:10). Inch states, however, that "one cannot hope to exercise his gifts effectively while neglecting to be filled with the Spirit."[115]

Where? The Field Is the World.

Priorities

In a world swarming with so much evil, how can God's people decide the best ways to devote their time in serving the Lord for the benefit of his creation? Good causes multiply.

Each of us has only one life of uncertain duration to give. Since Scripture indicates the Holy Spirit as the one who leads God's children (Rom. 8:14), he desires to guide consecrated people who trust him to set the best priorities. No one can do everything.

Central goal. The central goal toward which the Holy Spirit urges the Church is the exaltation of Jesus Christ. Jesus explained, "He shall glorify Me" (John 16:14).

"He is the center, which implies a more dynamic relationship than were He simply a model we might emulate."[116] Since it seems reasonable to think that some service more directly glorifies him than others, this central goal should have significance to praying, searching people who are ready to serve.

Central task. In unveiling his divine plan to the disciples shortly before the ascension, the risen Christ directed "that repentance for the forgiveness of sins should be proclaimed in His name to all the nations" (Luke 24:47). This he presented as a prime essential right alongside his own suffering and resurrection.

The worldwide witness remains the central task in service during this age. After two thousand years the assignment remains unfinished. Who will answer the Master's call to reach those people groups and individuals who have had no opportunity to hear the gospel? Workers who understand his heart and plan will keep first in their planning, praying, and giving this central task.

Did Jesus expand on how this herculean task could succeed? His promise and bidding follow: "Behold, I am sending forth the promise of My Father upon you; but you are to stay in the city until you are clothed with power from on high" (Luke 24:49). The central service task would require the Holy Spirit's power. He assured them of the fulfillment if they would remain in the place of receiving. Do we dare to undertake the central task with less?

Personal assignments

Not all have the opportunity to proclaim the gospel personally on a foreign mission field. Surely forces overseas would be greater if every Christian were fully obeying and God's will being done on earth as in heaven. In some segments of the church, leaders have rightly viewed this privilege as pressing.

Some believers, however, have felt wrongly pressured to volunteer for overseas service without any clear sense of a call from God. If a Christian has surrendered all to God and wants to serve him, surely God can adequately communicate where in the world he wants a person to serve. God's Spirit wants to guide believers who desire his direction rather than their own plans.

In interpreting the parable of the wheat and tares, Jesus explained, "The field is the world." Churches need pastors, staff personnel, and part-time volunteer workers. Christian organizations, colleges, and social ministries need full-time staff as well as volunteer assistants. The field is vast. All need to find and fulfill God's individual assignment for them.

In an army, not all who qualify as soldiers have identical tasks. In God's army, an infinitely wise Planner, who knew our capabilities before creation, prepares the assignment list. Enumerating tasks, Paul begins by illustrating:

We have many parts in one body, and these parts don't all do the same thing. In the same way, many as we are, we are one body in Christ and individually parts of one another. We have gifts that are different according to what His love gave us. If you can speak God's Word, do it according to the faith you have. If you can serve, then serve. If you can teach, teach. If you can encourage, encourage. If you share, be generous. If you manage anything, do it eagerly. If you help people in need, do it cheerfully (Rom. 12:4-8, Beck).

If we will submit to the Lord's wishes, we will discover that he knew better than we what we would most enjoy doing as well as what we can best accomplish. The Head of the Church suits the tasks to the individual. After all, he made the individuals!

Proper service must begin with total commitment, finding its initial impetus in an empowering by the Holy Spirit. Also proper service must do its continuing work through the continuing ministry of the Spirit to and through us. We must do God's work in God's way, drawing upon God's resources, for God's glory.

Part 3

The Heart of Sanctification: Romans 6

With two he covered his face (Isa. 6:2).

Thehe American Heart Association suggests using low-fat cereals. . . . Low sodium, low-fat cereals can be a part of a diet low in sodium, saturated fat, and cholesterol that may reduce the risk of high blood pressure and heart disease.

So reads the cereal box of a brand with no cholesterol or saturated fat and very, very low sodium content.

People in the western world have become highly health-conscious, especially concerned about preventing heart disease. In a comic strip I read this week, a young girl was carefully comparing the labels on food after food in the store. Rejecting offensive brands, she was seeking, in each case, the package containing the most healthful food. In the final picture, the girl commented that she will probably live longer but that she will need to spend all of that extra time in the grocery store.

In a *Modern Maturity* magazine cartoon, a husband and wife had just arrived in heaven. One commented on the outstanding beauty of the place. The spouse responded, "Yes, and just think, we could have been here ten years sooner if it had not been for that oat bran!"

People today often use "heart" as a figurative term, even as Scripture does. We use it sometimes as a figure for our spiritual selves, elsewhere of our emotional selves, and otherwise of the vital central core of anything. The title of Part Three refers to Romans 6 as presenting the central core of the issue. This biblical chapter provides the most vital unfolding of the New Testament Christological doctrine of dynamic sanctification.

When Isaiah noticed that the seraphim each had six wings, he disclosed that "with two he covered his face" (Isa. 6:2). Some commentators have suggested that such an action showed a humility, a desire not to draw attention to oneself.

In a sense this expresses in a capsule the heart of dynamic sanctification. The believer must come to the place of saying, "Not I, but Christ." I count myself dead, so that the Lord alone can be seen. Romans 6 centers here.

Having in Parts 1 and 2 looked *under* and *toward* sanctification to assess its foundations and the need for it, the reader now can gaze straight *at* the heart of the doctrine. Romans 6 comprises Scripture's most crucial doctrinal passage on sanctification.

10

An Invitation— to a Funeral! Past Historical Aspects

King Uzziah died (Isa. 6:1, NIV, KJV).

Political oppression in Cambodia, 1975-80, skyrocketed the death rate to four times the world average. While the most careful computation of Holocaust victims, 1941-45, stands at 5.8 million, the U.S. Judiciary Committee estimates that the Mao Tse-tung regime slaughtered between 32.25 and 61.7 million Chinese, 1949-65.

Such shocking records of massive human carnage stagger the imagination. Yet, according to Romans 6, when Jesus Christ suffered crucifixion, *every* single Christian likewise died.

As mysterious as it seems, Paul views this widespread execution as a marvelous advantage rather than a horrendous tragedy. The real death of which he writes occurs in the spiritual realm, not the physical.

Looking Back to the Calvary Events

Provision in Christ

Centering on past historical aspects of a death/resurrection theme, Romans 6 begins with Jesus' own crucifixion and arising.

His death. As already noted in chapter 4, Jesus' death affords provision for sanctification. Mentioning "His death" and "the death
that He died" (Rom. 6:3, 10), Paul affirms this as a *fact*: Jesus actually died. He is mentioning a literal physical death. Committing
his spirit to his Father, Jesus died. Jesus' heart stopped beating and
he stopped breathing. His mortal sufferings ended.

Why did he die? Spontaneously we reply, *"for* our *sins."* Romans
3:21—5:21 has taught us this. Yet a glance at Romans 6 divulges
that here Paul has injected an important new element into the
book. In this setting, a different *function* of his death hits the reader:
"He died *to sin*" (Rom. 6:10). Not only did Jesus, the Savior, die in
my place to buy me back from sins, but also he died to sin as a principle. This function provides release for me—from inner wrongness.

Scripture comforts the Christian with the *finality* of his death.
"Christ . . . is never to die again. . . . He died to sin, once for all. . ."
(Rom. 6:9-10). Since all human physical death marks a one-time
event, Christ died once. We will never lose our Sanctifier. Having
decisively defeated the foe, Christ accomplished the necessary
provision. Our present victory requires no additional triumph on
his part.

His resurrection. Like his death, Christ's resurrection stands as an
attested *fact.* "Christ was raised from the dead through the glory of
the Father, so we too might walk in newness of life" (Rom. 6:4).
God's glorious power comprised the awesome *force* behind it.

In his resurrection, *freedom* came to Christ, for "death no longer
is master over Him" (Rom. 6:9). Death retains no valid claim over
him since through his death our Redeemer rendered "powerless
him who had the power of death, that is, the devil" (Heb. 2:14).

Even as Christ died to sin, so also a *function* of his resurrection is
that now he "lives to God" on the new plane of resurrection life
(Rom. 6:10). His resurrection, however, powerfully ministers to
the Christian also.

"Christ was raised from the dead through the glory of the Father, so we too might walk in newness of life" (Rom. 6:4). Then,
his resurrection, as well as his death, provided for our present
sanctification. As an ambassador in a foreign land continually acts

representatively, so all that Christ accomplished, he did representatively. An ambassador represents his sovereign, acting as if he *were* his own nation. God was in Christ when he came to the alien land called earth, paying the price necessary for our sanctification. Unfortunately some imagine that sanctification relates only to the Spirit's advent at Pentecost. It issues, as well, from that preparatory redemptive package—Christ's death, resurrection, and ascension (Acts 2:23, 32-33; John 7:39).

Specifically because he arose, believers can habitually conduct themselves in a new sphere, quality, and way of living. Because Jesus died to sin, the plan calls for believers to behave toward sin like a corpse would. Because in Jesus' resurrection he lived to God, the plan leads believers likewise to behave constantly as in God's presence and by his power. Living to God sounds more delightful than living under sin's mastery!

Identification with Christ

As the U.S. Congress provides laws for the populace, so also they identify with other U.S. citizens. They are one with their constituency in certain respects. They share with those they represent the responsibilities and privileges their laws provide. They pay taxes. They enjoy freedom of speech and of the press. Some parallels teach us about Christ's relationship with the Church.

Whereas provision represents what Christ did for us, identification includes our union with Christ, a very prominent topic in Paul's letters. Even as God counted our sins as laid upon our Savior and his righteousness entered on our account, so also the saved form Christ's very body. We are in Christ—a constantly recurring theme in epistles like Ephesians.

Death. The believer's *union* with Christ includes participation in his death. "We have become united with Him in the likeness of His death" (Rom. 6:5). With loving concern, a Christian physician daily treated and prayed with his terminal patient. In a vivid sense the doctor emotionally united with him in his death. A daughter contributed one of her kidneys to her ailing father. In a new way she united with him physically.

It was in the spiritual realm, however, that Christ chose to unite himself with the sinner's deadness in trespasses and sins. He united himself with the race so fully as to acquire a human body and become a sin offering. Dying in our place, he provided our redemption. In sanctification also, God counts the believer as in Christ—sharing Christ's death to sin.

At what *time* did we die? Throughout Romans 6, Paul consistently paints the Christian's death with Christ as a past completed event, as Christ's death was. The logical inference here sees the time of our death as identical with the time of Christ's. The repeated message surfaces: "we who died to sin" (Rom. 6:2); "our old self was crucified with *Him*" (Rom. 6:6); "We died with Christ" (Rom. 6:8, Williams).

Regrettably, many speakers have missed the point. Well-meaning writers proclaim that Christians must now die out to sin. The adage that cats have nine lives persists because they recover from accidents that at first seemed fatal. Yet when tabby actually dies, she will not need to die out again—nor to die daily.

Ministers from opposite theological positions assert that we should "die daily" to sin—misinterpreting 1 Corinthians 15:31. The latter verse stands in an immediate context of persecution and the larger context of a chapter on a literal physical resurrection as following a literal physical death. The Williams translation accurately conveys Paul's thought: "Why too do we ourselves run such risks every hour? . . . I myself run the risk of dying every single day! . . . I have fought wild beasts here in Ephesus . . ." (1 Cor. 15:30-32, Williams). Romans 6 and a host of other passages overwhelmingly declare that the Christian has already officially died to sin.

This death concerns one's positional relationship to the warped nature. The Christian should affirm this stance: "When Christ died, I died. In Christ's death, I died. Oh carnal self, the sin principle, I choose to view myself as dead to you—refusing to respond to your allurements." Both in Romans 6:2 and 6, the death/crucifixion intends to release from bondage and lead to the resurrection life.

What *function* does this death with Christ fulfill? Somewhat different carnality figures occur in Romans 6 to illustrate the liberation in two contrasting ways. This phenomenon is not unique, however, for Paul elsewhere states that through Christ's cross, both the world had been crucified to him, and he to it (Gal. 6:14).

In verse 2, believers died to the principle of "sin"—sinfulness assumedly representing the inner wrongness. Here the emphasis lies on seeing oneself as the culprit that necessarily became dead so sin can no longer act as a controlling principle.

In verse 6, however, the "old man," or former person, experienced crucifixion with Christ, not "to" something—unless we are to infer to the body of sin. (See Figure 1 below.) The crucifixion of the former person should result in the destruction or rendering powerless of the body of sin. If one views "the body of sin" as roughly parallel to "sin" in verse 2, the dissonance vanishes and the verses appear quite parallel.

Figure 1

Dead with Christ: Romans 6

Vs.	Who Died?	To What?	Why?
2	we	sin	not to live longer in sin
6	our old self	[body of sin?]	no longer to be slaves to sin

Dunn reminds us that at each occurrence of the Greek word body, "modern readers need to be reminded that it does not denote the physical body as such, rather a fuller reality which includes the physical but is not reducible to it."[117] If the "body of sin" refers to the human body as a tool of sin, then the two aforementioned verses differ much more. Interpreters have noted several problems stemming from the notion that "the body of sin" equates fully or largely with the human body.

1. The translation does not read naturally if one says that the body is rendered powerless with regard to sin.

2. Favoring dualism, this interpretation can lead to gnostic de-preciation of the human body. Scripture fails to show the body as more wicked than the soul or spirit.

3. It supports ascetic thinking.

Origen and Grotius considered the expression "body of sin" to mean the totality of sin. Perhaps it personifies sin. In the Lange commentary, editor Philip Schaff mentions the idea here that "sin is personified as a living organism with many members (vices) which may be put to death."[118]

Although one cannot biblically declare that a Christian must now die out to self, it is biblical to speak of executing the individual members of one's life. Elsewhere Paul urges, "For you died. . . . Put to death, therefore, whatever belongs to your earthly nature: sexual immorality, impurity, lust, evil desires and greed, which is idolatry" (Col. 3:3, 5).

Bruce suggests comparing "the body of sin" (Rom. 6:6) to "the body of this death" (Rom. 7:24). He cautions that "this 'body of sin' is more than an individual affair; it is rather that old solidarity of sin and death which all share 'in Adam'. . . ."[119]

Nevertheless, he does not deny the individual aspect. He appears to equate it with "the 'flesh,' the unregenerate nature with its downward tendency, the 'old Adam' in which sin found a ready accomplice. . . ." He approves of the NEB translation's wording, "for the destruction of the sinful self" (Rom. 6:6, NEB). If this is a correct view, "body of sin" denotes the inner wrongness that this same verse also calls "our former person," although the connotations differ.[120]

Each has its own shade of meaning: our former person died so that the entire vexing body of sinfulness has potentially met its doom. Having lost its stinger, the hornet may startle but has been destroyed as a real threat.

Resurrection. Union with Christ in his death implies the certitude of union with him in resurrection. "For if we have become united with *Him* in the likeness of His death, certainly we shall be also *in the likeness* of His resurrection" (Rom. 6:5).

The New Testament teaches that because of his resurrection, Christ will transform our bodies when he returns to gather all his saints—whether deceased or still surviving. Christ's glorified body forms the pattern for our glorified bodies (Phil. 3:20-21).

In context, however, mentions of resurrection in Romans 6 surely concern sanctification. Union with Christ in his death focuses on the ruin of the power of inner wrongness. Union with him in his resurrection suggests power to live aright, conformity to Christ's holiness, and vigor to accomplish exploits in his service. Having died with him, "we believe that we shall also live with Him" (Rom. 6:8).

"Thoroughly dissatisfied with the lower life" of conflicts and defeats, Presbyterian pastor H. B. Elliot found power to live in victory. He experienced this relief from bondage to inner wrongness after a stranger on a steamboat invited him to attend a service. It was in one of Phoebe Palmer's Tuesday afternoon meetings where he learned of liberation.

Later he testified to "deliverance from that mixed, diseased state in which motives were conflicting, affections disordered, purposes contradictory. There is a oneness of direction which seems to me now as natural as I thought the former chaos was."[121] Can Christians enter then into a new resurrection life of spiritual victory?

Explaining the Christian's transformation in 1 Corinthians 2, Lewis Sperry Chafer, founder of Dallas Theological Seminary, notes that "the first experience, conversion, changes the 'natural' man into the saved man." On the other hand, "the second change is from the 'carnal' man to the 'spiritual' man . . . when a real adjustment to the Holy Spirit takes place."[122] This adjustment amounts to dynamic sanctification.

Looking Back to the Salvation Events

Conversion to Christ

Romans 6 is an excellent chapter to show the relationship between conversion and sanctification. Although conversion does not in itself bring the believer onto the highest plane of Christian living, it lays the substructure for the building of victorious living.

Conversion alters a person's allegiance. Paul rejoices: "But thanks be to God that though you were slaves of sin, you became obedient from the heart to that form of teaching to which you were committed" (Rom. 6:17).

Source. Consumers cannot purchase salvation at any supermarket—nor at any church! God, the great Provider, ultimately gives salvation without cost. Jesus serves as Savior. In the verse just quoted, Paul thanks God for the transformation of certain people at Rome, even as in Romans 6:23 he calls eternal life "the free gift of God . . . in Christ Jesus our Lord." To receive Christ includes receiving eternal life, for "this life is in His Son" (1 John 5:11). To receive the gift of a new car, one receives an engine.

Involving a personal decision, salvation requires heeding a divine message and committing oneself to obedience. As in a sweepstakes, the winner must play by the rules. Obedience to God's commands does not save, even as playing by the rules does not yield any prize for the vast majority entering a sweepstakes. The saved person has repented, however, implying a change in direction from disobedience to obedience (Rom. 6:17). Today too many suppose themselves Christians because they have, without repentance, mentally committed themselves to Christian principles and nodded mental assent to truth. The source of the commitment necessary includes an about-face to live in an opposite way, trusting Jesus Christ definitely to become one's Savior.

Rescue from sin's slavery. Paul characterizes all Roman Christians as formerly sin's slaves (Rom. 6:17). An unbeliever living in deep moral debauchery may readily understand this charge. When one has outwardly conformed to a government's laws and even to Christian principles, that person may have a harder time understanding.

Yet even pride in one's self-engineered rectitude represents a form of slavery. Pride led to Lucifer's downfall. Creating their own standards and striving to fulfill them, the outwardly righteous unbelievers have similarly made themselves gods. Presenting one's members to any evil brings slavery. Slavery to sin results in death (Rom. 6:16).

Various forms of impurity head several Bible lists of sins. Paul mentions one of the commonest areas in which the ungodly revel when he states that his readers have presented their bodily members to impurity (Rom. 6:19).

Today television, videos, and rock music lyrics blatantly recommend impurity. Pornography captivates many. Homosexuals justify their sin as natural and march to demand their "rights." Adultery has become a way of life as marriage vows seem trivial. Approving live-in arrangements, and assuming that dating involves the right to play at the marriage act, many youths flee *toward* fornication. It is no wonder that multitudes who eventually seek counseling have become slaves to lust without realizing the multiplied ways that impurity works havoc in a person's life. When society insists that the Bible advocates outmoded purity standards, it displays ignorance of the natural moral laws which God has written into his universe.

Another example of slavery is lawlessness. This word in the original language combines "law" and "not," so it refers to a refusal to keep a law. Moule explains lawlessness as "the hatred of holy restraint."[123] Vine identifies it as "the rejection of the law, or will, of God and the substitution of the will of self."[124]

At present, people insist on their own way. Refusing any or all standards at their own fancy, they practice rebellious insubordination against all authority. They absolutely do not want God to tell them what to do nor the church to interfere with their chosen lifestyle. Sometimes they follow only the governmental laws they like. As contemporary Americans express it, "laws are made to be broken."

Including even "contempt for the standard of right written in the law on every man's conscience," Godet perceives lawlessness as "life going beyond all rule." Scripture implies that lawlessness tends to reinforce itself and multiply. Lawlessness leads to more lawlessness, "lawlessness, resulting in *further* lawlessness" (Rom. 6:19). Godet interprets this phrase as "to do all one's pleasure without being arrested in the least by the line of demarcation which separates good from evil."[125]

Conversion rescues from this wretched slavery to sin. Although slavery under a slaveholder pays no wages, sin's wages consist of death, as Paul keeps warning (Rom. 6:12, 16, 21).

Commitment to righteousness' "slavery." Paul reasons that everyone serves something—whether sin or obedience. The way of obedience occupies the person with righteousness. Regeneration involves receiving a new nature designed for righteousness. When a person has received Christ, all life becomes absorbed in pleasing a new Master. This focus leads to sanctification, for that individual delights to offer himself or herself as a love slave to Christ. Desiring to grow consistently, that person will determine to overcome every spiritual foe. ". . . Now present your members *as* slaves to righteousness, resulting in sanctification" (Rom. 6:19). It seems clear that such demeanor culminates in eternal life; Paul writes, ". . . Enslaved to God, you derive your benefit, resulting in sanctification, and the outcome, eternal life" (Rom 6:22).

Symbolism in baptism

For the person who lives for Christ, four past historical elements, centering in Jesus Christ's death and resurrection, secure a firm foundation for living the sanctified life. Discussed in Romans 6, such elements consist of Christ's provision, the believer's identification with him, the fact of the believer's conversion, and the symbolism of baptism.

Furnishing a vivid object lesson, baptism associates the new believer with Christ. Baptism enables him or her to portray visually in a symbolic act both death and resurrection. It involves a moment of spiritual intensity that the Christian can pinpoint. Even as immersion exhibits death, and submersion represents burial, so emergence suggests resurrection.

How does baptism relate to the deeper life? In Romans 6, Paul promptly uses it to prove that when Christ died physically, the believer died to sin and arose to a new life. When in immersion a Christian plunges into the water, that believer voluntarily associates with a Christ who descended into the grave and arose.

Water itself never saves or sanctifies, but it depicts both Christ's provision and our participation in his benefits. The New Testament knows of no unbaptized believers. Baptism was both a privilege and obligation, which the new believer promptly experienced. Why condone carelessness today in obeying Scripture?

When does a believer experience sanctification? Provision remains complete due to Christ's finished work. Conversion brought victorious life within reach. Baptism, in holy dramatization, graphically encapsulates this provision and identification. In experience, however, we have only what we appropriate. Obedience to Romans 6 directions can bring satisfying results. Chapter 11 will examine future anticipated results before Chapter 12 treats present required actions.

11

From Today On: Expecting Future Results

Turn and be healed (Isa. 6:10, NIV).

After a minister had advertised a sermon on "Seven Ducks in a Muddy River," he preached about Naaman. As long as Naaman kept giving arguments on why he should not dip seven times in the Jordan, he retained his respectability—and his leprosy. Only when he obeyed God, including all seven splashes, did healing come.

Turning to the Lord's way should result in life restoration. If today you trust Christ's sanctifying provision, what future results can you expect—starting today?

Some people seek to claim dynamic sanctification without finding a satisfactory assurance. Later they remark, "I tried that once, but life remained the same." Sometimes this occurs because of inadequate information. At other times, the candidate fails to meet the biblical conditions.

Paul in Romans 6, however, anticipates a change when a person truly reckons, surrenders, and trusts. Paul mentions an emancipation, a cancellation, and a newness as a result of dipping into dynamic sanctification.

Emancipation

Returning home from work in the wee hours one morning this spring, a Christian youth who had intense struggles with sin suddenly perished when his car crashed on a curve. His loving family took comfort that at least his conflict had ended. "He who has died is freed from sin" (Rom. 6:7). Once he or she has physically died, indwelling sin—inner wrongness—has no more claim on a person. But, wait! We did die to its power in the spiritual realm when Christ died. As we count upon these truths, the self-life has lost its vitality. Christ makes us free.

When the Egyptian pharaoh oppressed the Israelites, God informed Moses, "I have surely seen the affliction of My people who are in Egypt, and have given heed to their cry because of their taskmasters, for I am aware of their sufferings" (Exod. 3:7). After Moses obediently began to press for relief, Egypt demanded that the brick makers find their own straw but still produce the same daily volume. How cruelly slave masters can treat other human beings! The fallen nature, under Satan's ultimate supervision, similarly keeps human beings in servitude—even Christians.

The sanctified can claim two complementary divine promises: (1) "We should no longer be slaves to sin" (Rom. 6:6) and (2) "for sin shall not be master over you" (Rom. 6:14). Imagine working 97 years for the same family like Susan O'Hagan did. The Hall family at Lisburn, Northern Ireland, employed her for three generations. Starting at age ten, she engaged in housework, still performing light duties at age 107.

Susan served as an employee, however, not a slave. It would be sad indeed to be sentenced to working for a lifetime as a slave. Never finding the spiritual liberty the Lord intends, in a real sense, people today suffer from such a predicament. As Jehovah called ancient Israel to freedom, so he calls Christians to free abundant living.

In support of his second promise, God affirms, "for you are not under law, but under grace." The principle of works or rule-keeping arouses the desire to do wrong. For example, a sign saying, "Wet Paint," in effect warns the reader, "Don't touch." The sign evokes, however, in many readers the desire to touch the newly painted surface to see whether it really remains wet.

Since we have died to law-keeping, law has no further rule over us (Rom. 7:5-6). Grace represents God's free gift. Under grace we need not finish years of service to earn God's love. Instead, we serve because God dearly loves us regardless of our deeds and because we love him supremely as well. Therefore, as recipients of grace from so dear a holy Father, we should avoid committing sin (Rom. 6:15).

Cancellation

After a postage stamp has accomplished its mission, it arrives on a letter bearing a black mark identifying it as used. No one can legally employ it to carry another letter. God has devised a means for the inner wrongness to bear a mark of his cancellation—so it cannot legally control the sanctified believer.

An anticipated result of a believer's entrance into sanctification is the cancellation of the force of the inner wrongness. If Chapter 10's earlier investigation was accurate on "the body of sin" in Romans 6:6, this phrase depicts that inner wrongness as a whole.

Previously it has pressured the believer day by day, inwardly drawing God's child to commit acts of sin. Yet if I have awakened to the reality that the person I used to be actually experienced crucifixion with Christ, I can live free. God's Word declares that this body of sin has been ruined, neutralized, rendered powerless, canceled!

Where is it? Is it still there inside me? Has God removed it? Has he destroyed it so that it has become a non-entity? Theologians have wrestled with such questions, producing various answers for a century.

Many enthusiastic Wesleyan holiness theologians in the nineteenth century adopted the doctrine of eradication. By this they meant that God had plucked up by the roots the inner wrongness. If so, God had totally extricated the person from the horrible inherited Adamic nature so it could never return. Though Satan could tempt externally, the person's inward desires should only seek for good. The person still had a human nature but without the twistedness. With no carnal nature, the person could surely hope to live without committing any intentional sin. Wesleyans define sin as only a willful transgression of a known law of God—very different from a Calvinistic stance that sin includes any slight deviation from perfect holiness.

Non-Wesleyans have generally rejected eradication as unbiblical and unworkable. In more recent decades, most Wesleyan theologians have also abandoned the theory as a poor analogy of what occurs in sanctification.

Although fellowshipping with those who differed with him, A.B. Simpson rejected eradication. He also shunned an opposite view called suppression, the idea that the Christian must throughout life keep holding down or counteracting the inner wrongness with the Holy Spirit's help. Neither position supplied the most biblical deeper-life theory. Instead, he saw habitation as the best way to account for our victory. Habitation means Christ so fully indwelling that he relives his holy life through the sanctified believer.

For Simpson, what happens to the carnal nature? Although he shunned focusing on the negative, he understood the old nature as dead and destroyed—but not obliterated. If that former self again appeals to the sanctified Christian, he or she should keep rejecting it, counting it as a dead thing, a ghost. Who believes in ghosts anyway? If a ghost tries to address us, we close our ears, ignoring him.

Perhaps this idea best explains Romans 6:6. As long as we keep realizing ("knowing this") that our former person became crucified with Christ, the whole body of inward sinful distortion for all practical purposes remains out of operation, annulled. Its effectiveness lies in ruins, destroyed. It cannot claim the victory.

The inner wrongness was not some separate entity injected into Adam that can later be eradicated; instead Adam's own very nature became polluted. We inherited his wrongness—it permeates and comprises our very person. God will not abolish our personhood. As we understand Scripture, nothing and no person will go out of existence, despite possible radical changes in condition or location.

Yet the nature can be cleansed from pollution and counted dead as the former self. Then Christ can occupy the heart's throne, supplying all needed authority against foes. Praise the Lord for a habitation that produces the foe's cancellation.

Newness

Entering sanctification produces newness. Two major Greek synonyms for "new" appear in the New Testament. "Newness" in Romans 6:4 relates to the adjective that connotes "unaccustomed or unused, not new in time, recent, but new as to form or quality, of different nature from what is contrasted as old."[126] The use of the noun, "newness" further underlines the quality of life involved.[127]

Regeneration brings new life into a human being, for Jesus claimed that a person becomes born again. In other words, at regeneration, a fresh, recently acquired new life and new nature arrive.

When we practice the sanctified walk, however, our newness of life bursts into action. The potential becomes actual. Likely it has not arrived recently. Although the Christian may have acquired the newness a long while beforehand, yet it has remained in mint condition—unused. It lies wrapped up like an unneeded Christmas present.

Too often we have failed to allow the new nature to overcome the old nature habitually. Positionally the new nature has been in place, but it has long laid dormant. God has been grieved that we ignored that gift so long, even as our relatives may have taken offense that their expensive gift found no appreciative user.

Finally, we begin to make use of this new quality of life. We wake up to see what a valuable gift Christ died to provide. Our appropriation of our union with Christ in his resurrection happens "so we too might habitually live *and* behave in newness of life" (Rom. 6:4, Amp.). Now, joy accompanies the new awakening. Now the sanctified Christian appreciates his spiritual healing.

Practically I have found that rejoicing in my new nature indwelt by God's Holy Spirit I receive power to literally starve the old nature — this happens as He helps me deny the old nature our time in my thoughts, pleasure time in my heart and body time in my behavior. Praise the Lord!

12

**No Time Like
the Present
for Presenting:
Present Actions**

*Turn
(Isa. 6:10, NIV).*

Drawing all its major concepts from Romans 6, Part Three has first considered the death and resurrection motif as the past historical aspect of sanctification—the things in history that provide a foundation for sanctified living. Second, it has peered into the future to see three benefits one can expect beyond one's entry into the sanctified life. The present aspect remains—how can the awakened Christian now enter the promised land of sanctified living?

Knowledge

A neighbor inquired of a physician's preschool son, "Is your dad a good doctor, Jeff?" "Nah," came the response, "He gets sick himself." Giving advice often proves remarkably easier than taking your own advice.

It is one thing to know what I ought to eat; it is quite another thing to adhere to my diet. Although knowledge avails little if I refuse to put it into action, yet knowledge forms a prerequisite for proper action. A person who needs to enter the deeper life, needs to understand a few things.

An item to recall

First, one cannot deepen something not possessed. A seeker for the deeper life needs to be able to recall that he has passed out of death into life. Romans 6 has mentioned how conversion affords an essential foundation for sanctification (Rom. 6:17).

Items to understand

How glibly passengers ignore the stewardess' pre-flight safety warnings in case the aircraft should encounter a severe emergency! Christians easily skip over vital directions on the sanctified life. God has given essential directions in Scripture. "Knowing this" introduces the Christian's union with Christ in his death (Romans 6:6). "Knowing that" precedes the mention of the permanence of Christ's resurrection (Rom. 6:9).

Furthermore, behaving as if they could gain greater grace by leading a substandard life, God's children must grasp the incongruity of continuing in bondage. Paul prods: "Are we to continue in sin that grace might increase? May it never be!" (Rom 6:1-2).

Isadore Zimmerman of New York City had spent 24 years in prison for allegedly murdering a police officer. Authorities found new evidence that cleared Zimmerman in the early 1980s. Upon his release at age 66, officials granted him a million dollars compensation. Do you suppose he refused to leave the prison, hoping to earn more cash by additional unjust incarceration if he remained? Such a suggestion seems as ludicrous as continuing in bondage to sin to build up a greater supply of God's grace.

Reckoning

Although a saved individual finally understands his union with Christ in the Sanctifier's death and resurrection, that knowledge per se fails to reprogram him to lead a holy walk. He or she must begin to count this crucifixion and resurrection as true and active in current experience (Rom. 6:11)! For most people this becomes a turning point.

Why did Zimmerman leave the correctional institution? His leaving did not clear his record; in fact, in a jailbreak, criminals illegally flee. Instead, his record now stood clear, paving the way for

Zimmerman's departure. The moment an authorized person granted permission, he could legally leave. Yet he needed to put one foot in front of the other or he remained behind bars. When he practically started to reckon upon the fact of his freedom, only then could he act out his freedom.

Verse 11 builds naturally upon verse 6. Earle helpfully explains:

> Our death to sin which was provisional and potential at Calvary we are to make experiential and actual now. Only as by faith we "reckon" ourselves to be dead to sin can we realize in our hearts what Christ's death has made possible.[128]

In a real sense reckoning does not legally liberate us from sin's grip, for we died when Christ died.

Yet, practically speaking, reckoning appropriates our union with Christ, so in this sense reckoning does make us free. Unfortunately, though, many Christians never leave their prison by reckoning upon the fact of their freedom. A highly important direction for entering the sanctified life involves starting the reckoning process.

This word "reckon" (KJV) does not imply that we guess something *may* be true, as colloquial English employs "reckon." When NASB translates it "consider," one should not think the word means to weigh various options as if to consider whether the notion has worth. Actually, the English word "logistics" ultimately derives from this word.

NIV's word "count" expresses well the technical commercial sense the original word sometimes carries—such as in verse 11. When you claim your layaway after paying its remaining cost, the clerk credits your cash to your account. Both you and the clerk account on the fact that you have paid the complete bill. You both count on it so fully that you receive both a receipt and the long-awaited merchandise. Do you as logically but eagerly count on the fact that you became dead to sin?

Dead to sin

Having once acted upon Romans 6:11, can we forget about counting? No, we have just begun a lifelong process, as implied by the ongoing present tense in the original language. Wuest's translation properly renders it, "you be constantly counting on the fact. . . ." Every day, we can profit from making such a declaration in prayer. Moreover, in the hour when special temptation hits, we will find great victory in firmly standing by the declaration.

What does it mean to treat oneself as dead to sin? The I.C.C. commentary strikingly paints: "In like manner do you Christians regard yourselves as dead, inert and motionless as a corpse, in all that relates to sin. . . ."[129] After a person has died and burial has occurred, sin has lost its attraction. The expression "in Christ Jesus" apparently accompanies union with Christ both in death and in resurrection.

Alive to God

Believers theoretically cannot answer sin's pleas, even as a dead person cannot answer the phone, spend money, or vote. When God calls, however, the Christian answers as fully alive to him. In fact, one now lives all aspects of life in God's presence and fellowship.

Beyond our bodily resurrection, pleasing God constitutes a full-time occupation. Although Lazarus experienced a temporary resuscitation, surely values seemed different. For the dedicated believer, things that once absorbed the energies lose their luster. On the other hand, the risen life of pleasing God right here brings deep satisfaction.

Presentation

Separation: from improper uses

The preservation of human life upon earth depends heavily on the few inches of topsoil that produce crops for food. Improper land use results in washing away valuable topsoil through erosion.

Before conversion, sinners similarly make foul use of the members of their human bodies. Surrendering their bodily organs to sin, they habitually respond to wrong stimuli. Hands steal and harm. Mouths lie, curse, boast, and partake of harmful substances. Feet lead to unwholesome places.

Paul reminds readers that they used to live constantly for sin—to please their carnal nature. Urging changed conduct, he calls Christians to cease allowing this habitual wrong "land use." "Do not go on presenting the members of your body to sin *as* instruments of unrighteousness" (Rom. 6:13).

Except for people enlisting in Satanism, a sinner ordinarily never hands the whole body over to evil in a decisive contract. Instead, as one opportunity follows another to try new ventures, organs and functions almost unconsciously join evil's domain.

First a young woman gives her eyes to watch an evil video, then her desires to covetousness, then her hands to stealing. Now a salesman surrenders his mind to improper fantasies, later his hands to pornography and his eyes to lust, then his mouth to alcohol, then his body to immorality. It is a gradual but a continuing process of submitting.

Because Paul was writing to Rome, a military metropolis, Lange understands "present" as involving enlistment for military service. An "instrument," an implement for accomplishing anything, can denote a weapon—especially in a military context.

Although Lange's idea has some merit, nevertheless, the word "present" itself seems slight justification for calling this a military passage. This same word "present" regularly occurs in the Septuagint, the Greek Old Testament, to refer to offering animal sacrifices to the Lord. The same word appears to have that same thrust in Romans 12:1, as Deissmann confirms.[130] That verse describes "a living and holy sacrifice," not military enlistment. It speaks of a "spiritual service of worship," not military service. Paul wrote Romans 12:1 to the Christians at the same Rome to which he was writing Romans 6:13. In the immediate context of the latter verse, the gratification of wrong desires, rather than war, predominates.

Thus, when a person gives over himself or herself piecemeal to sin, the very bodily parts become tools for the corrupt nature to manipulate, as this passage affirms. Since Satan masterminds the flesh's attack on humanity, bodily parts yielded to the flesh ultimately become tools for evil supernaturalism: "Do not give the devil a foothold" (Eph. 4:27, NIV).

Dedication: full surrender to God

In Romans 6:13, a person once presented bodily members to
sin, but Paul now urges a presentation to a new recipient. In bold
contrast to a gradual surrender to evil, God commands a speedy
and pointed surrender to himself.

Commentators frequently observe the change of Greek tenses.
Whereas the first use of "present" here is a continual present tense,
Paul next employs the aorist tense of the identical verb. Many have
seen in the second use a stress on the decisive yielding to God of
the complete person—as well as all its members. A later chapter of
this book will more carefully investigate the aorist tense. At the
least, one should notice that the aorist does not emphasize continuing action but may express a momentary action—especially if the
context implies this activity. In the verse being analyzed, the
scholarly I.C.C. commentary renders the expression, "dedicate
yourselves once for all."[131]

Greek professor Wuest translates the verse: "Moreover, stop
putting your members at the disposal of the sinful nature as weapons of unrighteousness, but by a once-for-all act and at once, put
yourselves at the disposal of God as those who are actively alive
out from among the dead, and put your members as weapons of
righteousness at the disposal of God. . . ." Similarly, the renowned
Greek grammarian, A.T. Robertson, emphasizes the tense contrast: ". . . do not be in the habit of doing so, 'do not go on putting
your members to sin. . . .'" but in presenting to God, "do it now
and completely."[132]

Trying by their own efforts to live victoriously, many Christians have never made this decisive surrender to God since their
conversion. Only a full surrender prepares us to be the channel
through whom the Holy Spirit can fulfill God's purpose.

The owner of a piece of property can decide whether to walk on
it, build a house on it, or keep it wooded. The will of the owner
must prevail within legal limits. In sanctification as in real estate,
property ownership remains a crucial issue. Although Christ
bought us at Calvary, he awaits our confirmation of this fact by
our willing commitment. That allows him to control the property
he purchased. Remaining unfulfilled without an act of full yield-

O Lord—You have already decided—once
and for all on Christ's priesthood. Christ in
me is continually assenting to this decision in
my own life. Praise Jesus Christ!

ing, human lives need to allow Christ to be Lord more than in name only.

Scripture commands a believer to present to God not only material goods or compartments of the life but one's entire being. The whole person, of course, includes the body's organs, desires, and potentialities. Romans 6:13 specifies the resignation of our individual members and the overall surrender of our person. Even as our continually counting ourselves alive to God rests on our having risen with Christ, so also this surrender recalls that we are alive from the dead. Christ wants to direct us as Christians in the use of all faculties.

Faith

Faith looks back.

Although a knowledge of Scripture's teaching on sanctification proves essential, yet we need more than a knowledge of facts, a reckoning of our position, and a full presentation of ourselves to God. Faith unlocks every spiritual benefit, including sanctification. Seeing the fact of our union with Christ in his death, "we *believe* that we shall also live with him" (Rom. 6:8).

Sanctifying faith builds upon the work of the cross and empty tomb. It cashes in on the victory potentially mine from conversion onward. Believing in the past divine provision, faith also believes in the present possibility of entering the victorious life.

Faith enters in.

Faith, moreover, believes that God accepts my offering of myself and my members, sets me apart, and consecrates all that I dedicate. Faith also trusts that the provision now meets my desperate need.

Perhaps Christians derive their very name "believers" from the current habit of believing God for every need, as well as the past act when we exercised faith to become God's child. Resting upon the promise that a faithful God will sanctify (1 Thess. 5:23-24), faith believes that I receive the desire of my heart—and of his!

Refusing

Romans 6 also shows how essential it is to refuse to be drawn back into the former life. Accounting yourself dead to sin but alive to God, "do not let sin reign in your mortal body that you should obey its lusts" (Rom. 6:12).

Since we died to sin, we should no longer let sin reign. With its authority shattered, we can and must refuse its desires. Entering through the gate into sanctification logically leads to a life of consistent triumph. No triumph comes automatically. When wrong desires arise, however, we can remember whose we are and in Christ can discover how powerful the reckoning process is.

Part 4

Use the Right Ingredients: The Elements of Sanctification

A burning coal . . . "Here am I" . . . . the holy seed
(Isa. 6:6, 8, 13).

Do you know which element makes up much more of our planet's crust than any other? Scientists calculate that over 60 percent of earth's outer layer's volume and nearly half its weight is oxygen. Whereas hydrogen is the lightest of over 100 known elements, uranium has a higher atomic weight than any element that occurs naturally in the world.

In chemistry, *element* denotes any of the fundamental substances that have only one kind of atom. As you probably remember, most substances we see around us are compounds—comprised of two or more elements. Beyond chemistry, *element* has several uses but especially refers to major components that make up anything—one of the parts of a complex whole.

What major elements make up sanctification? A. B. Simpson, the author of some 100 Christian books, on numerous occasions analyzed sanctification as including three elements—separation, dedication, and filling. Sometimes he explained this third element as habitation.

Study of Scripture shows the prominence of these elements in passages treating sanctification. Like oxygen in the world, they are prominent in the Word. In importance, like uranium, however, the elements of sanctification are weighty.

13

Keep Off the Grass: Separation

A burning coal (Isa. 6:6).

Importance of Separation

In contemporary life, what negative images the frigid word *separation* conjures! Sweet are the affections that the bride and groom lavish on each other. Neither has an eye for any competing lover. Yet, with the passing of time, misunderstandings have arisen. A lack of maturity has driven a deeper and deeper wedge between the lovers. Some leftover resentments from childhood hurts have emerged to create present friction. A critical spirit, harsh words, and unwillingness to resolve differences have turned a "forever" romance into a miserable rivalry to see who can hurt the other the most. Next, one decides that the final trump card is separation: "I'm not going to put up with your insults. I'm leaving!" With more maturity, patience, and a determination to put the mate's feelings and happiness first, most problems could find solutions. Separation brings pain.

By contrast, separation can be a pleasant term. Removing the husks before eating from the ears of corn results in a pleasurable experience. Likewise, excluding all rivals from one's affections leads to harmonious accord. "Forsaking all others," intones the minister in the traditional marriage vows.

To make a marriage succeed, both bride and groom choose to refuse to muse on another possible date or mate. Similarly, separation to the Lord involves separation from any opposing loyalty. Even as in commitment to a spouse, so "the Inward Christ . . . is the locus of commitment, not a problem for debate."[133] To be sufficiently in love with Christ should provide abundant motivation for separation.

Enlistment as a soldier involves an absolute separation from the enemies of one's own nation. Successful troops can never waver in loyalty. Despite David's past trustworthy record of valiant forays, the Philistine commanders refused permission to join them in attacking Israel. Surely former loyalty would compel defection to his native land's cause, they reasoned, winning his estranged monarch's favor (1 Sam. 29). Similarly, having forsaken Satan's kingdom to fight for the Lord, the Christian might desert—without drastic separation.

Evils to Avoid

Throughout history various Christian sects have adopted austere practices of one sort or another. For some it was black clothing, living in isolation, or required fasts. In one era a man would live for years on a small platform high in the air to avoid sin. Some individuals even beat themselves violently to kill tendencies toward sinning. Probably each of these far-out examples was practiced as someone's idea of separation from evil.

One current denomination split largely over whether men should wear neckties to church services. Those who opposed ties were not urging informality to attract outsiders to church; instead, they viewed ties as a mark of pride. Now both denominations allow ties. Some fine, Christ-honoring churches have set specific standards for female clothing, shoes, and hairdos. Often Christian groups forbid certain entertainments.

Surely it is not wrong to conform to the standards of a group that we feel led to join. Another vital criterion, however, is personal convictions on right and wrong. Yet the supreme Christian motivation for separation is the need to please Christ. What would

Jesus do? We should be willing to submit everything in life to his scrutiny. Surely in this permissive age, Christ is displeased with occult involvement, seductive clothing, unscriptural moral practices, and entertainments that make it easier to sin. A fine test, then, is whether or not we would or should be embarrassed if Jesus would return and find us in this entertainment, apparel, or habit.

Renunciation of the "right" to choose sin

Following Adam's lead, the sinner retains the possibility of sinning. In addition, the unsaved person finds it impossible to cease from sinning; he or she remains a sinner. One who has experienced the new birth, however, receives the new name "believer" rather than "sinner." Faith in Christ transforms the lifestyle.

Sad to say, some misinformed people today accept conversion as permission to keep on sinning safely. Finney complained against such people as "really seeking to be justified *in* sin. They ask God to pardon them, but they refuse to be sanctified.... They regard the gospel as an abrogation of the moral law."[134]

Scripture warns that "the one who practices sin is of the devil" (1 John 3:8). Practicing sin differs from stumbling into episodes of sin, to which, unfortunately, the Christian remains prone (1 John 1:10). Moreover, although sinning remains a physical possibility, it ceases to be a moral necessity. Now we walk in the light and enjoy continuous cleansing (1 John 1:6-7).

Does the Christian warrior retain the right to sin? No, God's Word urges that we make no provision for sinning—not even once. "... These things I am writing to you in order that you may not commit an act of sin" (1 John 2:1, Wuest). As noted in the previous chapter, Paul meets head-on the question, "Shall we sin because we are not under law but under grace?" With stern disgust he censures such thinking: "May it never be!" (Rom. 6:15). Separation involves a renunciation of the "right" to choose sin.

Severance from the self-life's control

At conversion, the newborn child of God delights in forgiveness, a new relationship with God, and newness of spiritual life. The young Christian enjoys assurance of a blessed eternity with the Redeemer. Generally this new believer, however, does not realize the struggles that lie ahead because the self-life retains control. As the hiker enjoys the level riverside trail, he little realizes how heavily his backpack will burden him trudging up rugged cliffs on the mountain beyond.

Some respected theologians even deny the existence within the Christian of an old nature alongside the new one. Packer, for example, writes: "A widespread but misleading line of teaching tells us that Christians have two natures: an old one and a new one."[135]

Andrew Murray, however, correctly sees the reality of this phenomenon. He observes how unaware one remains of the self-life: "At his conversion the Christian generally has no conception of the terrible evil of his nature. . . ." Carnality even volunteers for God's service, he notes.[136] As the infant Christian seeks to overcome sin problems, he or she spots that inner drive that pulls toward further failures and defeats.

When aspirations soar, a sudden disappointment plunges the struggler into a mucky swamp of defeat. Forgiveness has blotted out the record of sinful acts, but the heart requires cleansing (Acts 15:8, 9). Frederick William Faber begins his graphic poem, "Self-Love":

> Oh I could go through all life's troubles singing,
> Turning earth's night to day,
> If self were not so fast around me, clinging
> To all I do or say.
>
> My very thoughts are selfish, always building
> Mean castles in the air;
> I use my love of others for a gilding
> To make myself look fair.[137]

Before the new Christian can appropriate the new covenant of God's law written in the heart (Heb. 10:16), he or she needs a mighty separation from carnality's control. "It has been found that a deeper appropriation of the blessings of the Covenant must be preceded by a new and deeper cleansing from sin"[138] (Ezek. 36:25-27). Although some theologians see separation as related only to service, G. Campbell Morgan adequately shows that it must relate first to the self-life.

Abandonment to God is not merely the act of enlisting as
soldiers to fight battles—that is a secondary matter; it is
first the abandonment of self to the Spirit of God, that He
may purify and cleanse from everything that is unlike His
own perfection of beauty.[139]

Positionally and theoretically Christ's death and resurrection
have made full provision for victorious living. The Christian needs
to flip the switch to begin experiencing the dynamo of energy already there in the power lines. Continuation involves keeping the
switch open.

Our position in Christ is automatic; as in all aspects of Christian
living, however, one must appropriate the divine provisions. "Unused weapons do not inflict casualties on the enemy nor win
wars."[140] Counting oneself "dead to sin denotes, in the strongest
possible manner, complete separation through the death of Christ
from all sin."[141] Thus, a vital element in sanctification comprises a
separation from the self-life's control.

Detachment from the world system's pull

Separation also involves a decision and habit of detachment
from the world system's pull. Even as the devil uses an internal enemy, the self-life, to bring bondage, so he makes use of an external
foe—the world system. Paul wrote: "And do not be conformed to
this world" (Rom. 12:2). The present imperative verb carries the
connotation, "Stop being continually conformed."

The uncommitted Christian must put on the brakes immediately. Next, remembering where to find the brakes in daily living
remains vital. Since the world's values and the Lord's values mix
like oil and water, decisive separating proves essential. A sure way
to spiritual schizophrenia is the attempt to live by the laws of both
God's kingdom and Satan's.

J.B. Phillips vividly paraphrases this line in Romans 12:2:
"Don't let the world around you squeeze you into its own mold."
To form people according to his pattern, the enemy uses ploys like
peer pressure, employers and friends with dominant personalities,
and the godless lifestyle portrayed by secular media. We hesitate
offending an uncommitted mate or buddy.

The world system denotes the present age, a period of time and space under enemy control, as opposed to the kingdom of God. "By the *world*, John means human society apart from Christ and opposed to God. . . ."[142] As a magnet attracts a steel ball, the world attracts people, appealing to their twisted self-life.

Involving more an attitude than specific evil actions, the world focuses on wrong desire. John warns: "Do not love the world, nor the things in the world. If any one loves the world, the love of the Father is not in him" (1 John 2:15). Next he summarizes the world's attractions as "the lust of the flesh and the lust of the eyes and the boastful pride of life." Such toys represent transitory rather than permanent objects (1 John 2:16-17).

The lust of the flesh is human desire that springs from the fallen nature. It focuses on the wrong use of the sex, worship, ambition, drink, and food/pleasure drives (Gal. 5:19-21).

The lust of the eye includes any disobedience to the tenth commandment. Centering on an inordinate yearning for money and possessions, it impels us toward whatever God's law forbids. When she gazed on the forbidden tree, Eve found it pleasing to the eyes, even as Gehazi craved the clothing and wealth that Elisha had wisely scorned. David's look at Bathsheba led to other shocking sins.

The boastful pride of life uplifts self as the cause and hub of one's blessings. This pride egotistically prizes peer pressure, public image, status symbols, and keeping up with the Joneses—above God's praise.

God's remedy for worldliness involves separation, which releases the Spirit's power. "The power of the Spirit does not work like a steamroller: it does not crush but rather empowers human life. It liberates from bondage rather than sanctioning old bondages or introducing new ones."[143]

Renunciation of satanic compromise

Masterminding his constant war against God, Satan is the rebel who also marshals evil supernaturalism against all those made in God's image. In other words, he who uses the world system from without and the fallen nature within human victims, will add his personal word of appeal. Since Satan lacks omnipresence, he normally speaks through external demonic spirits who flash to a human mind thoughts of compromise and yielding. "Do it," they urge.

In the words of Ed Murphy,

> The church is revealed in Scripture . . . as a part of God's warrior kingdom in ongoing conflict with internal evil (the flesh), social evil (the world), and supernatural evil (the spirit world). I call this a multidimensional sin war.[144]

Do powers of evil operate in this way upon a believer? Yes, since they already clench an unsaved person securely in their grasp (Eph. 2:2), Christians are prime targets (2 Cor. 11:2-4). In Matthew's record, the same Peter who confessed Jesus as "the Christ, the Son of the living God" (Matt. 16:16), immediately sought to dissuade Jesus from the cross (Matt. 16:22). Jesus, who had just commended Peter's confession as divinely revealed (Matt. 16:17), turned and withstood Peter. Jesus commanded: "Get behind me, Satan! . . . for you are not setting your mind on God's interests, but man's" (Matt. 16:23). The director of Frontline Ministries writes:

> I believe the half-truths, the untruths, and the outright lies that undermine the word of the Lord eventually find their origin in the "father of lies." Satan injected into the minds of the first humans the poisonous power of mistrust, pride, unbelief, self-reliance, and shame in failure.[145]

Whenever humans unconsciously cede ground to him through wrong speech, actions, or attitudes, the enemy seeks to establish a beachhead through the forces of darkness at his disposal (Eph. 4:27). Despite his promises, his "irresistible" offers never provide lasting good for people.

In fact, he has adopted deception as his constant game plan. His henchmen prepare a studied strategy for defeating each individual human being. Although some tricks have proven widely effective, yet the traps that fool your neighbor may not fool you. Wicked spirits know our *own* weakest areas. They have been succeeding in the same work for thousands of years. Hence, our compromising with Satan is most foolish. It is never wise. It is always very dangerous. Only total separation from the evil kingdom is safe.

Sanctification mostly involves separation from the flesh—counting ourselves dead with Christ unto sin. When someone asked George Mueller his secret of being such a fruitful Christian, he replied: "There came a day when George Mueller died, *utterly died!* No longer did his own desires, preferences, and tastes come first. He knew that from then on Christ must be all in all!"

Hence, to live a fruitful, Christ-filled life, the first step for today's believer also involves the separation of death. Freligh helpfully explains that "the only way in which we can sanctify ourselves is in this negative aspect of separation."[146] One must set his or her mind against choosing sin and begin a lifelong reckoning process against control by the flesh.

Our chief opponent, however, constantly uses a triad of evil—the world and evil supernaturalism as well as the flesh. Thus, instead of conformity, a believer should practice detachment from the world system, its values, mores, methods, and lifestyle. "It is said that the ermine can be trapped by surrounding it with a circle of filth. It will die before it will sully its snowy coat."[147] Compromise with Satan must never seem an option.

14

Last Thing Someone Wants to Give Up— Oneself: Dedication

Here am I (Isa. 6:8).

In hockey, Gordie Howe remained devoted as a true athlete from the 1940s until the early 1980s. He distinguished himself as the first team athlete in a professional sport on the American continent to maintain a career through parts of five decades. After setting many records playing for the Detroit Red Wings for 25 years, he skated with other teams. As a grandfather at age 52 he attained honor as an NHL all-star for a record 22nd time. By contrast, believers appear to "play" the Christian life as flabby apathetic spectators—exerting effort only when it is convenient.

Discipline characterizes a true athlete. The worthwhile athlete has fully dedicated himself or herself without reserve to achieving success in playing and winning the game.

A life of dedication begins with a full surrender, even as an athlete makes a conscious decision to give himself to the sport of his or her choice. Although separation teaches us what to avoid, dedication prepares us to devote ourselves without reserve to God for a lifetime. Dedication forms an absolutely necessary part of sanctification.

Christ gave himself without reserve for us. Why should God accept less than every part of us—surrendered without reserve? A partial dedication amounts to no dedication at all. Only when he has every bit of a person can he or she live the Christ-life and serve selflessly as he intends through the power he imparts.

Motives

Why should the Christian present his or her body to the Lord in full dedication? Several inescapable motives provide just rationale.

God's revealed truth

Which is more vital—doctrine or lifestyle? The newest trends among our contemporaries tend to become soon impatient with theological issues. We hear questions like "Isn't how you behave more important than what you believe?" "If I behave properly, isn't that what God most desires?"

We should answer the contemporary inquirer, "Actually no; what *we* do cannot save or sanctify us since we already have both a sinful record and a sinful nature." A practice-oriented Christian society is in danger of falling into a works mentality all too similar to that of the cults.

The heart of the gospel is the truth that God has a righteousness to give us when we believe the divine message. Also, we cannot sanctify ourselves either; we must believe the truth and accept God's provision. Then we can depend on his holiness and power rather than trying to generate our own.

Paul refuses to sweep doctrine away as unimportant. He sees it as absolutely essential. Doctrine is the indispensable foundation for building a victorious lifestyle. Tozer warns his century of the necessity of understanding theology.

> The failure of contemporary Christianity to understand the vital importance of theology has greatly weakened the churches and given us a scrubby and degenerate type of Christian that can scarcely be distinguished from the sons of the world. A flabby humanism of the modern church, touched lightly with pale and bloodless Christianity, is not producing spiritual giants these days.[148]

In some of Paul's letters, one can easily discern that he expounds doctrine before beginning a highly practical application of truth to daily living. Romans is such a book.

In Romans 12:1, the word *therefore* appears to form a bridge between the doctrinal portion of Romans (chs. 1-11) and the practical portion (chs. 12-16). Having shown that all people as sinners lack the righteousness that God requires (Rom. 1:1-3:20), Paul has explained that God himself, through Christ's death and resurrection, has provided a righteousness to give the sinner who accepts it (Rom. 3:21-5:21). He called this good news the gospel (Rom. 1:16).

Furthermore, Paul has shown God's great concern about holy living. God himself has provided in the gospel and through the Holy Spirit's work of application that the justified person can escape the bondage of the sin nature (Rom. 6-8).   Sanctification is available.

After elaborating on sanctification, Paul has introduced the topic of the believer's future hope, which the theologian calls personal eschatology. Personal eschatology concerns what lies ahead for the individual beyond death (Rom. 8:15-25).

Paul next embarks on racial eschatology—a study of what lies ahead in world history at the end of the age and beyond it (Rom. 9-11). Racial eschatology concerns not only the human race but larger divisions within it, especially Israel, the Church, and the Gentile nations. Paul shows that God will again send Jesus "the Deliverer" at the end of the age (Rom. 11:26). God has a good future in store for his people, both individually and racially.

Thus, Paul has already built the necessary foundation of right doctrine (Rom. 1-11). As he introduces the practical implications of right doctrine to a holy, useful lifestyle, he uses *therefore* to bridge these two major sections.

In summary, his *"therefore* bridge" spans backward to God's (1) gift of righteousness to lost sinners, (2) provision of sanctification for struggling believers, and (3) glorious future plans for his people. The Romans 12:1-2 *therefore* bridge reaches forward to present and continuing obligations. Because of God's rich provisions, *therefore*, make sure to present your bodies to him to be able to live that holy, gifted, useful life, as he directs (Rom. 12:3-16:27).

One major motive then for presenting our bodies in dedication to the Lord is that this presentation is a key part of God's revealed truth. Without presenting ourselves in dedication, it is inconsistent to say that we have believed the doctrine in the New Testament's richest doctrinal book—Paul's epistle to the Romans.

What we truly believe we act upon. Paul writes that, in view of God's spectacular plan of redemption, each reader must be sure to present his body to God.

God's abundant mercies

The Bible's most familiar verse on Christian dedication promptly gives a motive for requiring it: "I urge you therefore, brethren, by the mercies of God, to present your bodies..." (Rom. 12:1).

In Romans 9-12, Paul focuses on racial Israel. He shows a bit of God's present treatment and—as shown above more generally—his future plans for them. Although most racial Israelites have not availed themselves of salvation through Christ, yet Paul marvels in God's mercy (1) in making salvation available to individual Israelites now and (2) in bringing the racial Israelites to repentance when Christ returns. Then living Israelites will take advantage of salvation because of God's great mercy (Rom. 11:26-27).

As many Gentiles now receive mercy, "so these [Israelites] also now have been disobedient, ... that because of the mercy shown to you they also may now be shown mercy. For God has shut up all in disobedience that He might show mercy to all" (Rom. 11:30-32). Thus, the immediate context reveals to what kind of mercy Paul was appealing in urging dedication. In response to God's abundant mercies shown to you, says Paul, be quick to present yourself in full dedication.

God's supreme love

God so loved the world that he gave his Son for our redemption (1 John 4:9-10). Christ so loved us that he gave his life to redeem us: "Christ also loved you, and gave Himself up for us" (Eph. 5:2).

As a husband's love should evoke love from his wife, so divine love to the believer should awaken a love response that gives itself without sparing (Eph. 5:25-28). You cannot trust just any stranger. You can trust yourself to the one who loved you so much that he surrendered his life to rescue you and provide for your sanctification.

God's supreme wisdom

Are you willing to trust your brand new Oldsmobile with a person whom you know to be a reckless drunkard, who is very irresponsible, unlicensed, and insolvent? On the other hand, if your careful, sober, responsible, licensed, solvent husband has lovingly given you that new Oldsmobile, would you consider lending it to him for a day?

The God who asks you to present your body to him is the one who made you and gave you life itself. Since he is humanity's creator and sustainer, no one should question his wisdom.   Since he had a plan for your life before your birth, why question whether he knows best where you should live or what you should do? He alone has the wisdom necessary for living the most fruitful life possible.

God's sovereign request

Secular humanists often hold that no creator exists since everything here somehow spontaneously evolved to its present state. Hence, no cosmic creator exists out there to care for us.

Others suggest that the immense number of human beings now in existence argues that no god could possibly have concern for each individual. To underscore this immensity one can travel to one of the world's huge metropolises to watch the throngs crowding onto mass transit lines at rush hour.

Yet Jesus assured us that not one sparrow falls without the heavenly Father's knowledge. Moreover, he affirmed that human beings are of much more value than sparrows and that he has numbered the very hairs of our heads (Matt. 10:29-31).

Scripture urges us to "fear God and keep His commandments." It affirms that this direction applies "to every person because God will bring every act to judgment, everything which is hidden . . ." (Eccl. 12:13-14). Hence, God fully knows every person, every act, and everything hidden by every person.

The psalmist wrote:

O LORD, Thou hast searched me and known *me*.
Thou dost know when I sit down and when I rise up;
Thou dost understand my thought from afar.
Thou dost scrutinize my path and my lying down,
And art intimately acquainted with all my ways.
Even before there is a word on my tongue,
Behold, O LORD, Thou dost know it all (Ps. 139:1-4).

An infinite God, who is sovereign over all things, exhaustively knows everything about each individual.

The very striking revelation that such a God desires our fellowship amazes us. The reason a Christian should refuse to consider himself or herself worthless is because such an all-knowing God yearns for our friendship. This sovereign God requests that we present our bodies to him. Paul guarantees that the body so presented is "acceptable to God." This appeal provides a strong motive for our dedicating ourselves.

The language of the inspired text is touching: "I urge you," Paul wrote, using the Greek verb related to the name *Parakletos*, our Paraclete, possibly a personal name of the Holy Spirit. English translations use such words as Helper, Comforter, Counselor, Advocate to express the word's shades of meaning to explain the Spirit's work. R.A. Torrey suggests constructing some compound English words to convey more fully its meaning, viz., Part-taker and Standbyer.[149]

The verb, *parakaleo*, used in Romans 12:1 etymologically means, "I call you to my side to make this earnest request." Some versions translate it "exhort," "beg," "beseech," "entreat," "appeal to," or "plead with." How can a sincere Christian refuse him?

God's practical goal

When children play boss, they sometimes order their playmates to do things to make them look silly. God does not order us to do things irrationally or for his fun. We are not his puppets on a string. His goal in asking our self-surrender is that we "may prove what the will of God is, that which is good and acceptable and perfect" (Rom. 12:2). Since he is all-wise and all-loving, he wants what is best for us. He wants to empower us to show forth his will in our lives.

Areas

Body

Why does Paul urge Christians to yield their bodies to God? Several responses are possible.

Some evangelicals today adopt a holistic or monistic view, believing that the human person in this life comprises one indissoluble whole—not two or three parts. If this view is accurate, then perhaps Scripture is not intending to distinguish physical from non-physical entities when it tells believers to present their bodies. Erickson, a conditional monist, sees sanctification as involving more than "one part of human nature, for no one part of man is the exclusive seat of good or of righteousness."[150]

If the holistic view is incorrect, then separable divisions exist. Even so, the body in Romans 12:1 may be a synecdoche—a symbol for everything that pertains to us. Weymouth translates the body as "all your faculties." Freligh comments: "Obviously if God has our bodies, He also has our whole being—spirit and soul as well."[151] After all, if the body dies, we cease from our current stage of existence so that we could no longer make earthly decisions. If the body dies, death affects the entire personality. Apparently the spirit leaves the body at death (James 2:26).

Why does Scripture command that we yield our bodies? If "body" is neither a word nor a figure of speech for the whole person, perhaps it occurs because the immediate context refers to presenting a sacrifice to God. Even as an offerer slew a lamb's body in Old Testament times, so now the believer must commit his or her human body totally to God.

A fourth possible view is that "body" simply means body since the surrender of the body forms a key role in sanctification. For one reason or another, many reliable commentators understand the word body here quite literally. Godet, for example, writes, "The victim to be offered is *the body* of the believer. Many regard *the body* as representing the entire person. But why not in that case say . . . *yourselves?*"[152]

In favor of this fourth position is Romans 6:12-13, that singles out the present mortal body as the place where the believer must refuse to let sin reign. Previously these Romans had each been pre-

senting the members of that body to sin. Now each must *present*
(the same Greek word as in Romans 12:1) themselves to God and
their *members* as instruments of righteousness to God. Although
some of the other arguments seem attractive, this scriptural parallel seems to tip the scales in favor of the fourth view.

Adopting the fourth view need not rule out the third view,
which helps to complete the picture. Every part of our body must
be yielded. Although we do not kill the body physically, we do
count it crucified with Christ to sin and alive to God. Thus we
present ourselves a living sacrifice. A person should live every
facet of life in the body for God's glory.

Soul

God desires to cleanse and keep free the entire personality—not
simply the physical body. Paul prayed for the Thessalonians:
"Now may the God of peace Himself sanctify you entirely; and
may your spirit and soul and body be preserved complete, without
blame at the coming of our Lord Jesus Christ" (1 Thess. 5:23).

Those who defend the idea that the human person has three essential parts often find support in this verse. Called trichotomists,
they distinguish the spirit from the soul. Often they understand
the soul as including the mind, emotions, and will.

Mind. Often writers have shown that thoughts lead to actions,
which in turn lead to habits, which combined form a person's
character. Scripture says, "As he thinks within himself, so he is"
(Prov. 23:7).

Satan accomplishes most—if not all—of his work through deception; the human mind becomes the major victim of this deception. It is no wonder that the enemy targets the mind to inject foul
thoughts, misconceptions, and wrong plans.

The unsanctified mind does not fulfill Christ's first commandment to love God with the whole mind (Matt. 22:37; Mark 12:30;
Luke 10:27). The unsanctified mind centers on self and remains
open to satanic suggestions. Jesus' stinging words to Peter, mentioned earlier, blamed Satan and Peter for the wrong control of his
mind: "Get behind Me, Satan! You are a stumbling block to Me;

for you are not setting your mind on God's interests, but man's" (Matt. 16:23).

Warning that the carnal mind remains hostile and insubordinate to God, Paul contrasts two mind-sets—carnal and Spirit-filled. "For the mind set on the flesh is death, but the mind set on the Spirit is life and peace" (Rom. 8:6-7). How does an improper mind-set work today?

Although Satan and the self-life use varied ploys, some of the most common include negative thoughts against God, against oneself as a Christian, and against other people. Even as the enemy told Eve, "Indeed, has God said . . . ?" instilling doubt about God's goodness, today he calls God unjust, uncaring, harsh (Gen. 3:1). The accuser of the brethren conveys doubt about a Christian's worth, salvation, and acceptance with God. The tempter fills the mind with sexually impure thoughts, calls attention to others' faults, and plagues the memory with brutal offenses sustained in childhood.

How does a person discard the deadly mind-set, breaking out of the dangerous habit of wrong thinking? The Holy Spirit wants to renew that mind (Eph. 4:23). When we deliberately set our renewed minds on the things above, we can let them dwell on positive, profitable things (Col. 3:2; Phil. 4:8). Sanctification's new covenant involves the inscription of God's very law on the human mind. "For by one offering He has perfected for all time those who are sanctified. . . . UPON THEIR MIND I WILL WRITE [MY LAWS]" (Heb. 10:14-16).

Emotions. God wants Christians to dedicate their emotions to him. Although Scripture does not seem to employ the collective word "emotions," it often warns against control by individual emotional sins. For example, Ephesians 4:31 directs: "Let all bitterness and wrath and anger and clamor and slander be put away from you, along with all malice." "Bitterness" suggests the way we allow hateful feelings to create pungent unpleasantness toward others and to chafe our own soul.

Whereas anger is the general term, wrath is "hot anger,"[153] and clamor suggests loud outbursts and tantrums. While slander refers to the evil speaking that often springs from angry feelings, malice as stored-up anger is the opposite of clamor. When one lets his or her rage loose, others are sometimes irreparably injured. Hoarding malice, however, we often blast others in some later argument plus hurting our emotional, physical, and spiritual health in the meantime. We gain no peace of mind by giving someone else a piece of our minds.

One should not deny the fact of angry feelings but should surrender them to Christ and then work toward practical solutions. Unfortunately some form of anger controls many Christians to one degree or another. Anger both gives the devil a foothold and grieves the Holy Spirit (Eph. 4:26-27, 30-31).

Since Scripture tells us 365 times not to fear—once for every day of the year—apparently God knew that fear is wrong rather than inconvenient. Irrational fear involves an unbelief reaction toward God. Supposedly something will happen in which God cannot protect.

Jealousy takes the self-life's attitude rather than the Christ-life's. Anxiety and worry show a stronger fixation on unknown troubles than on the Lord's mighty resources to keep his children.

Depression often results from harboring negative feelings toward ourselves, God, or others. Often it relates to self-deprecation (failure to accept what God says about us as Christians) or self-pity (resenting God's permitting our lot in life).

On the darkest night of Jesus' earthly life—the night of Gethsemane, betrayal, and unjust trial—he had enough inner joy to share. He told his disciples, "These things I have spoken to you, that My joy may be in you, and that your joy may be made full" (John 15:11). A bit later he prayed similarly for those disciples "that they may have My joy made full in themselves" (John 17:13). After years of unjust imprisonment, Paul wrote to the Philippians, "Rejoice in the Lord always; again I will say, rejoice" (Phil. 4:4; see 1 Thess. 5:16).

Controlled by wrong emotions, the carnal Christian usually finds little success in Christian work. Thus, surrendering our emotional life to the Lord's sanctifying power is an essential key to overcoming. God's plan includes our feeling what Christ would have us feel in addition to having the mind of Christ.

Will. The mind and emotions represent two of the soul's prominent features. Palmer correctly notes that "the Holy Spirit causes the *whole* of man to be affected in sanctification. . . . He sanctifies all of man: his will, his emotions, and his understanding."[154] The will represents the central decision-making function of personality. It stands in a much higher category than the title to the car or the deed to the property.

The surrender of the will is the supreme surrender. After describing presenting various members of her body to God—as well as possessions and the intellect—in earlier stanzas, Frances Ridley Havergal wrote:

> Take my will, and make it Thine;
> It shall be no longer mine.
> Take my heart; it is Thine own;
> It shall be Thy royal throne.

With the will fully surrendered to God, he can grant the believer freedom to claim the divine renewal. "The will boldly dares to do the deed and take the heavenly gift . . . and accept our heritage as a present possession."[155]

Spirit

Since some Scriptures appear to use "soul" and "spirit" interchangeably, many suppose that they are two words describing the same element of the human being. Those who distinguish them speak of the spirit as the part of us that possesses God-consciousness, the capacity for communion with God.

Logically, while the body relates us to the animal kingdom, the soul grants self-consciousness and relates us to fellow human beings. The spirit relates us to the realm of spirits, and supremely to God. Every unregenerate individual has bodily life discernible through medical examination. Although the unregenerate has a living soul—provable through self-conscious thinking, emoting, and willing, that person is spiritually dead. Jesus explained that "that which is born of the Spirit is spirit" (John 3:6).

The sorest and most recurring problem in the Old Testament was Israel's engaging in idolatry. Several prophets condemn this abomination as spiritual adultery. Hosea's own family experiences

form a vivid illustration of God's love for his people but his utter
disgust with their idolatry. The human spirit largely sins through
idolatry. Idolatry prefers some other source of power and information rather than Jehovah. Idolatry gives devotion and sacrifices to
the no-gods, whom Scripture calls demons (1 Cor. 10:20).

Many contemporary Christians have broken the first commandment by using occult objects and methods for deriving information about the future or power over some situation. More often
than not they have *played* with horoscopes, ouija boards, tarot
cards, Dungeons and Dragons, hex signs, magic healing practices,
fortune-telling, or séances for fun! Some have made a pact with
Satan at some point of frustration when God did not seem to be
answering their prayers as they desired.

Too often these Christians have never seriously repented of, renounced, and retracted ground from the enemy for these sins of
the spirit. At times such Christians minimize or justify such actions.

The dedicated spirit is spiritually alert to reject occult or
worldly practices that offend God. It longs for fellowship with
God in prayer. A. B. Simpson observes that:

> A dedicated spirit is thus wholly given to God, to know
> Him, to choose His will, to resemble His character, to trust
> His Word, to love Him supremely, to glorify Him only, to
> enjoy Him wholly and to belong to Him utterly, unreserv-
> edly, and forever. All its senses, susceptibilities and capaci-
> ties are dedicated to Him.[156]

Total personality and possessions

What does God desire of us in dedication? He wants our family,
our possessions, our "rights," our time, and everything that pertains to us. He wants our money.

Prussian King Frederick William III invited ladies to contribute
gold and silver jewelry to melt and make into money to save the
kingdom from financial collapse. Those who complied received a
crude iron or bronze souvenir reading, "I gave gold for iron—1813."
The King of kings gratefully receives our material wealth for world
evangelism, especially when it comes as a loving sacrifice. Full dedication includes dedication of all that we call ours.

Much more, though, he asks for ourselves, our total personality—for all we are. He wants our dearest idol—whether part of us or ours.

Often one hindrance will loom as insurmountable. At times it seems infinitesimal in contrast to everything already committed to God. Yet if it comes between a human being and God, it forms a massive mountain.

Sometimes this obstacle is a besetting sin, a bad habit never overcome, bitterness long hidden, a future aspiration, or some forbidden person. Perhaps God requires that person to rest on his altar—figuratively but as surely as Isaac at Moriah. Without this "single act of surrender, . . . faith could not lay hold of the blessing which was in full sight." One thing can become to a soul "the test of its surrender to obey in everything."[157] One comments that "the reason so few people are filled with the Spirit is that so few completely turn over to Him control of every realm."[158]

Future service

Beyond what we are, we need to present to him our unknown future, our potentialities, our decisions on where to live and what to do with our lives. Youth today in western cultures feel driven by a strong profit motive. Finances and personal security for the future are among the major motives for selecting an occupation. Most Christians have little thought of enlisting to reach unevangelized millions or to minister to urgent spiritual needs nearby. Families immerse themselves in their own needs.   Likewise most people who retire early do so for ease, not to minister.

If we are Christ's servants, however, then he is the Master who can send us where he will. Even today God is calling workers. Some respond favorably.

Distinguishing God's program (Go ye) from God's method (endued with power), Freligh explains. "Without an individual enduement of the Spirit," he asserts, "no person is prepared to be an effective witness."[159] If we allow His Spirit to lead and empower us, he will grant us the life that he knows is best for us and also best for the kingdom. He can supply the spiritual power to make that life and service effective.

Finality

When Paul begged his Christian readers to present their bodies, he intended that act to be a permanent commitment.   The verb used for "present" appears in the Greek version of the Old Testament at the offering of the required animal sacrifices to Almighty God. Worshipers solemnly presented these offerings for death. Although we may live for some time on earth beyond the moment of our dedication, the dedication has a serious finality in it.

After offering a lamb to God, no Israelite would have considered returning to the altar with a request like: "Say, priest, some guests just arrived at our house. My wife sent me over to see whether we can get a few lamb chops for dinner."

Sincere worshipers brought sacrifices to God with no reserve and no regrets. Our whole selves, too, must belong to God forever. In "The Acquiescence of Pure Love," Madam Guyon vividly cried:

> Love! if thy destined sacrifice am I,
> Come, slay thy victim, and prepare Thy fires;
> Plunged in Thy depths of mercy, let me die
> The death which every soul that lives desires.[160]

Thus, this presentation implies a desperate act—fully decisive. In many ways, dedication represents the last thing a person wants to give up—himself or herself. It is a voluntary act; it involves an act of the will. Not mere ecstasy, dedication connotes a practical act—an enlistment for service. Remembering all that Christ has accomplished for us, the act is reasonable, logical, right. God assures the presenter that this consecration is an acceptable act. Do you give up?

15

Jesus' Permanent Address— You: Habitation

The holy seed (Isa. 6:13).

The average time a person resides at the same address has been dropping remarkably. Mobility has emerged as a striking feature of contemporary Western culture. When someone asks a college student the part of the country he or she considers home, often the youth shows a puzzled expression. Employment shifts, military transfers and crumbling marriages all contribute to this condition. Third world emerging countries often experience much transition as multitudes flock to the cities from the countryside.

Where does the Lord Jesus Christ reside? "Everywhere," did you say? As deity he resides everywhere. "In heaven," someone else responds (John 16:28). Yes, and in the hearts of believers. His glorified, ascended body remains in heaven, but through the Holy Spirit, he makes the believer's heart his home. His purpose remains to abide forever (Matt. 28:20).

Beyond his omnipresence, habitation involves his choice of manifesting his presence in the hearts of those who have separated from evil and dedicated themselves to God. The Christian who concentrates on Christ's habitation

143

within has mastered a wondrous secret of the deeper life (Col.
1:27).

One of A.B. Simpson's favorite expressions for sanctification
was the Christ Life. Morris A. Inch correctly observes that "biblical holiness must always point beyond itself toward Christ. As
Christ is the center, holiness consists in approaching the center."[161]

Habitation refers to the indwelling of the Lord Jesus Christ
within the yielded believer through the work of the Holy Spirit.
Jesus shows that since the Day of Pentecost, each member of the
Trinity chooses to abide within every sanctified Christian (John
14:18, 23, 26).

In a Russian palace in an earlier period hung 850 portraits of
charming young ladies—all created for empress Catherine II by
the same skillful painter. Throughout Russia's provinces Rotari,
the artist, had traveled to find his models. The fascinating feature
is that Rotari deliberately crafted every painting to include a par-
tially-concealed resemblance of Catherine.

Similarly, God has conceived his plan of beautifying every
Christian to include the spiritual image of Christ. This can occur
as the believer allows the Sanctifier to live out his graces through
the yielded Christian.

Beforehand God planned that we should become "conformed to
the image of His Son" (Rom. 8:29). As Catherine lived in every
portrait, so also much more literally Christ desires to live within
every believer (John 15:4; 17:23).

Indwelling

Why separate? Logically, a believer separates himself from the
evil realm—and especially from the evil within—so he or she can
be dedicated to God—a *holy* living sacrifice (Rom. 12:1). Why dedicate? A believer dedicates himself or herself totally to the Lord
that Christ may establish his permanent address within the Christian.

What does it mean that in sanctification a believer allows Christ
to live his own holy life out through the separated, dedicated personality? Christ's thoughts fill one's mind. Feeling through one's
yielded emotions, Christ is acting through one's surrendered
body. It is not that we become helpless robots but rather that he

supplies the purity and power to make the believer's life victorious
and productive.

Implies an occupation by a whole person

It is not some thoughts, some energy, or some emotions of a person that want to abide in us sometimes. In habitation, a whole person occupies us—always. That person is God. Frederick W. Faber
poetically wrote on "The Holy Spirit":

> Thou art a sea without a shore;
> Awful, immense Thou art;
> A sea which can contract itself
> Within my narrow heart.[162]

Although the highest heaven cannot enclose God (2 Chron.
6:18), yet he chose to tabernacle among human beings in the very
person of Jesus Christ (John 1:14). The marvel of the nativity involves the arrival of God. Relating Old Testament prophecy to the
nativity account, Matthew explained, "'THEY SHALL CALL
HIS NAME IMMANUEL,' which translated means, 'GOD
WITH US' " (Matt. 1:23).

All the fullness of the Godhead dwelt in him in bodily form
(Col. 2:9). Now he chooses to make his permanent residence
within the human person who trusts in him. Paul wrote in a significant sanctification verse: "Christ lives in me" (Gal. 2:20).

Would I live just as I now do if I truly believed that the holy,
humble, divine Lord Jesus Christ is now living within me? Sanctification involves allowing him to enter every part of a believer at
all times. It involves intentionally behaving as though he is
there—because he actually is.

Implies an occupation of the whole human person

Human beings sometimes crave privacy. Perhaps we would suffer embarrassment around others because we sense that certain actions done alone are wrong. Surely those unkind words spoken
under the breath are wrong, and perhaps that idleness is wrong. If
moodiness or anger dominates the emotions, perhaps one would
suffer shame around people.

Some solitary individuals always feel inadequate around people. Surely, they say, people would not approve of my looks, my words, or my behavior. Perhaps aloneness insulates us from real or perceived criticism. Surely being alone allows us to do what we like—or to do nothing. Probably loners perceive being alone as less threatening than being in the company of others—at least at times.

Habitation, on the other hand, involves inviting someone to be with us every moment, constantly. We never breathe without Jesus' very presence. Do you really want Jesus to be living in you always—through joys, sorrows, disappointments, struggles, and victories? If they would think through the implications of the request, possibly many who keep praying for sanctification would instead beg, "Please Lord, do *not* sanctify me."

In reality, however, the Lord is present everywhere at all times whether or not we invite him to make his home within us (Matt. 28:20). He knows all we think, do, and say. He knows what we refuse or fail to accomplish.

Surely then, we ought to recognize his presence and allow that presence to transform us. Paul appeals to fellow Christians: "be transformed by the renewing of your mind, that you may prove what the will of God is, that which is good and acceptable and perfect" (Rom. 12:2). Habitation, then, involves a transformation to enable us to test, taste, and know the divine will. The person who trusts God for the Spirit's fullness can only then discern and show in life God's will—not one's own.

Implies constant residing, not a visit

Often moderns know how to grit their teeth and put up with an unpleasant predicament because they realize it will pass. If a person knows that a detour will result in a finer highway, he or she can suffer the inconvenience. If the supper guest in your home proves ungrateful and insulting, you manage to smile regardless—since he is your husband's boss. The evening will soon finish.

Habitation, however, involves a continuing constant relationship. By contrast with the insulting boss, Christ is the most desirable, most considerate companion. To the yielded Christian, his assurance of remaining provides sweetest consolation. The caller intends to remain as a permanent resident. He does not arrive and depart as an overnight tourist. Declaring, "I WILL NEVER DESERT YOU, NOR WILL I EVER FORSAKE YOU" (Heb. 13:5), our Lord will stay with us and stand by us.

Implies intended relationship/fellowship

In habitation we are inviting this our Master to share himself with us fully, to enable us to live to please him at all times in all ways. On the other hand, we choose to share our lives fully with him. In other words, we are asking, "Please live in me always. Help me not to grieve you. Help me not to get in the way of your doing in and through me all you desire."

If we invite guests to our home for dinner and proceed to ignore them, surely they would consider us rude. Never speaking to him and never consulting his wisdom, Christians too often ignore Christ.

He wants to occupy every single room in our daily lives. Habitation involves including him, fellowshipping with him, and honoring him.

Implies direction of life

The host would be shocked if an invited friend would ask him to remodel the dining room to her specifications, obtain new employment, and rework the family budget. Inviting company for a meal does not mean that the guest can begin to control every household activity. Yet when a person invites someone to move in and become a part of the life of the household, he or she often will eventually share in some of the family's decisions.

Christ, however, comes not as a temporary guest but a permanent resident, as already discussed. Since he is also Creator and Lord of the whole universe, the only wise decision will allow him to direct fully the person who receives him as a companion. I must not be a dictator even within my own life. I must not be part of a democracy in which my friends and I make a majority decision. I must not allow a partnership in which the Lord and I share the decision making. I must allow him to reign. He will not oppress.

Filling

Scripture uses several terms to describe the divine indwelling. Filling, a favorite Lukan term, enjoys wide usage today, by authors who approach the subject from varied theological viewpoints.

Touching on a crucial distinction that used to be taken for granted, contemporary professor Morris A. Inch accurately alerts readers to see that "believers *have* the Spirit indwelling them, but are not necessarily *filled* with the Spirit. To be filled with the Spirit is to be in submission to the Spirit. It requires that we yield to God's will without reservation."[163] "That there are scores of Christian people who are not filled with the Holy Spirit is an all too evident fact,"[164] G. Campbell Morgan explains.

Involves a level of control

Fullness implies control by whatever substance or person does the filling. A jar already filled with peanut butter cannot at the same time hold a pint of milk. The peanut butter already controls the volume within the jar, regardless of its size or shape.

Even as unhindered inhabitation by one who is Lord implies control, similarly, *fullness* of the Spirit necessarily requires his control. When a Christian remains full of self, he or she lacks the main qualification for the fullness of the Holy Spirit—emptiness.

A life totally filled with a new bride does not find time for lesser interests. When a person allows the Holy Spirit to fill the entire vessel, the Holy Spirit receives control of the human personality. It is not an ironclad control. He does not force us against our will. He does not wish to turn a person into an automaton. Instead, the Spirit enables the yielded Christian to do the things that please God.

Donald Grey Barnhouse views God as giver of a distinct necessity after conversion. "God offers salvation to the lost, through the death of Jesus Christ"; so also "to all who are true believers in Him He offers the fulness of the Holy Spirit." Ephesians 5:18 commands, "And do not get drunk with wine, . . . but be filled with the Spirit." Expounding on this contrasting parallel between drunkenness and Spirit-fullness, Barnhouse shows what the Spirit provides. A drunkard seeks the bottle for relief from a heavy heart, for positive happiness, and for conviviality while he babbles fluently and gives money away thoughtlessly. He finds reckless courage through strong drink. In bold contrast, however, the Spirit brings what spirits never can.

> ... He brings that which the world seeks and never finds: *quiet contentment* in the midst of any circumstances, *rich joy* even in the midst of sorrow, *true fellowship* with all of the Lord's own, *lips* that are open in His witness, *a purse* that is open in His cause, *a heart* that is strong to do great things for Him.[165]

Implies a time of filling

The term "filling" describes an activity that a person can perform only until the object becomes completely filled. If a pitcher of lemonade stands half filled on a table, we do not call it a full pitcher. We can notice that someone has added lemonade until it is 80 percent filled, but theoretically only when it stands 100 percent filled do we call it full. Often we use the term "level full" to describe such an amount.

On several occasions, Scripture records that people became filled with the Holy Spirit. When the early church sought qualified candidates for the original deacons, they looked for seven men who were "full" of the Holy Spirit (Acts 6:3). Not only does the New Testament call Jesus "full" of the Holy Spirit (Luke 4:1), but it also refers to Stephen and Barnabas as "full" (Acts 6:5; 7:55; 11:24).

Includes a renovation

If language has any meaning, to be filled describes a different condition from being empty or half filled. Can a person possibly be filled with Deity—the third Person of the triune God, and remain the same?

When one has separated from evil and dedicated all to God to be Spirit-filled, the renewing Spirit brings changes. His coming in fullness resembles a cool, refreshing shower after a blistering hot summer afternoon. He brings freshness. Although specific human needs vary somewhat in accord with previous lifestyle and growth, the Spirit comes in fullness only to improve us.

Implies abundance

Rich in meaning, fullness terminology suggests abundant living, not meager drop-by-drop Christian experience. When God's Spirit fills, his fruit should be growing toward a bounteous harvest. Jesus came so we might enjoy life abundant (John 10:10). He described not just fullness but overflowing with the Spirit. "If any man is thirsty, let him come to Me and drink. . . . 'From his innermost being shall flow rivers of living water' " (John 7:37-38).

Romans 12:1-2 is one of several passages that explain sanctification in terms of those three important spiritual elements—separation, dedication, and habitation. Whereas separation represents a negative human action and dedication a positive one, habitation refers to God's part. By his grace we can separate and dedicate, but only God himself can transform us by renewing the mind through living within.

Separation includes ideas like cleansing, renouncing, and setting apart. Dedication involves a full surrender, consecration, and yielding our bodies to God. Habitation, however, entails God's empowering and energizing through his indwelling and anointing. Through the holy seed indwelling and filling, we become holy.

Part 5

On Your Mark . . . Get Set . . . Don't Miss the "Go!"

He touched my mouth . . . and said, "Behold, . . . your iniquity is taken away. . ." (Isa. 6:7).

Excitement before a race exceeds description. After months of practice, each nerve seems tensed as the athlete coordinates every muscle for the opening gun. How tragic to morale to miss the starting signal! How disheartening to begin last—or never!

Many Christians sit about wishing their Christian progress were more rapid, realizing, alas, that they are running in place—or backward. After reading armfuls of Christian books and hearing countless deeper-life sermons and videos, some have never even begun to warm up.

Although an athlete must master the instruction book, yet if he never begins moving on the sound of "GO!" he'll never win a race. The entry point of dynamic sanctification represents step one—the vitally essential first move on "the highway of holiness" of which Isaiah wrote (Isa. 35:8).

16

A Crisis? Needing to Know and Knowing My Need

Lest . . . they under-stand; Woe is me (Isa. 6:10, 5).

Foundation

Even as a skyscraper requires a solid foundation, so does an important doctrine. Epistemology examines the grounds for believing, the source of knowledge. Since speakers, writers, and church traditions differ on the time of sanctification, it is appropriate to ask, "How can I know?" This chapter will explore this need to know. Next it will discuss whether or not human need for sanctification implies its reception at a point in time rather than gradually. First, where should one look for a foundation for beliefs?

The supreme place of Scripture

Adopting the words *sola scriptura* as his motto, Martin Luther proclaimed Scripture alone as the basis for theological beliefs. As the inspired Word of God, the Bible never misleads. Thus, this priest rejected the alternative that Roman Catholic tradition and councils should determine what all church people must believe. So much corrupt teaching had distorted biblical truth that Luther fought for a single pure source for doctrine. Does not *sola scriptura* sound like the safest route today? Surely Scripture itself must be primary in discerning what to believe.

The place of tradition

Some recent thinkers claim that Wesleyan theology, by contrast, esteems a quadrilateral as foundational for doctrine. Wesleyanism's fourfold underpinning allegedly includes Scripture, experience, reason, and tradition.

Historian Timothy L. Smith in *A Contemporary Wesleyan Theology*, however, forcefully argues that "the notion of a 'Wesleyan Quadrilateral' . . . will scarcely fit the facts."[166] Most non-liturgical evangelicals, in fact, would assert that they value tradition infinitely less than Scripture.

Although tradition tells what other people have thought through the centuries, yet in itself tradition establishes nothing for us.[167] Scripture does establish what to believe.[168] Admittedly, tradition sometimes provides additional support for truths we find in the Bible.

If Scripture is God's infallible Word and tradition is not, surely they do not deserve the same attention. In part, however, tradition can show how believers in past generations have understood and experienced the teachings of Scripture. No thorough interpreter today can safely ignore the work of past exegetes. Nor should he or she automatically afford them validity.

The place of reason

Although overdependence on reason, known as rationalism, proves dangerous, yet sound Bible study involves reason. Scripture mentions God's mind (1 Cor. 2:16) and his thoughts (Isa. 55:8-9). God invites his people to reason with him (Isa. 1:18). He values intelligible communication (1 Cor. 14:6-11). He surely expects us to treat Scripture rationally. Scripture itself is rational, not irrational. It is a message which God designed for us to read in human words—words he desires us to understand.

The place of experience

What part should experience play in establishing doctrine? What God has revealed in his Word must be the ultimate standard of truth—not human experience (John 17:17).[169] Scripture reveals the vital truth Christians must believe (Deut. 29:29; John 16:13).

Scripture, however, does not solve every problem that curious minds ponder—about mathematics, about the material universe, or about spiritual things. The God of truth who inspired Scripture also created the universe. Scrutinizing his universe can sometimes show us more of how God's laws operate—both natural and spiritual laws.

Thus, by examining God's truth in natural revelation in the universe, we can sometimes better understand what Scripture means.[170] Scripture is not only theoretically true; it is truly workable in the world outside of us and in our experience. Moreover, if we find that our interpretation of Scripture repeatedly does not square with human experience, a reexamination of our interpretation may prove necessary.

Searching for the ultimate determiner of truth, one must never elevate experience as superior to nor equal with Scripture. Human experience, however, supports truths in Scripture.

As honey tastes sweeter than vinegar and as people prize freedom above slavery, so God's Word juts upward as the Everest of authority. In summary, Scripture stands as the supreme source of proper Christian doctrine. Tradition calls attention to the thinking of Christians in ancient, medieval, and even contemporary times in relation to Scripture and theology. Reason can help in the use of Scripture and of doctrinal ideas. It can even aid our interpretation of what we observe in nature. Human experience can corroborate our interpretation of truth found in Scripture.

Do you enjoy solving a baffling mystery story or conquering a tricky crossword puzzle? What evidence shows that Christians can enter dynamic sanctification at a point in time? *Some exegetical, logical, and experiential evidence leads an objective searcher to understand sanctification as involving an instantaneous turning point after the moment of conversion.*

The remainder of Part Five will examine such evidences. Sifting through the evidences God provides in Scripture resembles solving a mystery. Spiritual benefits will prove much more rewarding than unraveling a mystery thriller. The value proves immense if, as a result of our search, we personally appropriate God's truth. If we teach others and lead them to freedom, the value of our successful search sometimes surpasses calculation.

Although not all evidences have equal weight, each deserves consideration. Some seem unmistakable. Other evidences are capable of very different interpretations. Still others are corroborating rather than directly teaching. In any case, when God's redeemed people search out his divine living truth with open minds and hungry hearts, truth has a way of commending its own worth to them.

Need

Lori's son and daughter had been attending a midweek service designed for children at a young church for a couple of years. When Lori visited one Sunday morning, the sermon understandably laid out God's provision of salvation in Christ. The Holy Spirit convicted her. As the pastor asked for raised hands if anyone present wanted to be saved, Lori responded. As soon as possible, he led her to a personal knowledge of Christ and began discipling her.

On the next Wednesday night, her children excitedly told people about the change in their mother. Lori attended another service at the church. Soon, however, she lost interest in attending. Was her newfound experience faulty? Why had life become so difficult? First steps in her recovery should assess how she views her conversion and help her understand exactly what has happened to her in conversion and what has not happened.

Requires awareness

What relief the sinner experiences after repenting and receiving the gift of eternal life! The well-intentioned counselor has portrayed conversion as an entrance into a calm life of abounding joy. Now the new Christian will enjoy victory over evil practices. Too seldom, however, does the soulwinner help the new believer to understand that foes still lurk. The new birth entails enlistment in a conflict with the enemy, fully as much as enjoying peace with God.

Who is that enemy? We earlier discovered it to be three-fold—the world system outside, plus Satan and his troops, and the ugly internal foe, carnality. Sanctification deals most directly with carnality. At the moment of conversion, the repenting sinner lacks awareness of his or her need of dynamic sanctification. A holiness evangelist, born shortly after the American Civil War, accurately explains the issues.

> Had God sanctified me when He converted me He would have done so without my having understood my need or privilege of the same and without my asking. No sinner feels his need of sanctification, nor thinks of praying God to sanctify him when under conviction for sin and seeking pardon.[171]

Instead, in Scripture, both prayers for sanctification and God's commands and promises of sanctification invariably relate to his own people (Rom. 6:19; 1 Thess. 4:3-5; 5:23-24).

Conversion—a beginning not a finish line. Conversion represents entering kindergarten, not receiving a college diploma. After falling soon and often into detested sins, a recent convert may arrive at one of several possible conclusions.

(1) "Conversion is an illusion; no one experiences it. I tried salvation but it did not work." Perhaps someone has misled such a seeker on what to expect. Conversion provides a real spiritual transformation—but without instant perfection.

(2) "Conversion would be a glorious benefit. I would have received it had I repented more fervently." God does not measure the length or the loudness of a prayer before responding. He requires a turning from evil and a simple trust in Christ for forgiveness. If we have met his conditions, God has kept his promises. The new birth has occurred with or without full understanding and with or without tingling emotions. Moreover, the powers of evil use discouragement and deception to convince a new convert of the falsity of his or her experience.

(3) "Conversion happened to me, but it must need to occur often—every time I sin. Conversion was marvelous but I must not

have worked hard enough to keep saved." Although conversion
constitutes a single event, yet the Savior offers daily cleansing to
deal with the defilements of the day. Furthermore, God keeps believers by grace, even as he saved them by grace. Jesus explained to
Peter, "He who has bathed needs only to wash his feet, but is completely clean; and you are all clean . . . (John 13:8-10). The same
Lord who provides for the bath of regeneration stoops to wash
away the daily defilement when we submit to him.

(4) "Conversion covers up my sin. Therefore, God turns his
head when I live in defeat. In other words, I know that when I
trusted Christ, God forgave all past, present, and future sins.
Hence, I need not concern myself about living victoriously. The
Lord will keep me even if I fail."

It is true that Christ's one death has provided atonement for all
sins. Even though conversion does wipe out our bad record, it does
not blind God to our current actions. He insists on victorious living (1 Cor. 6:8-11). It is not an option. Christ will preserve all of us
who make use of his power to keep us (2 Tim. 1:12). He has complete ability to keep his sheep permanently (John 10:27-29).

Dynamic sanctification—carnality's death blow. At conversion, God
imparts divine life and declares the sinner no longer guilty—for all
the *sins* he or she has committed.[172] By contrast, the singular word
sin represents our polluted carnal nature, as we learned in a previous chapter. Dynamic sanctification, not conversion, deals with
sin—not sins. Dynamic sanctification smites carnality.

Dynamic sanctification—demands readiness. A struggling believer
needs to learn God's open secret for abundant living. God has provided dynamic sanctification for the believer who needs victory
over carnality's bondage. Must a Christian wait for some length of
time or some stage of maturity before experiencing dynamic sanctification? No, the God who requires holiness and effective service
from his people also waits to supply purity and power to live and
serve effectively.

If dynamic sanctification required a certain quantity or quality
of works, then a candidate could not immediately enter it. God
justifies the sinner by grace through faith apart from human

works. Even so, he sanctifies the believer by grace through faith apart from human works.

Can a sequence of events lead up to dynamic sanctification even as it often leads up to conversion? Sometimes God brings or allows various influences into a life so that a sinner knows that he or she must receive eternal life. The candidate should understand God's instruction in Scripture about experiencing the new birth. Sensing a need and seeing both the divine solution and divine conditions, a person stands ready for an *immediate* entry into God's kingdom.

Similarly, various influences may lead up to dynamic sanctification. Often the believer must confront his or her own failures—admitting the inability to win. Misunderstanding, lacking clear instruction, hesitating to make a full surrender, or fearing to let God guide, a believer sometimes holds back. From God's standpoint, he is ready to sanctify a converted person immediately. Delay comes not because of God's reluctance but the person's.

Thus, even Wesleyan scholar Melvin Dieter contends that

> the critical point of this purifying experience need not be chronologically distinct from justification and the new birth, but logically it is distinct from them in the continuum of salvation. However, the scriptural exhortation to believers to pursue perfection in love, as well as the struggles they commonly have with a divided heart, indicates that believers typically appropriate purity of love in a distinct crisis of faith sometime subsequent to justification.[173]

Unfortunately, because of a lack of clear instruction, most new believers have no idea of their need of dynamic sanctification. Often years and years of up-and-down Christian experience intervene before a believer grasps the biblical solution and has courage to venture. Jon Tal Murphree perceptively observes that at conversion

> theoretically, a person could immediately enter the full release of completely surrendered motives, . . . but in practice few do so. . . . The notion of a "second experience" does not describe God's arbitrary formula as much as it describes human personality. It is *descriptive* rather than *prescriptive*. The need for a deeper working of God's grace does not in-

dicate inadequacy of God's initial grace. It simply reflects
the inability of the human personality to entertain an adequate love motive for Christ until His fellowship has been
consistently shared.[174]

Obviously, the unsaved person senses no need for dynamic
sanctification. In life, we look for no solution when we realize no
problem. We search for a remedy for carnality only after we have
joined God's family and discovered a personal inability.

We long to conquer overpowering temptations—but without
success. As soon as Christ saved us, people instructed us to start
witnessing. When we tried, however, our words seemed to pierce
unsaved hearts like a cotton ball hitting a steel girder. We discovered an inability to proclaim Christ with power.

Like the information gap of a sinner needing regeneration, so
also the believer needs to understand biblical possibilities of, and
conditions for, dynamic sanctification. If that Christian shows a
willingness for a full surrender to Christ's supreme lordship in all
areas of life, he or she can experience dynamic sanctification *immediately*. Faith unlocks the gate.

Anticipates a prompt remedy

Because God opposes carnality. What Christian wishes to have an
evil force dominating life? Billy Graham declares that "unless the
Spirit controls our lives, we will be dominated by our old sinful
nature."[175] The desperateness of the Christian's need cries for an
immediate solution. The unchecked twisted carnal nature threatens spiritual living even as ingested poison threatens physical life.

God has expressed his unalterable opposition to carnality. "For
the mind set on the flesh is death . . . because the mind set on the
flesh is hostile toward God; for it does not subject itself to the law
of God, for it is not even able to do so" (Rom. 8:6-7). Major Whittle
calls the flesh "the most dangerous enemy the new man has to contend with. . . ."[176]

Because carnality devastates true humanity. Not only is carnality
deadly because of God's opposition to it; it greatly devastates
our own aspiring redeemed humanity as Christians. Murphree
cogently explains that "the carnal nature is not something with

spatial dimensions that can be eradicated by radical surgery or specific acts." Instead, "it is more like a particular mind-set, a character condition, a moral warp or twist of a person's nature. ... subconscious selfishness." Its deadliness consists in "its ... cramping and hampering it [our own humanity], warping and twisting it, bending it toward oneself, preventing it from being straight toward God. It ... drives one ruthlessly, enslaving the selfhood. ..."[177]

Because gradualism proves inadequate. Since carnality so displeases God and sabotages our attempts at selfless Christian living and serving, should we not expect that God would provide a speedy remedy? Unfortunately some theologians advocate only gradualism—the idea that all practical sanctification is nothing less than a lifelong process. They blame those who teach a point of full surrender for advocating a quick fix, an easy way out. Since the mind set on carnality is deadly, we desperately need a radical cure.

Some people want their dog's tail short and submit it to surgery to accomplish their wish. Should the veterinarian cut it off a bit at a time over several months or years to prevent excessive pain in our pampered pet? No, the ridiculous suggestion horrifies us. Soon after birth the puppy experiences very little pain. Delay or repeated cutting would only multiply pain.

Nor does Scripture recommend our tapering off from the self-life's control. Like infection in a wound, mild, gradual treatment can prove as fatal as ignoring the contamination. Since carnality constitutes sin and rebellion, we must renounce it rather than trying to ease up gradually from its stubborn slavery. A revolution must overthrow carnality's reign.

Dubbing the existence of "carnal saints" as a "contradictory reality," the contemporary Baptist professor, Floyd H. Barackman, insists that "carnality in a believer should not be tolerated." As a cure he urges "the recognition of the lordship of Christ.... The total commitment of discipleship *follows* salvation" [emphasis his], citing Rom. 12:1-2; 6:11-13; Col. 3:1-3; 2 Cor. 5:14-15; and Luke 14:25-27, 33.[178]

W.T. Purkiser similarly argues for an immediate remedy for carnality based on human need.

If God wants to make His people actually holy and cannot, He is not omnipotent—the devil has succeeded in injecting into human nature that which God cannot remove. On the other hand, if God can cleanse the heart and will not, then He is not holy as we have thought Him to be, utterly opposed to all sin.[179]

17

Terms That Imply No Term

Your iniquity is taken away (Isa. 6:7).

In the phrase "his prison sentence," the word "sentence" flashes to our minds the concept of a period of time. By contrast, the word "release" suggests action at a point of time in the phrase, "after his release from prison." Do certain terms for dynamic sanctification imply that it occurs in a moment rather than throughout a lifetime? This chapter will explore this issue.

The Term "Crisis"

A *crisis* is a decisive point of change. A major use denotes the turning point in a disease—the hour when the sufferer's condition changes for the better or worse.

To communicate more readily with our contemporaries, some speakers who believe in a decisive entry into the deeper life have forsaken the term "crisis" in describing dynamic sanctification. "Crisis" misleads people in at least two ways today.

(1) In usual non-technical use, the word often notes a sudden unexpected emergency—when everything goes wrong at once. Instead, entry into dynamic sanctification is a crisis that we

163

choose to experience. It is a crisis of surrender, cleansing, and release.

(2) Since "crises" often strain the emotions, others think first of emotionality when they hear the word. Thus, they would interpret a crisis of dynamic sanctification as some dramatic upheaval that centers in ecstatic feelings. For average people, entry into dynamic sanctification involves a more rational and volitional transaction. An individual yields fully to the Lord and trusts that he accepts and empowers.

Cattell's elderly grandfather learned of dynamic sanctification from someone who had depended on feeling. He maintained that "when the Holy Spirit filled him it struck him like an electric shock going from head to foot. He was sure Grandfather ought to get the shock also." After six months of unsuccessfully seeking a shock, Grandfather realized his need of God's Spirit himself in fullness—not a sensation. How fortunate that during those months he got no shock! He might well have missed the Spirit himself.[180]

As in conversion, emotional joy may accompany the act of faith. Often it will instead come later—or never. One must remember that God sanctifies us by faith even as he justified us by faith. Faith constitutes trust that God now keeps his promise. Faith, therefore, stands in spite of emotional reaction—with it or without it. "But the Eternal Inward Light does not die when ecstasy dies, nor exist only intermittently, with the flickering of our psychic states."[181]

If it were not for linguistic baggage, "crisis" could continue as a descriptive, helpful term to identify dynamic sanctification as including a definite point of entrance.[182] The English word originates from a Greek word meaning "decision." Thus, it describes a decisive moment, a critical change in one's life or circumstances. Perhaps "turning point" should replace it—at least for a generation that grows impatient with theological jargon.[183] We have already noted that human need cries out—not for a lifelong struggle—but for immediate relief from carnal bondage. What more direct evidences mark dynamic sanctification as a point? Do the very terms employed in Scripture for dynamic sanctification imply action at a point of time?

Biblical Terms Denoting Dynamic Sanctification

Filled with the Holy Spirit

Luke places more emphasis on the Holy Spirit than the other two synoptic writers do. He notes that John the Baptist, Elizabeth, and Zacharias each had become filled with the Holy Spirit (Luke 1:15, 41, 67). He also mentions that after Jesus' baptism in Jordan, Jesus was full of the Holy Spirit (Luke 4:1). Ryrie explains that "from the viewpoint of practice and experience the filling of the Holy Spirit is the most important aspect of the doctrine of the Holy Spirit."[184]

In Acts, Luke singles out various groups and individuals as "filled with the Holy Spirit." Groups include the 120 at Pentecost, the early church after its size had grown to five thousand, and believers at Pisidian Antioch (Acts 2:4; 4:31; 13:52). The apostles charged the congregation to choose as the earliest deacons men "full of the Holy Spirit" (Acts 6:3). Apparently not every believer is automatically full of the Spirit, else the qualification is meaningless. Wuest correctly observes that

> the Holy Spirit possesses or controls the volitional, rational, and emotional activities of the believer who is said to be filled with Him. . . . The believer is not automatically controlled by the Spirit just because the Spirit indwells him. . . . The Holy Spirit does not control us in the sense of permeating our will, reason, and emotions, until we recognize Him as the One who has been sent by the Father to sanctify our lives, and trust Him to perform His ministry in and through us.[185]

Luke narrates that Peter and Paul were filled with the Holy Spirit (Acts 4:8; 9:17; 13:9). Moreover, Luke uses the phrase "full of the Holy Spirit" in describing both Stephen and Barnabas (Acts 6:5; 7:55; 11:24). Interestingly, except for Acts 13:52, every such use of "filled" in Luke and Acts appears in the aorist tense. This suggests that Luke was not stressing an elongated process to become filled with the Spirit. Moreover, the contexts show that becoming filled in each case occurred at a point in time.

At Pisidian Antioch, by contrast, most interpreters understand that recent converts "were continually filled with the Holy Spirit" on and on, more and more (Acts 13:52). Conceivably, however, the imperfect tense focuses on various believers one by one becoming Spirit-filled as they perceived their need and God's provision. The latter idea compares with the Samaritan incident: "Then they *began* laying their hands on them, and they were receiving the Holy Spirit (Acts 8:17).

Many of us have bought a couple gallons of gasoline when we suddenly realized a need but could not or would not buy a larger amount. If, however, you have completely filled the gas tank, no one can add more gasoline. In John 2:7, Jesus instructed the servants at the Cana wedding feast to "fill the waterpots with water." John recorded that "they filled them up to the brim."

By definition, "filled" means "full"—no one can add more. If one becomes Spirit-filled, we logically conclude that this person has fully committed his or her life to God for his control. It is commendable for a lady who understands her need to surrender her hands or lips to the Lord. In dynamic sanctification, however, God requires a surrender of our whole selves (Rom. 6:13; 12:1). "Meister Eckhart wrote: 'There are plenty to follow our Lord half-way, but not the other half. They will give up possessions, friends, and honors, but it touches them too closely to disown themselves.'"[186]

As the gas tank becomes one hundred percent full at a moment, so at a moment of full dedication a person becomes Spirit-filled. Murphree reasons, "At 99 percent surrender, my status with Christ was that of a not-fully-surrendered Christian, the same as at 10 percent surrender. . . . When I surrendered the last beachhead, I entered a new category."[187]

Gift/receiving a promise

Theodore M. Hesburgh, president of the University of Notre Dame, received 111 honorary degrees between 1954 and 1987. Universities and colleges bestow an honorary degree simply because they wish to honor a noteworthy individual, not because he or she enrolled in its programs and earned creditable grades in its courses. An honorary degree is a gift.

A gift may range from a paper clip to a ten-million-dollar estate. The recipient deeply appreciates some gifts. A person scorns other gifts. Inherent in the idea of a gift is the donor's intention to bestow something without pay. A true gift has no strings attached. In other words, no one can earn it.

Jesus implied that the Holy Spirit is a gift that the Father will freely give to believers. He reasoned, "If you then, being evil, know how to give good gifts to your children, how much more shall *your* Heavenly Father give the Holy Spirit to those who ask Him?" When we keep his simple conditions, the Lord invariably keeps his promises.

For a giving transaction to be complete, someone must receive a gift. Jesus promised the gift of the Spirit, but human beings must ask for and receive the promise. Christ died "in order that in Christ Jesus the blessing of Abraham might come to the Gentiles, so that we might receive the promise of the Spirit through faith" (Gal. 3:14).

In his farewell discourses, Jesus promised the Holy Spirit to believers—*not to the world* (John 14:14-24; 15:26; 16:7, 26). Later, as he sent them forth into the world to proclaim, it was to the disciples that Jesus gave the charge and privilege to "receive the Holy Spirit" (John 20:20-22). To those who repent and receive the forgiveness of sins, along with baptism, God promises "the gift of the Holy Spirit" (Acts 2:38).

Under usual circumstances a giver gives a gift at a point of time and a recipient receives a gift at a point in time. The gift of the Holy Spirit appears to coincide with the fullness of the Holy Spirit, which he consistently bestowed on believers—according to Luke, Acts, and Ephesians—not on unsaved people who at that point became believers.

Baptism

Water baptism, a literal ceremony with a symbolic significance, pointed to several ideas. Baptism recalls Jesus' sacrifice for sinners, our cleansing from sins, and a convert's testimony to regeneration and a new start in life. Although some theologians disagree, immersionists and many non-immersionists understand that Jesus' baptism in the Jordan River involved immersion.

The Bible regards water baptism as a once-in-a-lifetime ceremony. Jesus did not get baptized weekly or hourly—nor did anyone else in Scripture.

Water baptism relates the candidate to Jesus' death and resurrection. Paul reasoned,

> Do you not know that all of us who have been baptized into
> Christ Jesus have been baptized into His death? Therefore,
> we have been buried with Him through baptism into death,
> in order that as Christ was raised from the dead through the
> glory of the Father, so we too might walk in newness of life
> (Rom. 6:3-4; cf. Col. 2:12).

Thus, the Word mentions a baptism into Christ Jesus as a baptism into death. Even as water baptism is a one-time event, so there
needs to be a one-time entrance into dynamic sanctified living—ideally as soon after conversion as possible. Gradual baptism
would be an absurd notion. If we understand biblical baptism as
immersion, progressive continuous baptism could be a murderous
act! Surely the figure of water baptism should help us to understand dynamic sanctification as an entry event rather than a life of
progress without an entry point.

Gilbertson discovered that A. B. Simpson grappled more with
the interrelationship between water baptism and Spirit baptism
than Simpson's contemporaries did. He saw water baptism as
symbolizing a personal, voluntary surrender to die with Christ.[188]
If the term, baptism with the Holy Spirit, validly describes dynamic sanctification, it too connotes a plunging into the Holy
Spirit that Christ performed (John 1:33) at a point of time.

On the day of Jesus' resurrection, he had breathed on the apostles, saying, "Receive the Holy Spirit." On a later occasion, perhaps when mentioning the Spirit's power coming upon his
apostles (Acts 1:8), Jesus promised his hearers Spirit baptism.
"John baptized with water, but you shall be baptized with the
Holy Spirit not many days from now" (Acts 1:4).

On the day Jesus was speaking, the apostles had not yet become
baptized with the Holy Spirit; in a few days, however, this would
have occurred. Apparently the baptism was experiential, datable,
and empowering.

As Armin Gesswein reminds us, a wide variety of evangelicals accepted this term before its adoption by a new movement at the dawn of this century. He comments, "That term was used quite freely before the Pentecostals entered the field."[189] Unfortunately much of the contemporary opposition to the term is reactive—whether against Pentecostals, Charismatics, or the Wesleyan holiness movement. At any rate, the analogy of baptism in a baptism with the Holy Spirit, however one interprets it, does not portray a lifelong growth.

Biblical Terms Describing the Meaning of Dynamic Sanctification

Crucifixion/resurrection

Some biblical terms epitomizing central ideas in dynamic sanctification involve analogical or literal language that one can best understand as involving a point in time. "I have been crucified with Christ," Paul testified (Gal. 2:20). Also, in a definite dynamic sanctification context, Paul explains,

> For if we have become united with *Him* in the likeness of His death, certainly we shall be also *in the likeness* of His resurrection, knowing this, that our old self was crucified with *Him*, that our body of sin might be done away with, that we should no longer be slaves to sin (Rom. 6:5-6).

It would be unthinkable to speak of a literal crucifixion as a lifelong process that continues year after year. Jesus did not remain imprisoned for years while pursuing an appeals process. Instead, after an illegal overnight Jewish trial, the Sanhedrin sent Jesus to an early-morning (John 18:28) judicial appearance before the Roman procurator of Judea. That very morning soldiers nailed Jesus to the cross. Pilate expressed astonishment that Jesus was already dead six hours later. A person dies at a minute on the clock—not throughout a lifetime.

Likewise, a resurrection occurs at a point of time. Jesus arose on the third day. Although Jesus now lives forevermore (Rev. 1:18), God does not keep on resurrecting him.

As noted earlier, in a potential sense, we died and arose when
Christ did. If we have entered dynamic sanctification, however,
we can conceive of that entry point in time when we ourselves began to benefit spiritually from his sanctifying provision.

Representing a Reformed view of sanctification, Hoekema accurately writes, *"In one sense we died to sin and arose to new life when
Christ died and arose; in another sense, however, we died to sin and arose to
new life when by faith we grasped our oneness with Christ in His death and
resurrection."*[190] If so, a death/resurrection motif implies entering
dynamic sanctification at a point rather than a gradual process after conversion.

Put off/put on

Some of us would need to work several lifetimes to earn enough
money to purchase the suits worn by space shuttle crews from
1982. Each suit cost $3.6 million.

It is absurd, however, to imagine a person's taking a whole lifetime to put off a garment or to put on another garment. These are
actions that we normally understand to occur in a few minutes.

We have noted that God's Spirit inspired Bible writers to use
pivotal actions like fullness, gift, promise, baptism, crucifixion,
and resurrection. In addition, he likens the separation and dedication elements of dynamic sanctification to putting off the old self
and putting on the new (Eph. 4:22, 24).

18

Tense about Tenses: Communicating Sanctification

Touched . . . touched (Isa. 6:7).

Do you consider yourself a *foodie*? Are you particular enough to holler "*NIMBY*"? Linguists call words such as these two neologisms—brand new words that have won a place in the English language in recent years.

Perhaps you guessed correctly that the word "foodie" or "foody" identifies a gourmet, one boasting particular tastes about food. "NIMBY" or "nimby" stands for the slogan, "not in my back yard." People might use it to oppose the placement in their locality of such nuisances as a nuclear waste, a chicken-processing plant, or a landfill.

Language enables people to communicate with each other. In the English language, we think of a verb's tense as totally revolving around the time of an action or state. We call the verb *works* the present tense in a sentence like "She works at the bank." You get the idea, however, that she no longer works there when you hear a past tense verb. "She worked at the bank."

Although we have four additional standard tenses in English, we have no tenses called imperfect and aorist, which the ancient Greeks had. Not every Greek tense will receive treatment here. Instead, the present discussion seeks to point out a few prominent features of that language that have some application to sanctification. The writer's aim is neither to weary the reader with background nor to lure him or her into Greek studies. This brief treatment will not satisfy the expert linguist.

When we greet a friend with "How are you doing?" we are inquiring about kind of action. Grammarians often insist that the *kind* of action—not time—is most important in grasping the meaning of a Greek verb. Dana and Mantey, for example, uplift kind of action as "being the chief idea involved, for *time is but a minor consideration in the Greek tenses* [emphasis theirs]."[191] Although time has relevance to indicative Greek verbs, this statement is an excellent general rule in all Greek verbs. A respected current New Testament scholar agrees that "the primary significance of most forms of the Greek tense is not temporal signification."[192]

Stretching Out like a Line: Linear Emphasis

When you want to eat in a popular restaurant at a peak hour, you may stand in line for a long period. Even as a *line* goes on and on, the word *linear* pictures such a continuing idea. If you must stand in line, you hope that it will move along rapidly. One kind of action, then is continuation—action that is progressing or elongated.

Present tense

A major *emphasis* often found in the Greek present tense is this ongoing activity or state. For example, the sentence, "The line is moving," emphasizes that progress.

In English, it is one thing to say, "She works at the bank." The sentence gets a different and more specific twist, however, when you say, "She is working at the bank." Perhaps someone has just asked to speak to your daughter on the phone. If you answer that she is working at the bank, you likely intend to imply that she is continuing this activity right now. Therefore, she cannot come to the phone.

Imperfect tense

Another of your daughter's friends may reach her on the week-end with the complaint: "I kept trying to call you this week but you were never home." Her response might be: "I was working long hours at the bank all week." In this instance, ancient Greeks would best express both *kept trying* and *was working* by imperfect tense verbs.

Even as the present tense often expresses linear action, so does the imperfect. Although a verb in the imperfect tense conveys action in the past, it normally emphasizes that this action kept going on over some period of time.

All Systems Go—and Counting: Perfect Emphasis

At the launch of a spacecraft, when every preparation has been made for the imminent "blast-off," the message is "All systems go—and counting." In other words all preparations remain complete and the results of those preparations remain intact. The Greek perfect tense is like that—action has occurred in the past that affects the present moment—and assumedly the future.

In the illustration above about your daughter, suppose your daughter's friend responds, "Oh, I never knew that you worked at a bank." Your daughter might respond, "Yes, I have worked at the bank for over two years." Your daughter implies that two years have passed since she began to work at the bank and likely that she will continue in that work for the present.

"I have worked" might illustrate the way the ancient Greeks used their perfect tense. Normally it conveys past complete action with results continuing. Whereas both the present and imperfect show continuing action, the perfect tense points to its action as what has happened.

In photography, a time exposure illustrates the present tense. Likewise, a time exposure illustrates the imperfect tense. By contrast, a video that has captured past action portrays the perfect. One can now look back upon the latter activity as completed. In the example given earlier, two years have ended, but results continue—the daughter still works at the bank.

Viewing a Pinpoint: Aorist Emphasis

Unlike anything in English, the aorist tense conveys an action as undefined. Linguists think it was the original tense in Greek—usable to express all kinds of action. The aorist tense, however, *views* that action as simply a point whether it happened as a sudden event or a long process. Thus, scholars speak of the aorist as viewing the action as punctiliar—point action.

Instead of a time exposure or movie film, a snapshot represents the aorist. A snapshot can capture your baby's innocent winsome smile for years to come. His happy mood may have lasted a long time, but the snapshot at least views it as a single glimpse. Even as proud grandmothers take great numbers of snapshots of their first grandchild, so New Testament Greek uses great numbers of aorists in comparison with other tenses.

Traditional view

Experts both in classical Greek and in New Testament Greek have pointed to the aorist tense as customarily conveying *action* at a point in time. As a result, multitudes of ministers and highly respected authors have applied this principle in their books, articles, and sermons. They argue that an aorist verb in a given verse assures us that a completed action happened in a moment, once for all.

Daniel Steele, a Greek, theology, and philosophy professor, taught at Genesee College, Syracuse University, and renowned Boston University. He distinguished himself as a minister, reformer, and denominational leader before his death about the time World War I began.

In his book, *Mile-Stone Papers*, Steele wrote a pivotal chapter, "The Tense Readings of the Greek New Testament." Citing esteemed grammarians and biblical expositors, he examined a large number of New Testament texts. Steele concludes that

> when we come to consider the *work of purification* in the believer's soul, by the power of the Holy Spirit, both in the new birth and in entire sanctification, we find that *the aorist is almost uniformly used. This tense*, according to the best New Testament grammarians, never indicates a continuous, ha-

bitual, or repeated act, but one which is momentary, and done once for all. . . . Our inference is that the energy of the Holy Spirit in the work of entire sanctification, however long the preparation, is put forth at a stroke by a momentary act [emphasis his].[193]

Doubtless building on Steele's foundation, Olive Winchester, a well-educated Greek professor, amassed additional evidence for Steele's position.[194] She noted many Scripture verses on regeneration—admittedly something that occurs at a point of time. Likewise she called attention to many verses on dynamic sanctification that fit the same pattern.

Many writers who do not share the Wesleyan theology of Steele (Methodist) or Winchester (Nazarene) argue from the aorist. They see it as indicating decisive action—whether in regard to dedication or very different matters in Scripture.

Contemporary challenges

In recent decades, several writers have contended that Greeks used the aorist to express any kind of action—not just punctiliar. Thus, they have challenged earlier interpretations, noting that certain uses of the aorist surely do not demonstrate that the action itself had occurred immediately, at a point of time, as completed action, or once for all.[195]

These critics cite numerous evidences to substantiate their claims. One example will suffice here.

John used an aorist tense to report the Jews' words, "It took forty-six years to build this temple. . ." (John 2:20). Forty-six years of intermittently continuing work do not suggest an immediate action at one point of time. Moreover, temple-erection did not constitute completed action, for the lengthy process did not end until several decades after those Jews spoke to Jesus. Nor did the temple even at its completion stand as a once-for-all construction, since the Romans soon destroyed it in A.D. 70.[196] Furthermore, prophetic Scriptures seem to anticipate a later rebuilt temple in tribulational and millennial times (2 Thess. 2:4; Ezek. 40:5; Zech. 14:9, 20-21).

Validity of evidence

Like most iconoclasts, the aorist reformers, use strong language—as well as strong arguments. Stagg cleverly diagnoses those who draw unadvised theological points from aorists as afflicted with "aoristitis."[197] If the aorist reformers have drawn correct conclusions, many writers—even famous, careful scholars—draw unwarranted inferences based on aorist verbs. In addition, occasional wild interpretations based on an inconsistent use of the aorist tense, to be sure, exist. Some find their way into fervent sermons by well-meaning expositors.

Some aorist reformers confidently accuse the most respected grammarians of inconsistencies. Charles R. Smith, for example, writes that ". . . almost every standard grammar may be faulted at this point—even those which in other contexts clearly state the matter."[198] One keeps wondering whether such critics fully understand *how* those grammarians intended certain statements.

Affirming that this Grace Seminary professor has gone too far, Carson objects. He insists that Smith is "linguistically naive" in his criticism. Stripping the aorist of its distinctiveness, Smith claims that an author used an aorist when not wanting to use a tense with "more specifying force." By contrast, Carson contends:

> . . . All that such counterexamples [like those of Smith] prove is that not every aorist is used in such a way, not that no aorist is used in such a way. . . . A tense is not infinitely plastic, but brings a certain broad semantic range with it before it is shaped by the context outside of which range the meaning of the tense will only rarely move.[199]

Carson's distinction is quite important.

Stagg has made some illuminating points. If an unprejudiced observer studies all sides, Carson's chapter, along with articles like one by Maddox, prove more convincing than Smith's. One of the keys surely is that *an aorist essentially does not always concern itself with whether the action is extended or instantaneous.* The aorist states the fact as a fact not as a process. Maddox warns that one must never confuse "(a) speaking of something as a whole in the simplest possible manner, and (b) actually implying that the event is instantaneous."[200]

Instead, when one used an aorist, that writer was *viewing* the action as a point, whether or not it *occurred* in an instant. For example, as John saw it, Jesus' Jewish antagonists were compacting forty-six years of constructing into a single thought.

Stagg correctly calls understanding the aorist as "point action" "serviceable" if one rightly understands it. He explains that "careful grammarians make it clear that the 'punctiliar' idea belongs to the writer's manner of presentation and not necessarily to the action itself."[201] A.T. Robertson states that the aorist "always means point-action." He adds, however, that "the tense has nothing to do with the *fact* of the action, but only with the way it is stated."[202] If a person will keep this distinction in mind in examining Stagg's and Smith's counterexamples, most of them disintegrate as no longer "countering" the basic thrust of punctiliar action.

Application to dynamic sanctification

Since the aorist does not automatically show that an action happens at a point of time, how can one know a writer's intention? How can a person know, for example, whether to interpret an aorist used of sanctification as a punctiliar *action*? Stagg accurately asserts that "contextual factors are primary for any attempt to go behind the aorist to the nature of the action itself."[203] If we accept reformers' conclusions, the aorist

> cannot be used in and of itself to prove that an action was of a crisic nature. While the presence of the aorist makes such an interpretation possible, it becomes probable only when the meaning of the verb and the context support it.[204]

In Romans 12:1, Paul employs an aorist verb in his appeal to believers. "Present your bodies a living and holy sacrifice, acceptable to God," he urged. In such a passage the verb appears to be an ingressive or inceptive aorist—that is, one depicting the entrance into a state. The context *demands* that one understand the action as a point in time.

Recalling that the Septuagint uses this verb *present* for offering animal sacrifices to God, one sees clearly that God expects a drastic, permanent dedication. The Old Testament animal was not coming back from the dead to romp in the fields. Christ's sacrifice of himself was permanent, irrevocable, and irreplaceable. Likewise, God asks us to surrender so fully to himself that we become a sacrifice—although physically we still live on. Thus, the kind of aorist, the verb's meaning, and the context impel us to understand the need for a definite action point.

Similarly, Paul's use of the same tense of the same verb in Romans 6:13 surely urges the believer's immediate action. Paul's argument here insists on a decisive, permanent commitment to God, including the whole person and the individual members of the human body.

The striking contrast in the same verse with an imperfect tense of the same verb seems to confirm this. The contrast underscores our previous decision to understand this dedication as decisive. As you formerly were habitually presenting yourselves to sin, so now at this point present yourselves to God. Such a full dedication results in dynamic sanctification (Rom. 6:19).[205]

One other principle deserves mention here. We have learned, of course, that an author who uses the aorist might not necessarily intend to express point action. As Stagg insists, however, "aorist is well suited to action which in itself is punctiliar whereas some other tenses, for example, the imperfect, are not."[206]

As noted above, both the present and the imperfect tense normally emphasize that the action is continuing over a period of time. When, therefore, a biblical writer used the aorist, likelihood is great that he was *not* intending to *emphasize* progressive, continuing action. This fact can help to some extent in examining any activity or doctrine, including dynamic sanctification.

19

Illustrative Events: Types

With a burning coal in his hand. . . . "Your iniquity is taken away" (Isa. 6:6-7).

God has revealed truth in many ways in the Bible. Both symbols and simple figures of speech commonly occur in our own conversations—as well as in Scripture. The burning coal from the altar in Isaiah's vision pointed forward to the fulfillment in Jesus Christ's blood. That sacrifice alone actually removes sinfulness (Heb. 9:12-14).

Biblical scholars refer to various Old Testament persons, objects, ceremonies, places, and events as types because they portray or enact spiritual truths beyond themselves. A type normally occurs in the Old Testament with its counterpart, the antitype, in the New Testament. The antitype is the New Testament person, experience, or other truth toward which the type pointed. Many types, though not all, foreshadow Christ and his atonement.

Proper hermeneutics cautions against *building a doctrine* on a short figure of speech, type, symbol, or parable. A doctrine should instead stand on clear direct passages of Scripture. Such a principle safeguards readers from fanciful interpretations.

If, however, Scripture teaches a doctrine in clear passages, then illustrative events, parables, types, symbols, and other figures can *confirm and illuminate that doctrine*. Since several clear Scriptures proclaim the doctrine of dynamic sanctification, illustrative and typical material can substantiate this teaching.

Adventures Portraying Sanctification

Jacob at Peniel

Bible students sometimes discern Jacob's strange experience of wrestling with the angel at Peniel as illustrating the doctrine of dynamic sanctification. When, twenty years earlier, the trickster Jacob had fled from Esau's just wrath, he used a stone for a pillow his first night.

Dreaming of a ladder to heaven, with God's angels climbing up and down it, proved a startling revelation. The Lord was standing above the ladder (Gen. 28:13). The Lord was *here*, too, not just back home. Jacob named that spot "Bethel," which means "God's house." Perhaps the ladder suggested the possibility of Jacob's access to God's eternal home.

At least it implied safety. God was supernaturally assigning angels to watch over Isaac's unworthy son. God was sparing him from lurking wild beasts—and from a wild brother. Listening, he heard the Lord promising, "I am with you, and will keep you wherever you go. . ." (Gen. 28:15).

God made a series of promises to Jacob, including the family, land, and messianic promises he had earlier made to Abraham. Calling the place awesome, Jacob accepted the promises and vowed that if God kept them, he would give tithes to God.

Whether or not we can classify what happened in terms of New Testament theology, surely this occasion marks a noteworthy personal encounter with God. Involving divine revelation and mutual commitment, this encounter brought him into direct communication with the God of his fathers.

Did Jacob's conversion occur that hour at Bethel? Probably it did. Interpreting some informative parts of the dream, Davis seems to imply this. "The stairway symbolized the genuine and uninterrupted fellowship between God in heaven and *His people on earth.* The angelic messengers reflect God's constant care *of His own.*"[207]

Having spent many years at Haran in the service of his Uncle Laban, Jacob sensed both God and life's circumstances leading him back to his homeland. As he neared that area, through messengers he informed Esau of his return, beseeching his favor.

Hearing the disconcerting news that Esau was approaching him with 400 men, Jacob prayed earnestly. When he had sent droves of animals as a gift to appease Esau, he divided his sizable family and hoard of possessions. So that half might escape in case of attack, they formed two groups. Next he waited—alone.

The "man" who wrestled with him throughout the night appears to have been God himself—apparently a theophany, that is, a preincarnate appearance of Christ (Gen. 32:24-30; Hos. 12:3-5). Jacob refused to let the Lord go unless he blessed him.

When the Lord inquired, "What is your name," he admitted he was Jacob, a name that meant swindler, crook, supplanter. The Jews considered names of special significance. To confess Jacob's name meant to confess his nature.

> All his years of chastening had not taught him the danger of the self-life. The time had come for Jacob, the supplanter, to die . . . a spiritual death. . . . The angel of the Lord weakened him physically to show him the futility of the flesh.[208]

Before the Lord could bless Jacob as he desired and would change his name to Israel, he must confess his name (although God already knew it). When God renamed him "Israel," that new name signified God's fighter,[209] or one who has striven with God, or God strives. No wonder Jacob now called this place Peniel, "God's face" (Gen. 32:30).

Without doubt, this episode at Peniel comes as Jacob's second recorded major experience with God. Wrestling with God, Jacob did confess his sinfulness. When Jacob asked the other wrestler's name, Scripture recounts this reply: " 'Why is it that you ask my name?' And he blessed him there" (Gen. 32:29).

This evidence convinces many that sufficient parallels exist here to consider the account as illustrating an actual experience of dynamic sanctification. If so, Jacob's years of struggling ended in a one-night wrestling match, which climaxed at dawn with a point of full surrender. Talbot explains that "the angel changed his name to symbolize the spiritual transformation in Jacob's life. . . . He was convinced that . . . he was a changed man."[210]

Jacob's sudden surrender supports the doctrine of a clear entry point into dynamic sanctification. Charles Wesley compressed into a hymn the thrust of this striking event as a full submission for dynamic sanctification.[211]

Crossing Jordan into Canaan

After 54 hours of continuous labor with almost no sleep, a Houston area mother recently delivered a lovely baby girl at home with the assistance of two midwives. Following the ordeal, imagine her need for rest. When a person completes a day full of enervating work under constant pressure, the body craves rest as well.

When God had created our universe, including plant, animal, and human life upon earth, Scripture asserts that he rested on the seventh day from all his creative activities (Gen. 2:2). No doubt He was not weary like human beings get. "Do you not know? Have you not heard? The Everlasting God, the LORD, the Creator of the ends of the earth does not become weary or tired" (Isa. 40:28). Scholars surmise that "this rest of God, however, cannot mean complete inactivity, for the administration of the universe and the work of man's salvation must continue."[212]

At his special call to the father of the Israelite race, God promised Abram a land (Gen. 12:1). Later God informed Abram that after years in a foreign land, his descendants would return to the Promised Land (Gen. 15:13-16).

The Hebrews writer reviews the wilderness generation's failure to arrive there because of unbelief—despite God's promises of rest. He recounts the renewed promise of rest through David a few hundred years after the conquest of Canaan under Joshua. Hence, the earthly Canaan rest did not begin to exhaust God's full intent. The writer proclaims, however, that a rest remains *now* for God's people (Heb. 3:7-4:11). What does God mean by the last statement?

At least two views predominate. Hebrews 4:9-10 anticipates a keeping of the Sabbath when we have ceased from our works—as God ceased from his works on the seventh day. Some see the "rest that remains" as dynamic sanctification; others as the experience of heaven forever—God's ultimate reward.

Schneider, for example, thinks that the present era represents the work week, and heaven will be our supreme Sabbath. He calls "the promised rest of God" "the end of all earthly labor, suffering, and conflict."[213] Commenting that rest follows both our entrance into salvation and our entrance into heaven, Hewitt opts for the latter suggestion because of the context.[214]

Kistemaker, a contemporary reformed author, focuses repeatedly on a heavenly but "spiritual rest," that "has become a reality for the believer. . . . Believers, because of firm faith, enter God's rest." How does one enter? ". . . This rest is attained by the believer in personal repentance and an ardent dedication to obey God. When the believer rests from his evil works, he enters the Sabbath-rest granted to the people of God."[215]

The writer to the Hebrews promises, "For we which have believed do enter into rest. . ." (Hebrews 4:3, KJV). He mentions "believing" as a past action, using an aorist active participle. People sometimes call this the "now generation." Something that can now happen to believers shines through in the main verb, "enter into," a present tense verb.

Helen Bartlett Montgomery's version, *The Centenary Translation: The New Testament in Modern English*, vividly renders the verse: "We are actually entering into that rest, we who have believed." If the promise were pointing to heaven, one might logically expect a future tense, "we will enter." The question also arises whether the author would speak with so much doubt about whether or not those who are surely believers would enter into heaven.

The noted New Testament scholar, B.F. Westcott, wrote:

> The writer seems to say, "I speak without hesitation of a promise left us, for we enter, are entering now, into the rest of God,—we who have believed." The above verb is not to be taken as a future, but as the expression of a present fact.[216]

If the verse alludes to a present entrance into rest here and now, it refers to the Christian life rather than to future rest in the heavenly city. Walvoord, a contemporary dispensationalist, states that the Promised-Land motif fits much better as a type of abundant Christian living rather than as a type of heaven.[217] John Owen argued:

> The rest here spoken of (4:1) cannot be the rest of heaven and glory, as some have affirmed, wholly misunderstanding the argument of the apostle, which is the superiority of Christ over Moses. The rest here intended, is that rest which believers have entrance into by Jesus Christ in this world.[218]

Wiley understands this passage as teaching a crucial entry-point into the promised rest for believers in the present life. After all, the Israelites crossed the Jordan and marched into the Promised Land at a specific time. Denying that it depicts entering Canaan, Wiley sees it as entering dynamic sanctification. God requires "the ceasing from those works which flow from our own self-life." Dynamic sanctification comes at "a yielding up of our own wills that the works of God may be wrought in us."[219]

Although many have treated the Promised-Land theme, A.B. Simpson was one of the nineteenth-century-born authors producing an entire volume. His *Land of Promise* expounds a deeper-life stance. Twentieth-century Alliance writer, Robert Meredith Stevens, wrote *Promised Land*, supporting a fresh approach to a similar view.[220]

In early Israelite history, the crossing of the Jordan to enter Canaan marked a definite turning point. If this river-crossing typifies forsaking the self-life's domination, a believer can reach the promised rest of sanctification. The figure supports a crisis entry into dynamic sanctification.[221]

Ceremonies Acting Out Sanctification

Circumcision

God required circumcision of Abraham and his descendants as a sign of the covenant he made with the Chosen People (Gen. 17:7-14). It affirmed God's selection of Israel and his promise to be their God. It formed "the mark of that nation's separation to God."[222]

Since circumcision happened to one individual at a time, the rite suggests a person's separation to God. Because shedding blood comprised "an essential part of the rite," can anyone escape the conviction that circumcision consecrated the baby to God? The consecration focuses on "the fact that" when a person received circumcision, "his life (*i.e.* under the symbol of blood) was offered to God."[223]

In various passages, however, God portrays in circumcision a truth more penetrating than his initial selection of Abraham and the differentiation of his descendants from Gentiles. Alexander Macalister, a Cambridge University anatomy professor, explains this. "Among the Jewish teachers circumcision was regarded as an operation of purification and the word foreskin has come to be synonymous with obstinacy and imperfection."[224]

In this light, one finds Deuteronomy 10:16 arresting. God directs his own stubborn people, "Circumcise then your heart, and stiffen your neck no more." Accusing "all the house of Israel" of being "uncircumcised of heart" (Jer. 9:26), God admonished them. He revealed their need of spiritual circumcision to deal with that perverted heart. Without this removal of the heart's foreskin, God warned of his wrath—because the Jews could only remain ensnared in deeds of wickedness (Jer. 4:4).

Moreover, God promises to some post-exilic Jews (Deut. 30:1-4) who would commit themselves to obey him fully, that *he* would then perform a heart circumcision. This would enable them, as he explains, "to love the LORD your God with all your heart and with all your soul, in order that you may live" (Deut. 30:6). Thus God's work within his people supplies the power to fulfill the greatest commandment—total love of God. The relation to dynamic sanctification appears almost inescapable.

Furthermore, the Holy Spirit sanctifies God's people. Paul confirms that true "circumcision is that which is of the heart," adding, "by the Spirit" (Rom. 2:29). James Dunn remarks that

> God looks for . . . the circumcision of the heart, what the prophets had called for (Deut 10:16; Jer 4:4) and promised (Deut 30:6; Ezek 36:26-27; *Jub.* 1:23) . . . something which could be fully accomplished only by the Spirit of God. . . . It is Paul's distinctively Christian claim that this hope has

been already realized, . . . the eschatological hope of the gift
of the Spirit. . . .

From Paul's words Dunn sees the "'Spirit,' as the divine agent of
renewal and enabler of a life acceptable to God. . . ."[225]

Likewise, Paul contrasts "worship in the Spirit of God" by "the
true circumcision" with confidence in the self-life for success. "We
. . . put no confidence in the flesh" (Phil. 3:3).

Again, writing to Colossae, Paul vividly relates circumcision to
dynamic sanctification. ". . . You were circumcised, not in a physical sense, but by the stripping away of the old nature, which is
Christ's way of circumcision" (Col. 2:11, REB). Coates, a Plymouth Brethren writer, calls the eighth day "the circumcision
day—typically the day when the flesh is seen to be cut off in the
death of Christ."[226]

Oesterley beholds in Christ's circumcision "the highest significance, . . . a parable of the Crucifixion. . . ." We noticed earlier that
Christ's death made provision for our sanctification (Heb. 13:12).
Citing Romans 6:3ff, the same author reminds us that "both circumcision and baptism were a figurative death, by means of which
a new spiritual life was reached."[227] As noted in an earlier chapter,
dynamic sanctification comes through identifying ourselves with
Christ in his death and resurrection, as illustrated by baptism.

Regeneration involves the new birth. Carradine argues that

> . . . circumcision always *follows* birth. . . . The child grew
> and strengthened before it was circumcised. Indeed, God,
> in order to distinguish the two facts and their spiritual ap-
> plication to experiences in the kingdom of grace, separated
> them by a dash or interval of eight days.[228]

Hence, spiritual circumcision occurs later than the new birth, concerns heart purification, and impairs the carnal self. Enabling
wholehearted love of God, it implies identification with Christ in
his death. It constitutes the sign of a covenant with God, and involves the promise and internal working of God's Spirit. It includes a separation to God from evil and a dedication to God.

Does one enter sanctification in a moment or in a lengthy process? If the figure of circumcision offers any implicational evidence, it happens at a point of time. A surgical procedure,

circumcision never occurs throughout 80 or 90 years, though its result may endure that long. The ceremony of circumcision confirms a crisis of dynamic sanctification.

Leper's cleansing

During the wilderness journey, Israelites must have dreaded leprosy. Ostracized from the camp and segregated from human contacts, lepers had to shout: "Unclean! Unclean!" if people approached (Lev. 13:45-46).

Disagreeing on specific identification, scholars agree that leprosy in Bible times could differ from the Hansen's disease that people today call leprosy. Coleman states that leprosy in Leviticus 13-14 "does not in every case refer to the disease known by this name at the present time. On the other hand, true leprosy is most certainly included. . . ."[229] Schreiner, however, writes more recently: "The word *leprosy* in the Bible refers to various kinds of inflammatory skin diseases, and not necessarily to Hansen's disease." Chamblin goes a step further: "probably excluding Hansen's disease."[230]

Martens argues that Israelites unquestionably did not limit the Hebrew term to what we call leprosy since it also described "mildew or mold in clothing (Lev. 13:47-52) or in houses (Lev. 14:34-53). . . ."[231] In a most informative article, Browne, a leprosy researcher in Nigeria, states that "doctors and laity" in Israel today use this same Hebrew term. They use the word one finds in the Old Testament for "any repulsive skin condition, including leprosy."[232]

Vine identifies the New Testament term as "primarily used of psoriasis, characterized by an eruption of rough, scaly patches."[233] The *NRSV Exhaustive Concordance* explains the term as "scourge; a cancer-like disease."[234]

Regarded as hopeless in Bible times apart from divine intervention, the disease rendered one ceremonially unclean. Perhaps this is the reason that Scripture usually speaks of the leper's cleansing, rather than healing. Hence, Scripture seems to make it a symbol of sin, which also requires cleansing.

The sinner lives for sin and self—using the body's members for evil purposes. The ears listen to foul things from human beings or

from the tempter. The sinner uses hands to hurt, steal, or work for
wicked causes. The feet take the sinner to dens of iniquity where
people blaspheme God and lead others astray. All this changes
when people trust the Savior to justify their standing and revolu-
tionize their lives. In Scripture, the leper's experiences symbolize
leaving sinfulness to become the Lord's.

Involved in the ceremony when the priest pronounced the leper
clear of his affliction was a *double ritual* on the eighth day. After the
priest had slain the guilt offering lamb, he *first* applied some of its
blood to the leper's body. He placed blood "on the lobe of the right
ear of the one to be cleansed, and on the thumb of his right hand,
and on the big toe of his right foot" (Lev. 14:14). The New Testament makes clear that a believer receives justification through
Christ's blood (Rom. 5:9). Because of Christ's provision at the
cross, the saved person has found God's forgiveness for wrong listening, working, and walking.

The *second* ceremony in the double ritual concerns the oil that
the priest had just presented to and sprinkled before the Lord
(Lev. 14:10, 12, 15-16). Bonar discerns that this oil declares that
the leper, " . . . now cleansed, offers himself as a consecrated one to
serve the Lord who dwells within that veil."[235] Dipping his finger
into the oil in his palm the priest next applied it directly on top of
the lamb's blood. He placed it on the former leper's right ear lobe,
right thumb, and right big toe (Lev. 14:17). "The oil is put on the
man's ear, as if to say, 'Lord, I will hear for You,'—and on his right
hand as if to say, 'Lord, I will act for You,'—and on his right foot,
as if to say, 'Lord, I will go up and down, to and fro, for You.'"[236]

After this, the priest put all the rest of the oil in his palm on the
former leper's head (Lev. 14:18). Bonar continues:

> He then pours all that remains on his head that as it ran
> down in copious streams over his whole person, he might
> hear every drop cry, "You are His that save [sic] you."
>
> And inasmuch as the oil was to be put upon the blood of
> the trespass offering, there was implied the glorious truth
> that the blood which cleanses also sanctifies. . . . Jesus
> cleansed away the guilt that there might be a fair table on
> which the Spirit might re-write His holy law. . . . You are

handed over to the Lord to serve Him in holiness and righteousness.[237]

Oil in Scripture often symbolizes the Holy Spirit, so expositors usually speak of his work in dedication when explaining this ritual. In dynamic sanctification, the Holy Spirit wants to permeate, fill, and equip the entire person.

> . . . What answers to leprosy in a believer comes about by ignoring the Spirit of God. I should not fulfil the lust of the flesh if I walked in the Spirit. . . . Then there is the Spirit to give character to his hearing, action and walk. His members are to be held as dead in regard to his own will, but the Spirit comes in as life to control them for God. . . . The perfection of the divine pleasure is only to be brought about in the power of the Spirit.[238]

Writers from many schools of thought see sanctification symbolized in the application of oil to the former leper. The moot question is whether the ceremony implies that a person enters dynamic sanctification at a point of time. Without doubt, the priest applied the oil at a divinely appointed moment. Beyond this, people tend to respond pro or con because of previous doctrinal convictions, from other Scripture, or from experience.

If applying the blood represents justification and applying the oil represents the fullness of the Holy Spirit, then the blood came first and the oil afterward—very soon afterward. Carradine notes "a distinct interval of time between the two transactions in order to punctuate clearly the two works of God."[239] Thus, the oil applied to the leper reinforces the idea that dynamic sanctification occurs at a point after one's appropriation of salvation.

New Covenant

Imagine marrying atop an 18,640-foot mountain. Having met in Washington, DC, Pat and Dorothy Cardiff finally decided to marry atop Mt. Kilimanjaro in Tanzania, the nation where Pat teaches.

The couple selected the unusual site to symbolize their realization that achieving success in marriage involves an uphill climb. They chose as an inscription inside their wedding bands: "18,640

feet and climbing." Whether a wedding convenes in a home, cathe-
dral, little chapel, or on a mountain peak, it involves one of the
most solemn covenants into which two humans can enter.

Committing oneself to any covenant involves solemn obligations not to be treated lightly. When the patriarchs covenanted
with God, they meant business. The ancient Hebrews did not
speak of making a covenant, but of cutting a covenant—perhaps
with the idea of cutting into stone the enduring pledge. Also, in the
ceremony of covenant-making, an animal sacrifice solemnly involved cutting a beast apart and dividing the parts (Genesis
15:9-10, 17).

Although God attached severe penalties for disobedience, his
covenants centered in a grace principle. He himself assumed the
full obligation for saving his people. "In contradistinction to . . . a
mutual undertaking between two parties or more, each binding
himself to fulfil obligations, it [the biblical word *covenant*] does not
in itself contain the idea of joint obligation. . . ."[240]

Even as grace underlies God's covenanting, so God sanctifies
his people by grace. Although many will disagree with facets of
Toon's book on sanctification, yet four major statements in his
conclusion deserve widespread acceptance.

> The way of self-sanctification cannot ultimately be suc-
> cessful. God's sanctification is the only sure way of sanctifi-
> cation. God's sanctification in and through Christ is wholly
> free, and only faith can receive it. God's sanctification of
> our lives in space-time by the Holy Spirit requires the obe-
> dience of faith, dedication and commitment.[241]

God entered into a specific covenant relationship with Israel at
Mount Sinai. Speaking the Ten Commandments in their hearing,
he also wrote them on tables of stone. This chapter earlier discussed circumcision as a sign of that Israelite covenant with God.

As Gilchrist notes, "the primary requirement of the covenant
relationship" centered in "complete consecration to Yahweh in
one's innermost spirit. God's demand for exclusive lordship is
based on the covenant relationship established at Sinai."[242] Undoubtedly the terms "consecration," and "exclusive lordship,"
number among key concepts in studying sanctification like ham in
a ham sandwich. Thus, Israel's failures to attain first-covenant

goals showed need for a new covenant where grace would seem even more inescapable.

Because the chosen people broke God's covenant, he promised to provide a new one. "'Behold, days are coming,' declares the LORD, 'when I will make a new covenant with the house of Israel and with the house of Judah. . . . I will put My law within them, and on their heart I will write it. . .'" (Jer. 31:31, 33).

Likewise, God agreed to remove their hearts of stone. He promised, "And I will put My Spirit within you and cause you to walk in My statutes. . ." (Ezek. 36:27). The writer to the Hebrews spoke of dynamic sanctification when quoting from the Jeremiah 31 passage. God chose to replace the first covenant with a second.

> Then He said, "BEHOLD, I HAVE COME TO DO THY WILL." He takes away the first in order to establish the second. By this will we have been sanctified through the offering of the body of Jesus Christ once for all. . . . For by one offering He has perfected for all time those who are sanctified (Heb. 10:9-10, 14; cf. v. 16).

The new covenant involves not only forgiveness of sins. It includes God's taking the responsibility for giving us the ability to do his will—an invaluable aid. "A new power was needed and is supplied under the new covenant. This power is not impersonal, but is . . . the Holy Spirit, who enables the believer to resist the attractions and overcome the power of evil."[243]

God's commandments no longer stand as external foreboding words on tables of stone—words that we prove incapable of obeying. Instead, with God's Spirit implanted within to purify and empower, we can live to please God. We do so not because we must but because we love his will.

Despite a little boy's mischievous behavior, his Christian father may never once entertain the thought of murdering him. Why not? Is it because of the first covenant's commandment against committing murder? No, it is because of love within the father's heart. Similarly, God wants to implant his love in the Christian heart to enable him or her to keep all his commandments.

Paul shows that the plan for victorious living includes the righteous requirement of the law fulfilled in the believer who walks according to the Spirit (Rom. 8:3-4).

The new covenant will be written deeply into the wills of the Israelites, who will obey it by choice rather than by compulsion. . . . Because allegiance to this covenant would be motivated internally, it would be of permanent validity and duration for the people.[244]

God originally guaranteed the promise to Israelites, but by strong New Testament implications broadened it to include any human being who accepts its terms.

At Sinai, the people verbally declared their commitment to obey God's commandments (Deut. 5:2, 24-27). God had adopted Abraham and his descendants corporately as his covenant people. In one sense, however, people must obey individually.

When Moses addressed the *new generation* reared in the wilderness, he reminded them of the Sinai events some forty years earlier. He announced, "The LORD did not make this covenant with our fathers, but with us, *with* all those of us alive here today" (Deut. 5:3). R.K. Harrison, noted Old Testament authority, sees personal responsibility as conspicuous.

In acclaiming this new form of covenantal relationship both Jeremiah and Ezekiel saw that it changed the older concept of a corporate relationship completely by substituting the individual for the nation as a whole. . . . When the new covenant was inaugurated by the atoning work of Jesus Christ on Calvary, this important development of personal, as opposed to corporate, faith and spirituality was made real for the whole of mankind.[245]

God established the first covenant at a specific time—when the Israelites gathered at Mount Sinai and God gave the law through Moses. Individual Israelites comprised part of the body that obligated itself to obey the covenant requirements. It was a decisive event. Amid lightning flashes, thunder claps, thick clouds, deafening trumpet blasts, fire, smoke, and an earthquake, God spoke intelligible words (Exod. 19:16-19; 20:1).

God's establishment of the New Covenant at Calvary also occurred as a decisive event (Luke 22:20).[246] While Jesus was dying, however, people did not gather at Golgotha to covenant with God. Despite his prior attempts to prepare them, Jesus' disciples poorly understood the spiritual significance of what was occurring before their eyes.

Now, amid three hours of darkness, an earthquake, and opening graves (Matt. 27:45, 51-54), God addressed humanity. In communicating he used no words, but a magnificent object lesson of love. Thereafter, entrance into covenant provisions became an individual responsibility.[247]

Although the connection of the New Covenant with sanctification seems clear, the New Covenant also provides for justification through Christ's actual death (Heb. 8:12; 10:17). A person receives forgiveness of sins at the turning point of justification.

Carradine inadequately asserts that "the new birth brings one into the first covenant, and baptism with the Holy Ghost and fire ushers us into the second covenant. . . . In sanctification, which is the second covenant, the promises are all better."[248]

No doubt people living under the first covenant could experience justification (Gen. 15:6). The second covenant paid the bill, however, for this divine forgiveness (Heb. 9:15; Rom. 3:24-25). So, without doubt justification has a great deal to do with the *New* Covenant (Rom. 3:21-22).

Also, surely some individuals living under the Old Covenant experienced dynamic sanctification—as we will explore in the next chapter and as we noted earlier in Jacob.[249] Through his New-Covenant death, Christ purchased both justification and sanctification and offers the benefits of both. Therefore, it seems hazardous to insist that the mere fact of a second covenant *proves* sanctification as a turning point beyond conversion. On the other hand, several probable inferences follow.

(1) God instituted the Old Covenant at a point of time—the Sinai giving of the law. (2) The initial participants in the Old Covenant entered into the covenant at a point of time—the Sinai giving of the law. (3) God inaugurated the New Covenant at a point of time—apparently at Christ's death that purchased both justification and sanctification. (4) A person experiences justification at a point of time—as did three thousand initial converts after Spirit-filled Peter's sermon (Acts 2:38, 40-41). (5) Folks apparently become Spirit-filled at a point of time—as did 120 believers who experienced the awesome power of the New Covenant when

they became filled with the Spirit just before Peter's aforementioned sermon.

A later chapter will examine Pentecost more fully. People normally associate the fullness of the Spirit with sanctification. Some
understand this filling at Pentecost as the first phase of the answer
to Jesus' prayer for the dynamic sanctification of his people (John
17:17).

This chapter has probed several Old Testament items that illustrate the doctrine that believers enter into dynamic sanctification
at a point after conversion. The list has included Jacob's wrestling
at Peniel, the crossing of Jordan into Canaan, circumcision, and
the leper's cleansing ceremony. God's provision of the New Covenant may not provide a positive proof. A person can, however,
build a case from it, suggesting the probability that one enters dynamic sanctification in such a turning point. The case built here
depends on a series of parallels.

20

Pre-Pentecost Experiences

Your iniquity is taken away (Isa. 6:7).

The Bible describes the highly committed lives of various believers. Does it ever narrate the circumstances that led them to a deeper life? Can a searcher discover details in Scripture on how a saved person arrives there? If so, one might expect to find some light to confirm the way into sanctification. If Scripture shows that way to involve a point of entry, do any biblical biographies confirm this concept?

Do believers begin sanctified living intentionally at a point of time? Or, do the righteous imperceptively progress into the deeper relationship with God gradually without any moment of focused faith? The most reliable source for answering is inspired Scripture.

Instead of investigating a large number of Bible characters before the day of Pentecost, this chapter will examine the experiences of two Old Testament individuals as well as a husband and wife who became filled with the Holy Spirit a short time before Jesus' birth. Next, it will close by considering whether or not to expect the history of the early church in Acts to supply experiences pertinent to this quest.

Job

Genuine upright believer

At the start of the biblical account of Job, God refers to this patriarch as "blameless, upright, fearing God, and turning away from evil." God holds up Job to Satan as "exhibit A" of integrity (Job 1:1, 8). Such high commendation surely does not portray Job as absolutely sinless or perfect as God (Rom. 3:23).[250]

The Book of Job epitomizes lofty moral standards. It espouses virtues. It condemns such wrongs as lying, deception, stinginess, greed, idolatry, injustice toward the oppressed, and adultery—even in the heart.[251]

Need to deal with self

After Job's three friends ineffectively attempted to comfort him, Elihu sought to minister to him. Then, God spoke to Job. Though he did not directly answer Job's complaints, the patriarch felt overwhelmed by God's self-revelation. Job finally saw the flaws in his own outlook and his very nature.

> It was the heat of trial that melted Job's nature in the crucible of affliction and brought the dross to the surface. . . . This added trial was bringing out the pride, the self-vindication, the self-glorying that was so indigenous to his nature.[252]

God had accepted Job long beforehand as a righteous man, and Job clung tenaciously to that righteousness throughout the book. Yet, to show Job his creaturely weakness, God used severe trials to contrast with the Creator's immense wisdom and power.

Only when Job admitted his "comparative insignificance," that he was "of no weight" (Job 40:4), could God remold his nature. Job surrendered so

> that he practically canceled himself entirely. . . . Thus the language of Job was that of complete submission to God. . . . Man rises to the ultimate dignity, grandeur, splendour of his own life when he . . . yields himself in complete submission to that [i.e., God's] will.

Jesus insisted that people "deny, not the essential fact of their personality, but the sum-total of their thinking about themselves, resulting from their sin and rebellion against God."[253]

Freligh thinks that behemoth and leviathan depict pride (Job 41:34) of "creature power" and "the hideousness of self, even good self, in God's sight. He (Job) could not tame these wild beasts; neither could he tame his own desperately wicked nature." Recalling the book's contents, this professor continues to explain.

> Job has been stripped, stripped of his possessions, stripped of his friends, and now stripped of himself. In naked reality he stands before the great I AM and knows himself as he truly is. The deep-seated need of which he has until now been utterly unaware at last becomes articulate.[254]

Beginning to realize the deeper needs of his nature, Job trusted the Almighty to make him a different man. Andersen correctly notes that Job "has gained knowledge of God and of himself. . . . There seems to be contrition, for Job says *I despise* (and the translations usually supply *myself* as the object not found in the Hebrew)."[255]

Gill, a renowned Baptist Hebraist wrote prolifically before the American Revolution. His major theological work contains a chapter entitled "Of Sanctification." There he asserts that "one that has the principle and grace of holiness, loathes his sin, and himself for it; and, with Job, abhors himself, and repents in dust and ashes."[256]

Sudden arrival of a deeper experience with God

God brought Job to see his need of sanctification. Did he find the divine provision? Morgan likens Job's experience to Paul's familiar testimony to having been crucified with Christ (Galatians 2:20). "Christ had brought him to the exact place that Job had reached, with the difference that Job at the moment only realized the negative. . . ."[257]

Job had come to some sense of divine provision, which we now understand to be Calvary's provision for our sanctification. "Job had been to Calvary. There he had seen the cure for his innate loathsomeness." "The Lord turned Job's captivity when he prayed for his friends, . . . the final and evident proof that Job abhorred self, and had left it on the cross."[258]

The evidence examined shows that Job appears as a genuine believer in the true God when the book starts. In the latter chapters, however, God revealed himself so profoundly to this suffering patriarch that he acknowledged his wrong in challenging him.

Obviously, Job's repentance (Job 42:6) involved no admission that his afflictions originated because he had committed sinful acts. If Job were guilty of wrongdoing, his friends judged accurately. Instead, he repented at least of impugning God's justice and at most of self-righteousness and pride—central self-life traits. He surely did find a richer experience of God and a teachable spirit (Job 42:4-5). Job's new experience arrived at a point rather than gradually throughout the lengthy illness.

Isaiah

Personal need shown in the vision

Isaiah's name means that Jehovah is (the source of) salvation, a major theme of his book. In the Isaiah 6 vision, Isaiah heard a seraph calling out, "Holy, holy, holy, is the LORD of hosts." Sensing his own impurity in contrast to God's utter holiness, Isaiah received instant purging from *iniquity* and *sin*—words connected with what God deals with in dynamic sanctification.

His lips most impressed him as vile—a tragic admission for a man God was calling to proclaim the divine message. ". . . The lips are singled out . . . because the spoken word was a prophet's business—thus Isaiah acknowledged his unworthiness to be a prophet. . . ."[259] After his cleansing, the prophet heard and accepted a special call to service—using his clean lips for God.

A believing worshiper before the vision

Assuming a chronological arrangement of his book, one sees that Isaiah received divine revelations during the reigns of Uzziah and three later kings (Isa. 1:1). Both Vine and Kilpatrick, for example, seem to hold that Isaiah was exercising some ministry as a prophet before the vision in chapter 6.[260] Apparently Isaiah already had experienced the Lord's saving grace when the book commences.

His spectacular vision of God as supremely holy came in the year of Uzziah's death. People speculate on whether the demise came before the vision or a bit later (Isa. 6:1). Noting that a Jewish tradition identifies Isaiah as Uzziah's cousin, Fitch thinks the vision happened in this way.

> Isaiah hears of the death of king Uzziah and thereupon, with some sense, it would seem, of national sorrow in view of the difficulties and hazards that the nation must now face, he enters the courts of the temple that he might seek after the Lord. It was then that the vision recounted in this chapter breaks upon him.[261]

Some writers, however, view chapter 6 as chronologically earlier than the first five chapters.[262] Some suppose the prophet delayed relating his call so he could plunge immediately into his urgent theme—warning against sin.[263] In either case, chapter 6 appears to portray a believing worshiper of Jehovah in the temple, overwhelmed by God's utter holiness (Isa. 6:3). "This vision of God's holiness, majesty, and purity paralyzes Isaiah with the knowledge of his and his people's sinfulness."[264]

Decisive moment of purification during the vision

The flaw that then smote him with conviction was iniquity, sin, impurity—the bent inward nature. God, by way of a seraph, sent the remedy—ruin of, and purification from, carnality, based on atonement (Isa. 6:5-7).

A.B. Simpson saw the live coal as "the baptism of fire . . . that consumes and cleanses intrinsically and utterly." He believes that "its effect was to cleanse his lips and purge away his iniquity, that he might be fitted for his great commission."[265] Moreover, "inner purification had resulted in a new ability to discern and do the will of God."[266] Van Gemeren understands Isaiah as a representative of the chosen people. "Israel and Judah will not be able to experience the lovingkindness of the Lord until they have been cleansed and sanctified," he comments. "Only then can they experience the presence of the Holy One of Israel."[267]

As Isaiah experienced a decisive moment of purification from iniquity, so may believers today. Such a sanctification point prepares for further service as well as for holy living.

Elizabeth and Zacharias

Circumstances surrounding the fullness

When did the parents of John the Baptist become filled with the Holy Spirit? When the expectant Virgin Mary arrived at their home and greeted her relative, Elizabeth's baby leaped in her womb. Then and there "Elizabeth was filled with the Holy Spirit" (Luke 1:39-41). This occurred suddenly.

Earlier, while Zacharias, the priest, was burning incense in the temple as assigned, the angel, Gabriel, suddenly appeared to him. Fear gripped the priest. When the angel informed him that he would become the father of John, he doubted. He and Elizabeth were elderly and childless. Because he asked how he could be sure, Gabriel stated that he would lose his power of speech until John's birth (Luke 1:8-20).

Rejoicing with the couple at the circumcision, the neighbors and relatives thought they should name him for his father. Elizabeth disagreed. When they consulted Zacharias, he wrote on a tablet, "His name is John." Suddenly Zacharias could speak. He praised God. At once he became filled with the Holy Spirit (Luke 1:57-64, 67).

Suddenness of the fullness

Each parent became filled suddenly rather than throughout a period of growth. Although some teach that the Spirit's fullness should arrive during a gradual process, it did not happen that way for John's parents.

As in nearly every occurrence of this phrase, "filled with the Holy Spirit," Luke chose an aorist passive verb to express the idea of "filled." Earlier we discovered that an author who uses an aorist tense at least views the action as happening at a point. The context here confirms that the action really happened at a point.

Correct Use of the Acts History

When anyone experiences regeneration, the Holy Spirit automatically enters and begins to abide. The Holy Spirit automatically unites the person to the universal body of Christ. Potentially the convert has everything ever needed for successful Christian living.

Does Acts history contain only exceptions?

It is both interesting and disappointing, however, the way many current evangelical and fundamentalist theologians treat the Acts history. They believe every fact in the paragraph above. Often, they hold a strong view of full inerrancy. They, nevertheless, resist seeing *most* Acts accounts as normative examples of the Spirit's deeper work in people's lives in the present age. They admit that Acts contains absolutely accurate history. *They think, however, that Acts records only exceptions to what one ought to expect of the Holy Spirit's working today. Does this make good sense?*

Admittedly, Jesus spoke to multitudes in parables so his elect would learn much while those rejecting him would remain puzzled and stumble (Matt. 13:9-17). Hearing, they did not hear nor understand. Even as Christ wanted his own followers to understand truth, however, surely God today desires born-again believers to grasp his truth.

Would the God of history who wants his Church to understand truth do everything possible to deceive them? Would the Holy Spirit inspire Luke to describe only exceptions to the rule in regard to receiving the fullness of the Holy Spirit?

Can Acts speak for itself or must we reinterpret?

Unfortunately many contemporary writers see no current relevance in the Acts passages on groups who received the fullness. Because of the presupposition that all Christians already have the Holy Spirit, such writers approach these Acts passages with the assumption that the people described lacked regeneration.

The reinterpretation proceeds as follows. At Pentecost, God first gave the Holy Spirit to his followers, so they first became regenerate at that point. What Scripture states this? None.

Proceeding, the "reinterpreters"[268] claim that Pentecost involves God's pouring out the Spirit upon his Church once for all forever. Thereafter, all new believers automatically receive at regeneration all that the 120 received at Pentecost. What Scripture states this? None.

When we read Acts 10, however, we discover a new outpouring on the household of Cornelius. The "reinterpreters" tell us that this is an exception because here the first Gentile converts believe. Here is the "Gentile Pentecost."

If we mention Acts 8, such writers forbid Christians today to expect to receive the Holy Spirit's power as the Samaritans received. Why? Here stands another exception, reinterpreters *claim*. Since the Samaritans formed a hybrid race with mixed Jewish and Gentile elements, did they actually need an additional Pentecost? If so, the false foundation crumbles. God surely did not intend the fullness at Pentecost as an unrepeatable once-for-all-forever enduement of all who would ever become believers.

Examining Acts 19, we discover twelve men whom Luke and Paul depict as believers, but believers without the Holy Spirit. After interaction and teaching, at the laying on of hands the Holy Spirit came upon them. Here is yet another exception, according to our reinterpreting opponents.

This time the problem allegedly arose because the converts lacked instruction. Shall we assume that every convert today has thorough instruction? Or shall we assume that the Holy Spirit has decided to come in fullness regardless of human ignorance since the original apostles have died?

Having originally received water baptism at the hands of a follower of John the Baptist, the Ephesian believers needed to learn of Christ's resurrection. Not understanding the Holy Spirit's arrival at Pentecost, they needed to receive the Spirit later. Therefore, "reinterpreters" inform us that the Spirit had not come when they originally believed because the new birth awaited Paul's arrival. Acts, they insist, forms a transitional book. The "reinterpreters" hasten to explain that no such exceptions could possibly exist today.

Does Acts show a consistent pattern for *this* age?

An honest student needs to consider carefully the historical background of each incident and treat fairly all the details. The next few chapters will give attention to several of these Acts incidents. Did you ever suspect, however, that God is showing us in Acts, the only inspired *history* of the early church, a very valuable consistent pattern for the present age, which began at Pentecost? An open-minded examination may show us that the Acts history really is not a string of exceptions quite irrelevant to us.

One wonders whether Scripture may be seeking to inform us that God truly has available for each believer a fullness of the Spirit over and above his initial automatic regenerating and incoming? If he wanted us to believe this, how could he have done a better communication job than what he has already done? He has supplied us with the Acts history where person after person and group after group entered into the Spirit's renewing after conversion? In that history an empowering fullness became available as soon as possible after a person's initial trust in Christ for salvation. Do we not live in the church age, even as the early church did?

Inch correctly discerns a distinction that other contemporaries need to hear:

> Believers *have* the Spirit indwelling them, but are not necessarily *filled* with the Spirit. To be filled with the Spirit is to be in submission to the Spirit. It requires that we yield to God's will without reservation.[269]

21

Experience of 120 at Pentecost

Your iniquity is taken away (Isa. 6:7).

A Momentous Day

The day of an Allied invasion of France would become "the longest day" predicted Erwin Rommel, Hitler's Normandy commander. An American news agency referred to it as history's greatest overseas military operation.

Suspecting an imminent invasion, Axis intelligence could only guess exactly where and when the axe would fall. A successful invasion would likely torpedo the Nazi dream of world domination. Amid most unfavorable weather on June 5, 1944, Germans retained their patrol craft in port, "sure" that the Allies could not then attack.

"OK, we'll go," sounded the predawn decision of Allied Commander Dwight D. Eisenhower, beginning the June 6 D-Day invasion of Normandy. An Allied armada—700 warships, 2700 support ships, and 2500 landing craft converged on 50 miles of beaches on France's northwest coast. Envisioning the liberation of Europe from oppression, 326 thousand Allied invaders landed with vast stores of vehicles and supplies the first six days.

The British had broadcast cryptic messages to the French un-
derground resistance to prepare them for the D-day invasion.
When God had long been planning a remarkable invasion of Satan's territory with trained troops, he, too, sent information. God
had sent forecasts by ancient prophets and rather explicit directions to his people through Jesus Christ. This chapter probes the
significance of God's D-day after wrestling with its relevance to
today's Christian's need for sanctification.

A Relevant Day

Scrutinizing opposing views

Many sincere Christians today consider the experience of
the 120 as supplying no evidence about whether dynamic sanctification begins at a point in time. They seek support from several ideas listed in italics, numbered, and weighed below. The
issue fully concerns Pentecost, often applying to groups later in
Acts as well.

Does Acts provide a historical account?

Opponents assert: (1) *The biblical account of Pentecost appears in
Acts, a historical rather than a doctrinal book.* The New Testament
epistles provide a highly essential foundation for building one's
theology. In proving doctrines, Jesus and Paul constantly appeal to
Old Testament writings throughout the Law, the Prophets, and
the Hagiographa. They do not restrict themselves to one genre of
biblical literature. They never avoid historical literature.

One epistle, however, verbally shows the proper sources for
building doctrine as wider than the epistles. "All Scripture *is* given
by inspiration of God, and *is* profitable for doctrine, for reproof,
for correction, for instruction in righteousness" (2 Tim. 3:16,
KJV).

Wherever in Scripture teaching occurs, it instructs both in what
to believe and how to behave. The whole Bible, not just one part, is
profitable as the source of Christian teaching.

What is the principal meaning of Pentecost?

Opponents assert: (2) *The day of Pentecost focuses on the start of the Church rather than on the sanctifying of individuals.* God lives everywhere at once. Theologically, the previous sentence means that each Person of the Trinity possesses omnipresence. Yet the Son and the Holy Spirit have unique ministries implying unique manifestations of their presence.

Citing Augustine's expression that Pentecost was the *dies natalis,* the Holy Spirit's birthday, Gordon explains well. As Jesus arrived in a body in Mary's womb, so the Spirit uniquely arrived at Pentecost to indwell human flesh. Of course, the church is neither deity nor absolutely perfect like Jesus was.

"The Christian church throughout all this dispensation stands as the home of the Spirit as truly as heaven, during this same period, is the home of Jesus Christ."[270] Since Pentecost, the Holy Spirit has made his unique home within believers on earth. Within believers also he has established his place of work. Jesus explained that when he himself would depart, he would send the Holy Spirit to his believing followers. Through these believers, the Spirit would "convict the world concerning sin, and righteousness, and judgment. . ." (John 16:7-8).

Christians understand that the significance of this day of Pentecost included several important features. Many would list the body of Christ begun, the birthday of the universal Church, and the start of a new divine-grace era.

One must not deny the importance of these three features, the birthday of the Spirit, the birthday of the Church, and the dispensational beginning. Speaking just before his ascension, however, Jesus disclosed *none* of them. Judging from the New Testament, Jesus explained just before departing to heaven *one* immediate result of Pentecost only—his troops must experience empowering. They must be "clothed with power from on high." (Acts 1:5; Luke 24:49).

Virtually all Christians would point out that at Pentecost God launched an unprecedented world evangelization offensive. Through committed troops he liberated a vast throng enslaved in Satan's oppressive kingdom. Jesus spoke of this as an *effect* of clothing his troops with divine power (Acts 1:8-9; Luke 24:47-49).

Southern U.S. clothing mills worked nonstop around the clock to produce uniforms and parachutes for World War II Normandy invaders. Similarly, God provided the Christian's essential clothing for battle.

Peter afterward remembered another effect of Pentecost as dynamic sanctification. "Cleansing their hearts by faith" concerns both "us"—the 120 at Pentecost and "them"—the household of Cornelius later (Acts 15:9).This dynamic sanctification radically transformed Peter from a denying, wavering recruit to a committed, fearless soldier ready for the invasion of planet earth with the gospel.

In what sense is Pentecost unrepeatable?

Opponents assert: (3) *Whatever occurred at Pentecost happened once for all for the entire Church, so we should not expect its empowering to be repeated now. Our individual lives form part of that Church.* The key to a correct answer, however, lies in differentiating *which* features Scripture shows to be unique at Pentecost. Other features reappear in scriptural history and throughout later Church history.

In a sense, the Holy Spirit uniquely came into the world at Pentecost even as Jesus came into the world at Bethlehem. This *part* of what occurred at Pentecost did happen once for all for the entire Church. The universal Church began once, not over and over again. Nevertheless, other individuals and groups elsewhere did receive a special empowering by the Holy Spirit for holy living and effective service.

Did the 120 become born again at Pentecost?

Opponents assert: (4) *At Pentecost the 120 received regeneration rather than dynamic sanctification.* No, the 120 were already believers. The 3,000 to whom the 120 witnessed are the ones who received regeneration that day. This witness of newly empowered believers resulted in a highly fruitful spiritual harvest on this Jewish harvest festival day.

We infer from Scripture that when a human being believes on the Lord Jesus Christ in any era, that person experiences both justification and regeneration. In other words, God declares that person to be righteous because of the divine provision in Christ.

Furthermore, God imparts divine life into the person through the Spirit's work.

Even as God justified Abraham through faith before the cross (Rom. 4:3), so Jesus spoke about a repentant man as able to go down to his house justified (Luke 18:14). Very early in his ministry Jesus taught Israel's chief Sanhedrin teacher that a person could become born of the Spirit (John 3:3). Jesus insisted, "You must be born again" (John 3:7). Jesus never said, "Oh, by the way, it will be several years before anyone *can* become born again."

Early in his ministry, Jesus had said that "whoever believes in Him" will "not perish, but have eternal life" (John 3:16). Regeneration involves receiving eternal life. Moreover, John explained that those who received Jesus by believing on his name became born of God (John 1:12-13). Having authority to forgive sins during his earthly ministry, Jesus did so on various occasions, sometimes adding that the person had now experienced salvation (Luke 5:20-26; 7:47-50).

During Jesus' earthly ministry, many people "believed in him" (for example, John 2:11; 4:39; 11:45). Jesus told the seventy to rejoice that heaven's roster of the redeemed included their names (Luke 10:20).

Just before sending out his disciples two by two, he assured them. "For it is not you who speak," he affirmed, "but it is the Spirit of your Father who speaks in you." God was their Father and the Holy Spirit was speaking in them. How can anyone treat with fairness such statements and call these unconverted men? The kingdom of God belonged to them (Luke 6:20). Concluding his ministry, Jesus directly described his disciples, excluding Judas Iscariot, as clean because of the Word he had spoken to them (John 13:10-11; 15:3).

Moreover, Jesus stated that although he would send the Holy Spirit to his disciples, yet "the world cannot receive" him (John 14:17). Again, just before his betrayal he prayed for the sanctification, not of the world, but of those whom the Father had already given him out of the world (John 17:9, 16-17).

. . . He does not ask that they be "justified," "saved," for they already were His. . . . *They did not need to be saved, but they did*

need to be sanctified. . . . But that is not all. See verse 20: "I do
not ask in behalf of these alone, but for those also who believe
in Me through their word" (the children of God, the saved,
the justified of all time—us) [emphasis his].[271]

Surely Christ's prayer found an initial fulfillment at Pentecost.
Those whom the Holy Spirit filled were already believers.

Regarding Pentecost, "the central point or main purpose of the
whole miraculous event is . . . that all the *believers* were filled with the
Holy Ghost. . . . all the believing people who were present, without
distinction. . ." (emphasis mine).[272] Davids believes that "all of those
in the upper room were believers in Christ and baptized. Only the
empowering for mission in the Spirit was missing."[273]

Does the fullness make one a Pentecostal?

Opponents assert: (5) *To concede that all contemporary Christians
need to become filled with the Holy Spirit opens the door to Pentecostal and
charismatic excesses.* No doubt some excesses exist in various groups
who overemphasize signs, feelings, and experiences. Scripture
never advocates excesses, nor should we. Believers need to exercise caution. If Scripture teaches, however, that Christians must
become filled with the Spirit, it will not please God if one substitutes caution for obedience. Swindoll reminds us that ". . . we are
clearly commanded to 'Be filled with the Spirit!' Therefore, it is
something we are to obey."[274]

At Pentecost, in Dunn's words,

> the experience should neither be reduced to nor seen solely
> in terms of its phenomena, ecstatic vision and glossolalia.
> For those involved, so far as we can tell, these latter were
> only the concomitant circumstances of the invasion of di-
> vine power from without. . . .[275]

The evidence doctrine states that a person who has received
baptism in the Spirit, will manifest as initial evidence speaking in
tongues. When Pentecostals and charismatics advocate the evidence doctrine, they appear to go beyond Scripture. Of the many
individuals and groups in Acts who became Spirit-filled, Scripture
mentions only three groups who spoke in tongues.

Since the Spirit keeps "distributing to each one individually just as He wills," he must not intend tongues for all Spirit-filled believers (1 Cor. 12:11). Even when writing to a church that seemed overzealous for tongues, Paul inquired, "All do not speak with tongues, do they" (1 Cor. 12:30)?

Paul never mentions tongues in other epistles. Paul devotes a whole chapter to explaining tongues' relative unimportance—in contrast to prophecy—even in the apostolic period (1 Cor. 14). It is perilous to insist on tongues contrary to God's will. It seems equally perilous to doubt that God has filled me with his Spirit unless I speak in tongues.

Americans enjoy the warning: "Don't throw out the baby with the bath water." Although one must throw out unscriptural excesses, no one should throw out a scriptural command because excesses exist. God calls us not to excesses but to obedience. Graham sternly insists that

> "Be filled with the Spirit," is binding on all of us Christians everywhere in every age. There are no exceptions. We must conclude that since we are ordered to be filled with the Spirit, we are sinning if we are not filled.

Does fullness come at conversion?

Opponents assert: (6) *If every Christian in the present age automatically has the Holy Spirit living within, we enjoy Spirit-fullness from the moment of conversion.* It is true that the Holy Spirit now lives in every born-again believer. The above objection, however, mistakes the biblical use of language. No Scripture uses "full of," or "filled with the (Holy) Spirit," to describe a person's experience at the moment of conversion.

Although Wayne Ward (incorrectly) thinks the 120 experienced conversion at Pentecost, he correctly sees all later uses as describing post-conversion experiences. "After the initial coming of the Spirit, the word 'filled' is never used again for the beginning of the Christian life. . . ."[276] Figure 2 on the next page shows New Testament uses. In the Old Testament as well, this terminology speaks of special empowering or enabling rather than conversion.

Figure 2

N.T. Uses of "Filled with the Holy Spirit": Saved or Unsaved?

PERSON	SCRIPTURE	ALREADY SAVED	AT THE POINT OF CONVERSION	UNIQUE CASES
Elizabeth	Lk 1:41	X		
Zacharias	Lk 1:67	X		
The 120	Ac 2:4	X		
Peter	Ac 4:8	X		
Jerusalem Church	Ac 4:31	X		
Paul	Ac 9:17	X		
Paul	Ac 13:9	X		
Pisidian Antioch "Disciples"	Ac 13:52	X		
Ephesian Church	Eph 5:18	X		
John the Baptist	Lk 1:15			Unborn!
†Jesus Christ	Lk 4:1			Jesus
†Deacon Candidates	Ac 6:3	X		
†Stephen	Ac 6:5	X		
†Stephen	Ac 7:55	X		
†Barnabas	Ac 11:24	X		

† *"Full" rather than "filled"*

If the expressions, "born again" and "filled with the Holy Spirit," were interchangeable phrases, then Paul surely would not command believers to "be filled with the Spirit" (Eph. 5:18). Walvoord argues persuasively and correctly:

> In . . . that Christians are commanded to be filled with the Spirit, it is clear also that it is possible to be a Christian without being filled. No Christian is ever warned to seek the other ministries of the Spirit because in their nature they are wrought in salvation. It is apparent, then, that the filling of the Holy Spirit, while possible only for the saved, is not a part of salvation itself.[277]

At conversion a sinner stops trying to save himself or herself. At the fullness one stops trying to live the Christian life by his or her own strength. In conversion, someone dead in trespasses and sins (Eph. 2:1) receives God's gift of eternal life. At the fullness, one alive in Christ receives an enabling to spend life in a consecrated fashion. Life now becomes abundant life.

In conversion, God forgives acts of sin, but at fullness, God cleanses the nature that enslaves a Christian to Satan's program. At conversion, a person senses the need to witness, though at fullness, a person receives a divine dynamic enabling an effective witness and service. Swindoll correctly differentiates conversion from fullness.

> It is one thing to become a Christian. It is another thing entirely to become a Spirit-filled Christian. The tragedy is that so many are converted and so few Spirit-filled. When this happens, a person misses the best God has to offer us on earth.[278]

Summary of evidences

In summary, all Scripture is profitable for doctrine—not just the epistles. When correctly used, historical literature like Acts can help our search for truth. Other features of the Pentecost event must never eclipse the empowering of the individuals who initially made up the Church. Although the Holy Spirit came only once to begin the age of grace, individual Christians keep needing the empowering God promised.

Much evidence suggests that the 120 had experienced conversion sometime previous to Pentecost. The errors of extremism must never prevent our taking a balanced scriptural view of the fullness of the Spirit. Scripture uses terms like "filled with the Holy Spirit" to denote a degree of surrender and empowering beyond conversion.

Thus the fullness of the Spirit at Pentecost has much direct relevance to today's Christian. Even as the 120 needed special divine power for holy living and for the worldwide witness they were undertaking, so do we.

A Preparatory Day

A predicted event

Shortly before the Ascension, Jesus had directed that his assembled apostles must not leave Jerusalem until after God had fulfilled "the promise of the Father" (Acts 1:4, Greek, NASB mg., and KJV) in their lives. Clearly this expression refers to the promise made by the Father that centers in his giving the Holy Spirit. This event was one that could afterward be dated; it was no lifelong process. Thus, adding that this event would occur "not many days from now," Jesus equated this promise with the baptism with the Holy Spirit (Acts 1:4-5).

In so doing, Jesus reminded the apostles that he himself had earlier told them to anticipate this special baptism, contrasting it with John's baptism. John the Baptist had himself drawn the same contrast.

Location of the event

After Jesus had ascended, some 120 of his followers met in Jerusalem. Luke gives the number as approximate (Acts 1:15). Christian tradition from the fourth century, based on Acts 1:13, has located the outpouring at Pentecost in an upper room. Campbell Morgan, however, cautions readers that this theory does not fit the facts.

> . . . The upper room was merely a place of tarrying for some of the fellowship; but their meeting-place day by day was

in the temple [Luke 24:52-53; cf. Acts 2:46]. . . . There were at least one hundred and twenty of them together; and moreover, presently more than three thousand people were gathered about them.[279]

One problem with Morgan's attractive view is that Scripture locates the sound of the wind as filling "the whole house" where they sat (Acts 2:2). In this context, we might expect a different word if Luke had intended a part of the temple. Although he wishes for the outpouring in the very upper room where Jesus had made the promise to the disciples, yet Swete opts for a house since they needed privacy.[280]

The 120 were obeying Christ's command to wait in that city, Jerusalem. Likely they did not realize how long they needed to wait. They remained together in one place (Acts 2:1) during the ten-day interval at least until the Jews celebrated the feast of Pentecost. This proved to be D-Day. Before launching the invasion, however, that would liberate so many from their sins, they must await the arrival of the designated clothing (Luke 24:49)—the Holy Spirit's empowering.

An event with wind and fire

Suddenly, the 120 heard a sound resembling a violent wind, and they saw tongues that appeared like fire, each descending to rest on the head of one worshiper. The original words for "Spirit" and "wind" are identical—both in Hebrew and Greek. Thus, God's use of wind and fire in the immediate context of Acts 2:4 surely cannot be accidental. Both symbolize the Holy Spirit.

John the Baptist had predicted that Jesus would baptize his hearers with wind (the Spirit) and fire (Matt. 3:11; Luke 3:16). In context, as people hurl unfruitful trees into the fire, so Christ will thoroughly purge his threshing-floor. He will burn up the chaff (Matt. 3:10, 12; Luke 3:9, 17). Illuminating the early verses of Acts 2, Blaiklock reminds readers that "*wind* (2) and *fire* (3) were an accepted symbolism for the powerful and cleansing operation of God's Spirit. In this event God was manifesting Himself uniquely at a vital moment in history."[281]

> ... On the day of Pentecost, when the fullness of the Spirit
> was imparted ... amid visible and audible signs, ... these
> signs evidently possess an emblematical character, and re-
> fer to the promise that the disciples shall be baptized with
> the Holy Ghost and with fire. ... The Holy Ghost is a di-
> vine fire, purifying the heart, consuming all that is sinful in
> it, elevating it to God, and sanctifying it (Quesnel).[282]

Thus, the Lord prepared for the day of Pentecost, predicting
beforehand its arrival and its significance. The day itself, however,
was preparatory. It prepared committed believers with spiritual
virtues and skills for service. It clothed God's picked troops for the
invasion of Satan's territory for the liberation of multitudes.

The troops were ready. The offensive began—immediately.
That preparatory day became also the start of the mighty offensive
as three thousand then and there found the Lord Jesus Christ in
saving power. Through prepared troops the Holy Spirit snatched
three thousand from bondage to freedom.

A Crisis Day

A crossroads of human history occurred. D-day arrived. The
time arrived for the fulfillment of God's promise. Believers must
have power to live victoriously, to proclaim God's message convincingly, to do God's work proficiently.

Regarding the crisis moment, Luke records that "they were all
filled with the Holy Spirit,"—the cleanser and "empowerer" (Acts
2:4). Since the word "filled" does not occur here in the imperfect
tense, Scripture's emphasis is not on an ongoing lifetime or
month-long process of becoming filled. Instead, the aorist used
views the action as punctiliar, at a point of time.

The context surely confirms this idea. A few days beforehand
these people had not received the promised filling (Acts 1:5).
"Suddenly" on the day of Pentecost the wind sound and fire sight
appeared and they became filled at once. Hence, the experience of
the 120 confirms that dynamic sanctification comes to believers at
a point of time.

22

Post-Pentecost Experiences: Petrine Period

*Your iniquity
is taken away
(Isa. 6:7).*

Most striking is the transformation of the blundering, boasting, Christ-denying Peter in the Gospels into the new Peter after Pentecost. After receiving Spirit-fullness, Peter stood amid persecution as the unflinching, unconquerable witness for Christ. Acts 4:8 mentions Peter's Spirit-filling as the reason for his bold penetrating reply to the Sanhedrin under interrogation.

Was the Spirit-fullness restricted to the 120 or did God intend that the three thousand converts that day should receive the same promise? When the church grew to five thousand, could the additional people converted receive the fullness? Was the fullness limited to Judea or could people in Samaria who came to trust Christ also acquire the fullness? This chapter will examine selected events in the period of Peter's major influence in the early church after Pentecost.

Early Jerusalem Multitudes

After filling the 120 with the Spirit, God amazed Jews gathered in Jerusalem from all over the Roman world. He miraculously allowed them to hear of "the mighty deeds of God" in their own languages (Acts 2:5-11). Asking the meaning of this, stunned listeners that same day learned about Jesus' death, resurrection, and ascension from Peter's Spirit-anointed preaching (Acts 2:12-35).

Three thousand listeners

A promise must be fulfilled.

When Peter charged his listeners with Jesus' death, conviction seized them so that they cried: "What shall we do?" (Acts 2:36-37). Peter responded by urging each to repent and accept baptism in Jesus Christ's name. They needed God to forgive their sins. That very day three thousand repented, received baptism, and joined with the 120 as part of the Church (Acts 2:41).

Peter had added the promise: "and you shall receive the gift of the Holy Spirit" (Acts 2:38). Since those convicted Jews had observed the surprising results of the Holy Spirit's arrival, Peter had encouraged them to believe that God had not limited "the promise of the Father" to the 120. Telling his hearers that the ascended Christ had poured forth the promise of the Holy Spirit, he assured them, "the promise is for you" (Acts 2:33, 39).

A gift must be received.

He explained that by becoming believers, they too "became candidates"[283] to receive "the gift of the Holy Spirit." Calvin grasped the occasion for this promise. ". . . Wondering when they saw the apostles suddenly begin to speak with strange tongues, . . . he promiseth them the gift of the Spirit. . . ."[284]

The gift of tongues, an external sign, had attracted attention. *The gift of the Spirit*, by contrast, was the internal essence causing the transformation of the 120. God, a bit later that day, was promising this gift of the Spirit to the thousands of convicted unsaved Jews listening to Peter preach. The sermon prescribed prerequisites. First they must receive forgiveness of sins. Then the promise was available.

As Robertson correctly shows, this is the gift that *is* the Holy Spirit, an example of the "genitive of identification."[285] Too many readers, however, jump to the conclusion that this reception of the gift who is the Holy Spirit is automatic. A child must receive the gift of a frog from a playmate, or else he (or she!) has no frog. Likewise, though God has promised salvation, I do not have salvation until I accept it by receiving Christ (John 1:11-12). Similarly, although God has promised the Spirit in fullness, I have no gift if I accept nothing. Morgan writes,

> . . . They might share in all they had seen, as they fulfilled the conditions thus stated. . . . That which is permanent is the fullness of the Holy Spirit, placed at the disposal of the children of God. If there be any lack, it is found in us, in some reserve . . . holding back from complete surrender.[286]

That phrase, "the gift of the Holy Spirit," also appears in Acts 10:45. "All the circumcised believers . . . with Peter were amazed, because the gift of the Holy Spirit had been poured out upon the Gentiles *also*" (emphasis mine). "Also," in context, implies that God had bestowed "the gift of the Holy Spirit" on the 120 as well as on Cornelius' household.

Apparently, then, God gave "the promise of the Father," also called "the gift of the Holy Spirit," not just once in history. Instead, over and over again in various places and times God fulfilled the same promise. Peter promised "the gift of the Holy Spirit" to all who would meet the conditions—his audience, their children, and future believers whom God would call to himself (Acts 2:39).

God bestowed the gift who is the Holy Spirit upon those lives properly prepared as the 120 had been. Is this not the answer to Jesus' prayer? Jesus had prayed for the dynamic sanctification of those whom the Father had given him out of the world. He had included also others who would believe in him through their word (John 17:9, 14-20).

Jesus keeps fulfilling this promise, bestowing this gift, and sanctifying believers since the original outpouring. It seems apparent, then, that Christians do not automatically enter into the fullness of the Holy Spirit at conversion. It occurs, however, at a point of time.

Experience of additional thousands

After Pentecost, when three thousand people had converted to Christ, the number of believers kept increasing. Swete correctly observes that "Luke does not say that the three thousand who were baptized that day received the gift of the Spirit immediately. . . ."[287] By Acts 4:4, the number of male members alone in the Jerusalem church had reached five thousand.

After God healed the man in his forties at the temple gate, the Council threatened Peter and John (Acts 4:1-22). They insisted that the apostles cease speaking in Jesus' name.

Returning to the company of believers, they reported their experiences, and engaged in an earnest spontaneous prayer meeting with the group (Acts 4:23-30). Luke emphasized prayer more than the other synoptic writers, giving attention to prayer in Acts as well. In Jesus' prayer instructions, when Matthew used the phrase "good gifts," Luke substituted "the Holy Spirit," perhaps implying that he is the best gift. Apparently Jesus used both expressions (Matt. 7:11; Luke 11:13).

The intense early church prayer season proved most effective. God answered this time with a miraculous sign in addition to inward spiritual power for effective living. ". . . The place where they had gathered together was shaken, and they were all filled with the Holy Spirit. . ." (Acts 4:31). Since the Scripture states that God filled "all," this probably included a refilling of people already filled at Pentecost.

On the other hand, in this place assembled multitudes—conceivably thousands of people converted since Pentecost. In the face of rising persecution and pressing needs for evangelization, they greatly needed a divine equipping. Here they received the fullness of the Holy Spirit. Results included unity, love, unselfish generosity, and evidence of great grace in their lives along with boldness in witness (Acts 4:31-33).

In this incident also, the infilling amounted to a sudden action at the point of time when the building shook after their praying. As Lechler observes, "The believers could not have been filled with the Holy Ghost, if they had not previously offered this prayer."[288] The Scriptures indicate point action not only by an aorist verb for "filled," but also by the context of a specific prayer meeting. An apparent earthquake, perhaps localized, quickly ensued.

New Samaritan Believers

When China fell to communist rule, overseas missionaries necessarily left. Discouragement caused missions activists to wonder whether Christianity could survive in China. Information during this decade, however, proves that the church multiplied astonishingly well during those decades of persecution.

Jewish persecution likewise threatened the Jerusalem church, slaying Stephen and ousting other Christians, except the apostles (Acts 7:58-8:3). As in China, so in Judea and Samaria, sufferings resulted in the gospel's wider dissemination.

Powerful evangelization

Philip, apparently the Spirit-filled deacon introduced earlier (Acts 6:3, 5), heralded the gospel in a Samaritan city with remarkable success (Acts 8:5). Textual scholars and commentators have trouble knowing which city Luke intends. Was it the Old Testament city, Samaria, that had borne the same name as the later province, or an unnamed city within that territory?[289]

Traditional animosity between Samaritans and Jews did not prevent large numbers of Samaritans "with one accord" from believing the message. They proceeded into the waters of baptism. By impressive signs, God kept confirming the validity of Philip's preaching ministry. Luke relates that *many* demonized people in the city experienced deliverance from evil spirits. God was curing *many* paralyzed and lame people. No wonder great joy flooded the city! (Acts 8:6-8).

When the apostles at Jerusalem learned about the gospel's progress in Samaria, they sent Peter and John. Perhaps the presence of such respected leaders would allay latent fears in the new church. Previous racial antagonism must not prevent full acceptance into the body of Christ.

Peter and John engaged in immediate spiritual ministry. Apparently the new converts had not yet entered into the fullness of the

Spirit. Praying that they might receive the Holy Spirit, Peter and John laid hands on the Samaritans (Acts 8:14-17).

Peculiar puzzle or proper pattern?

Issue of new birth: Had Philip led only half way?

Opponents of the idea that a person enters the fullness of the Holy Spirit after conversion labor diligently. Digging beneath the obvious meaning of words, they seek to show that this incident did not happen as the New Testament account reads. Their main strategy attempts to convince people that Philip's converts remained unregenerate until Peter and John arrived to pray for them.

Examining denials of new birth under Philip.

Assuming that "in NT times the possession of the Spirit was *the* hallmark of the Christians," Dunn sees the Samaritans totally without him. He concludes that they *could not possibly* have been born again before the apostles came.[290] Thus, he seems to beg the question, assuming the conclusion, rather than allowing this and other Acts passages to speak for themselves.

He entitles his chapter "The Riddle of Samaria." If one disposes of theological presuppositions, however, Acts 8 harmonizes with the rest of Acts. The riddle melts away. Countering Dunn's arguments, Ervin, for example, entitles his own chapter, "Samaria, Riddle or Pattern of Pentecost?"[291]

Most Keswick, Wesleyan, and Pentecostal writers agree that the Spirit lives in every Christian, allowing however for the Spirit's deeper ministry beyond conversion. Many Christians from varied theological backgrounds, moreover, have also long understood the Samaritans as true believers before Peter and John arrived. Centuries ago, Calvin sensibly distinguished Philip's ministry from the apostles'.

> It is the Spirit by whom we are washed with the blood of Christ. . . . Therefore, we must not deny but that the Samaritans, who had put on Christ, indeed, in baptism, had also his Spirit given them; and surely Luke speaketh not in this place of the common grace of the Spirit, whereby God

> doth regenerate us . . . but of those singular gifts wherewith
> God would have certain endued. . . .[292]

Noting Acts 2:16, Calvin explains that

> they were only endued then with the grace of common adop-
> tion and regeneration. . . . As for this, it was an extraordinary
> thing that certain should have the gifts of the Spirit . . . that
> every one might profit the Church according to the measure
> of his ability.[293]

By contrast, Dunn argues that Samaritans (1) expected a Messiah to exalt Samaritans while crushing Israel's enemies, (2) remained superstitious and emotional, (3) believed facts without
trusting the Savior, (4) had no deeper faith than Simon, and (5)
early bypassed full faith because of racial animosity.[294]

Admitted Samaritan messianic expectations (John 4:25), nevertheless, had not prevented the woman of Sychar's acceptance, and
effective testimony, of Jesus. "And from that city many of the Samaritans believed in Him. . ." (John 4:39).

Moreover, Jewish messianic expectations had centered more in
a king who would throw off the Roman yoke than in a crucified
Redeemer. If messianic misunderstanding did not deter thousands
of Jews from becoming regenerate believers, how would it invali-
date the Samaritans' faith recorded in Acts 8?

Though a person needs to guard against dependence on feelings
for assurance of regeneration, emotionality need never serve as a
barrier to true faith. A gleaming white lily sparkles more in contrast to the black soil out of which it grows. Lechler thinks that regenerating faith shines the brighter in contrast with the
Samaritans' superstitious background.

> The faith with which the Samaritans listened to the
> preaching of Philip . . . was the more honorable and blessed,
> as it took the place of a superstition. . . . The conversion . . .
> was the fruit of the preaching of the word.[295]

Faith in Jesus Christ proves an indispensable prerequisite to becoming God's child. Dunn correctly sees that a frequent Acts ex-
pression for saving faith in the Greek is believing $\varepsilon\iota\varsigma$, "into" or '$\varepsilon\pi\iota$,
"upon" the Savior. Dunn oversteps, however, in limiting the verb

"believe" with a dative object to signify only "intellectual assent to a statement or proposition." Thus he rejects the idea that this construction could denote "commitment to God" "except perhaps" when someone uses it with "Lord" or "God."[296]

(1) In the first place, Dunn fails to document how one determines that the dative turns commitment into a mere intellectual exercise. Michael Green points out Acts 16:34; 18:8 as where Luke employs this verb "believe" with a dative to show true faith in the Lord, not merely intellectual assent.[297]

(2) Dunn's rule fails to work at times. For example, John writes, "And this is His commandment, that we believe in the name of His Son Jesus Christ. . . ." The case of "name" is dative. John uses neither "into" nor "upon" with "believe." To follow Dunn, one must consider this divine command as implying nothing more than intellectual assent to a proposition. It would say nothing of a Christ-centered lifestyle commitment.

(3) Even if the rule that the dative refers to intellectual assent were valid, what right has Dunn to prop it up with exceptions? Does sound grammar require uncertain exceptions? After saying, "except perhaps," Dunn in a footnote suggests possible exceptions to the exception. Refuting Dunn, Ervin offers some convincing arguments.[298]

In three New Testament passages showing that God justified Abraham by faith, Scripture uses the dative form of "God." "AND ABRAHAM BELIEVED GOD, AND IT WAS RECKONED TO HIM AS RIGHTEOUSNESS" (Rom. 4:3; cf. Gal. 3:6; James 2:23). Surely no sound exegete would affirm that Abraham was simply giving mental assent to the fact that a God existed. The occasion was when God justified him.

(4) Dozens of Scriptures express true conversion by simply stating that a person or group "believed"—with no additional phrase (I count some 22 times in Acts alone.).

Dunn uses his rule in probing the Acts 8 passage, trying to prove that "the Samaritans' response was simply an assent of mind." Supposedly the Samaritans mentally found Philip's message acceptable and acquiesced to the course of action he advocated. Dunn contends that the Samaritans lacked that commitment distinctively described elsewhere which alone deserves the name

"Christian."[299] He further holds that the Samaritans remained as much without true faith as Simon the sorcerer.

Weighing evidence for new birth under Philip.

Against Dunn, however, since Scripture affirms that the Samaritans "believed Philip preaching the good news," they apparently placed trust in that gospel. That gospel concerned the kingdom of God and the name of Jesus Christ. Hence, the Samaritans surely did not merely believe in the evangelist as a person (Acts 8:12). He had been "proclaiming Christ to them" (Acts 8:5).

Convinced that the Samaritans had truly believed, Spirit-filled Philip baptized them, literally "into the name of the Lord Jesus" (Acts 8:12). Comparing Acts 19:5, F. F. Bruce notes the common ancient use of "into the name" in property transfers. "The person baptized 'into the name of the Lord Jesus' bears public witness that he has become the property of Jesus and that Jesus is his Lord and Owner."[300] Arriving, Peter and John expressed no doubt of the reality of the Samaritans' faith in Christ nor of the validity of their baptism.

This stands in bold contrast to their treatment of Simon, whose actions betrayed a fraudulent faith. Peter saw Simon in danger of perishing, lacking true participation in the truth, and manifesting a heart not right with God. Needing repentance from his wickedness, Simon remained "in the gall of bitterness and in the bondage of iniquity" (Acts 8:20-23).

Believers received Spirit-fullness

Luke records no such words directed to the Samaritans. Assuming the reality of their faith, the apostles laid "hands on them, and they were receiving the Holy Spirit" (Acts 8:17). This is the simple, normal thrust of the passage. Citing the noted Calvinistic scholar, Ned Stonehouse, Bruce distinguishes the latter action from conversion:

> The proper operation of the Spirit in regeneration and faith is not in view here. "To us that may seem baffling because the theological questions are of paramount and perennial interest. But one may not insist that the writer of Acts had to reflect upon these questions in our terms . . . in a volume . . .

centering attention upon the extraordinary miraculous
power of the Spirit. . . ."[301]

Thus, despite the resistance of many contemporary theologians
on doctrinal grounds, the biblical evidence shows a later reception
of the Holy Spirit's empowering. Although the Samaritans received a new birth through Philip's preaching, a short while later
they found the Spirit's fullness. Before the apostles' arrival, they
had not the fullness. Both verse 17 verbs appear in the imperfect
tense, emphasizing the process of laying hands on individuals in
this crowd—and the result. As Peter and John placed their hands
on person after person, one after another was receiving this empowering (Acts 8:17).[302]

Therefore, even this disputed passage lends support to our previous discovery. People receive the fullness of the Spirit at a point
in time. This point logically follows conversion. If Acts is a safer
guide than some present-day theologians, that point often comes
chronologically later.

23

Paul's Remarkable Conversion— and Empowering

*Then I heard the voice of the Lord.
. . . And He said,
"Go. . ."
(Isa. 6:8-9).*

Seeing a dazzling light in his room at 4:30 A. M., teenaged Sundar found his home had not caught fire. When he gazed into the light, the form of Jesus spoke in Hindustani. "How long will you persecute me? I have come to save you; you were praying to know the right way. Why do you not take it? I am the Way."

Stricken with the thought, "Jesus Christ is not dead," Sundar Singh dropped to his knees. He trusted Christ instead of putting his head on the rail over which the 5:00 A.M. express would soon thunder. Those railroad tracks ran just behind his father's garden. In black depression, he had been planning for three days this morning's suicide—unless someone answered his prayer: "Oh, God, if there be a God, reveal Thyself to me." Christ did, and Sundar became his mighty witness in India, Tibet, and around the world.

Before all this, life had shattered when his beloved mother died. From a Sikh family in India where Hinduism also played a powerful role, Sundar had incited people to hurl stones at Christian preachers. Joining a gang, he urged them to destroy the Christian

school and drive the missionaries from town. Three days before
his vision of Christ, Sundar had climaxed his hateful antagonism
by buying and burning a kerosene-soaked New Testament in a
blazing wood fire.[303]

Location of the Conversion

Sundar's encounter with Jesus resulted in one of history's most
startling conversions. Saul of Tarsus, the Pharisaical pious persecutor became the self-sacrificing missionary, Paul the Apostle in
what also proved to be a startling conversion. In each role he evi-
denced strikingly ardent zeal.

Judas' house?

Some who hold that the fullness of the Spirit really constitutes
Saul's conversion defend the idea that he was an unregenerate
seeker until Ananias prayed for him (Acts 9:17). Hence, by this
view his conversion occurred in Judas' house on Straight Street,
Damascus.

On the Damascus Road?

Most speakers and writers disagree with that conclusion. In
Maclaren's words, "He marched out of Jerusalem, breathing
threatenings and slaughter; he stumbled into Damascus, a devoted
servant of Him whom he had hated an hour before."[304]

This usual view locates Paul's conversion point as on the Damascus Road as he neared the latter city on a 200-mile trip from Jerusalem. "Almost all Bible scholars agree as to the validity of his
conversion at that time."[305] Actually, "critics, both hostile and
friendly to Christianity, admit that Saul" experienced conversion
there.[306] Tradition locates the place about a mile east of the extremely old city.

Identification of the Speaker

Paul's whole journey normally would require at least six days or
considerably more. Overwhelmed at noon by a blinding light and
by a voice that all heard but only he understood,[307] Saul fell to the

ground. "Saul, Saul, why are you persecuting Me?" he heard (Acts 9:3-4, 7-9). To a knowledgeable, devout Jew, the brilliant light from heaven could only represent God's Shekinah glory.[308]

When Saul responded, "Who art Thou, Lord?" such a theologically educated Jew could only assume that the voice originated from Deity (Acts 9:5).[309] Therefore, although Greek-speakers employed the same word for "sir"—a human being—and "Lord," Deity, yet no translation but "Lord" suffices here because of the context.

Unfortunately the Contemporary English Version evades the issue by entirely omitting the word, as follows: "'Who are you?' Saul asked." Surely the word is not inconsequential, so as to justify ignoring it. Baker, by contrast, reasons: "Saul's answer, 'Who are you, Lord?' (v. 5), in all likelihood implies recognition of the divine presence, since the words had come from heaven. . . ."[310] Clark, an articulate apologist and staunch Calvinist, convincingly scorns Dunn's interpretation that Paul simply addressed Jesus as "sir."

> But in opposition to Dunn's conjectures, we should note that Paul addressed the person in the vision twice. Maybe (hardly maybe) the first time *Kurie* could mean *Sir.* But then the vision answered, "I am Jesus whom thou persecutest" (Acts 22:8-10; 26:14). To which Paul answered trembling, "Kurie, [sic] what will you have me to do?" Simply a polite Sir? Hardly.[311]

Two of the three major words for the true God in the Old Testament become "Lord" in the translation into Greek and English. When New Testament writers use it of Deity, however, "Lord" ordinarily refers to Jesus Christ, unless the context requires another Godhead member.

Submission to a Sovereign

Moreover, this word suggests Saul's radical submission to the speaker. He was admitting that the Speaker was a Sovereign with full right to command him. After the appearance, his eyes saw nothing for three days. Paradoxically, "the vision had struck him blind" (Acts 9:8-9).[312] A Being with such glory as to blind his eyes and such power as to strike him down could claim his full obedience.

The heavenly Speaker introduced himself as Jesus, the real object of Saul's persecution campaign. Nevertheless, Saul immediately queried, "What shall I do, Lord" (Acts 22:10)? At once, Saul complied with the commands *Jesus* was giving (Acts 9:6). Baker views this obedience as "evidence of conversion or confessing Jesus as Lord (Rom. 10:9). Obedience results from this confession of faith and serves as evidence of the reality of Saul's faith (James 2:14)."[313]

The vision convinced Saul that Jesus had risen from the dead, since a corpse could not appear in blinding light (1 Cor. 15:8-9). Since the appearance came from heaven, Jesus had ascended. Since he appeared in Shekinah glory, he must be Jehovah as he had claimed. What an education one brief glimpse of Jesus had provided! What repentance it had produced in him!

Furthermore, Saul suddenly learned that Jesus sustained such an intimate relationship with his followers, that Saul had been persecuting Jesus! Although Jesus must exercise immense divine power and though he justly arrested Saul's furious aggression, he must want to forgive him.

Jesus went on to speak of appointing him a minister to bring *others* to divine forgiveness (Acts 26:16-18). This latter passage helps readers understand that Christ had divulged enough to Saul right on the road to make possible his conversion there.

At Saul's conversion, Jesus Christ appears more conspicuously than elsewhere in Acts, Pierson thinks. "There is a special reason. Christ is now *calling a new apostle,* and the call must be direct and personal."[314]

Was Paul a Christian Brother When Ananias Arrived?

Praying Saul

It is true that even desperately wicked scoundrels pray in emergencies. Torrey believes, however, that Jesus' words to Ananias, "behold, he is praying," show that Saul was already a true believer

(Acts 9:11). He calls the expression "an evidence of conversion here."[315] The Lord further explained that he considered Saul as "a chosen instrument of Mine," which also likely indicates a believer (Acts 9:15). By contrast, God refers to the ungodly as "vessels of wrath prepared for destruction" (Rom. 9:22).

Brother Saul

When Jesus divulged Saul's whereabouts to Ananias, that disciple trudged along Straight Street—a long, straight east-west thoroughfare apparently still surviving. Reaching Judas' house, Ananias greeted the persecutor as "Brother Saul" (Acts 9:17). He used a term that the New Testament often reserved for believers—not just fellow-Israelites.

Fellow-Israelite? Paul did use the term for fellow-Israelites occasionally. Good examples of this latter usage include plurals, "brethren," in the narration of his conversion before the angry Jerusalem Jews (Acts 22:1, 5).

Arguing from statistical frequency in Acts, Dunn, predictably, holds that Ananias by "brother" simply intended friendliness to a fellow-Jew. Claiming that "brother" refers to Christians in thirty-three of fifty-seven Acts occurrences, he thinks direct address examples are more significant. When Luke records "brother(s)" in directly addressing someone[316] (as in Acts 9:17), thirteen uses refer to Jews and only five relate to Christians.

He contends "it is unlikely that he [Ananias] would call 'Christian' one who had neither yet received the Spirit nor yet been baptized." Wavering between brother as "racial kinship" and as "*in the process* of becoming a Christian," Dunn forsakes sound logic. He cannot reasonably keep both senses. Surely precedents are lacking in Scripture for the use of "brother" for an "almost Christian."[317] Moreover, although in this age every believer has the Spirit within, historical accounts in Scripture normally focus instead on the Spirit's distinctive empowering.

Fellow-Christian? Ervin argues from contextual exegesis and other statistics, predictably, that "brother" here means a Christian. He shows that every Acts use of "brother" in direct address is plural except three passages about Saul (21:20; 9:17; 22:13). Since two of these relate Saul's conversion, the very passages in dispute, Ervin sees Dunn's argument as impotent. Ervin bolsters his own proof since the third passage (21:20) indisputably calls Saul "brother" as a believer.[318]

Ervin properly insists that in every Acts usage, an interpreter must discover the meaning of "brother" from the context. Ervin sees two related matters as confirming his view. "Ananias' natural fear of Saul/Paul as the persecutor of the Christians required divine assurance of the change in Paul before he ventured to go to him." Second, God reassured Ananias that Paul was a chosen instrument. This "would naturally predispose him to receive Paul as one already sharing a common commitment to Jesus."[319]

It seems impossible to make a foolproof argument for either of the main positions on the word "brother." Without question Paul was a Jew, and without question he became a Christian. Some sense of Paul's keen mind and tumultuous feelings during his Damascus Road experience may aid the investigation a bit.

If he understood "brother" as "Christian brother," Paul might sense considerable comfort as he groped with blinded physical eyes. Might "brother" terrify him, instead, if the speaker proved an unconverted Jew? What if Paul surmised that some anti-Christian former accomplice mouthing the word had got wind of his sudden turncoat allegiance to Jesus?

It would be thrilling, however, if "one whom he had come to persecute now accepted him as a brother in the Lord."[320] "In calling him 'brother,' Ananias not only addressed him as a fellow-Israelite, but welcomed him into the new fellowship," writes Bruce.[321] Barnes, the noted Philadelphia Presbyterian, with no theological axe to grind, calls "brother" "an expression recognizing him as a fellow-christian [sic]."[322]

Had God Cleansed Paul's Sins before Baptism?

One also should examine Ananias' direction to Paul, "Arise, and be baptized, and wash away your sins, calling on His name" (Acts 22:16). Dunn employs this argument to show that Paul had not experienced regeneration on the Damascus Road.[323] *If* baptismal regeneration were defensible as true biblical doctrine, Dunn would be writing correctly.

Instead, however, the Acts record seems consistently to require evidence of repentance and faith in Christ before baptism. Acts shows people receiving baptism shortly after their conversion rather than as the conversion itself. Baptism significantly symbolizes washing away sin through Christ's blood. Water does not save. Hence Paul's baptism proclaimed a testimony of what Christ had earlier accomplished in him.

Why does Ananias lay hands on Paul? It has nothing to do with regeneration. Since he received baptism soon *after* regaining his sight, apparently the imposition of hands did not relate to that ordinance either (Acts 9:18). Instead, Calvin explains: "partly that he may consecrate him unto God, partly that he may obtain for him the gifts of the Spirit."[324]

Sometimes this rite signified the Lord's power in healing (Mark 16:18; Acts 28:8). Sometimes it concerned the fullness of the Holy Spirit (Acts 8:17; 19:6). Sometimes it pertained to ordination for ministry (1 Tim. 4:14; 2 Tim. 1:6). Perhaps Ananias had at least two or three of these latter three purposes in mind.

Conclusion

Remarkable indeed was Saul's conversion through a sudden arrest by a blinding light and an accusing authoritative voice. In addition, however, Saul's divine empowering through the fullness of the Holy Spirit also proved remarkable. Overcoming his natural hesitancy to visit a murderous opponent of Christianity, Ananias only dared to approach Saul because the Lord clearly ordered him to go. The resulting physical healing and empowering fullness of the Spirit came suddenly to one whom Ananias' Master had identified as a chosen vessel—now miraculously transformed into a Christian brother.

Regardless of background, numerous scholars interpret Saul's becoming filled with the Spirit as consecration or empowering for service rather than as regeneration. They understand conversion as having occurred beforehand. Bruce, e.g., asserts that "such filling was necessary for the prophetic service. . ." to which Christ

called him (Acts 9:15).[325] Baker offers a perceptive observation
about Paul's experience.

> This "filling" may not necessarily be the reception of the
> Holy Spirit for the first time, if filling and reception are dis-
> tinct concepts. At any rate, it serves to prepare Saul for his
> ministry of the gospel, something that seems consistently
> to be involved with the filling of the Spirit.[326]

The above evidence favors the idea that Saul became regenerate
on the Damascene road three days before receiving the fullness of
the Spirit. "There is no evidence that he experienced a gradual
change of attitude toward Christianity."[327] On that road, "it was
conversion, shattering and sudden, and an act of God."[328] Although God probably used such incidents as Stephen's martyrdom to prepare him, his regeneration represented a sudden
turning point.

Likewise, his healing from three days of blindness and his entrance into the Spirit-filled life mark actions at a point in time. Before Ananias prayed, Paul could not see. Afterward, he could.
Before Ananias prayed, Paul was not Spirit-filled. Afterward he
was. In Paul's case, the context confirms the aorist verb to underscore that the fullness of the Spirit arrived at a turning point.

Almost immediately Paul began to preach Jesus Christ with
anointing in the synagogues. Studying Luke-Acts without distort-
ing presuppositions would likely reveal the most fre-
quently-recurring initial evidence of Spirit-fullness as a gift of
evangelism.

Dunning calls mission "the motif that dominates Luke's thinking from the beginning to the end" of Acts. "This means that he
would stress the gift of the Spirit as endowment."[329] Paul especially needed the empowering inherent in Spirit-fullness for the
witness assignment Jesus had immediately given him. Opportunities to proclaim Christ came very quickly.

24

Twelve Other Disciples

"I live among a people. . . ." And He said, ". . . Tell this people. . . ." (Isa. 6:5, 9).

Among the handful of dependable saints committed to beginning a church in the quiet bedroom community were Henry and Mary, an older couple. No one could prove more faithful in attendance, giving, and encouraging. I was a new single young pastor fresh out of graduate school.

In launching a new congregation, how helpful it is to find a nucleus with whom to begin! When Paul returned to Ephesus (Acts 18:19-21; 19:1) more than twenty years after Pentecost, his enthusiasm for Christ radiated. How excitedly he must have discovered about a dozen male believers! Here in the principal city of the province called Asia, Paul was ministering early in his third missionary journey.

Spiritual Background

Perhaps he found something different about these twelve—something lacking. Asking whether they had received the Holy Spirit, he noticed that they professed considerable ignorance.

After he questioned them further, he learned that they had already received baptism. Someone had administered the baptism of John the Baptist. Instructing them more fully, Paul thought it necessary to rebaptize them. Following this, he laid hands on them, and the Holy Spirit came on them.

Two discernible gifts followed—tongues and prophecy. Bruner observes that "neither in Acts 2 nor in Acts 8, 10, or 19 . . . are tongues recorded as *sought*." He calls these passages "the primary Pentecostal texts for tongues as evidence."[330]

Some elements making Acts 19:1-7 unique include the following: (1) puzzling prior spiritual background, (2) ignorance about the Spirit, and (3) the only biblical rebaptism.

Unknown elements

Luke provides no details on who guided these dozen men to the truth. Writers, therefore, offer such guesses as (1) John the Baptist in Judea, (2) some unknown disciple of John, or (3) Apollos. Luke had just mentioned Apollos as "acquainted only with the baptism of John" until Priscilla and Aquila instructed him further (Acts 18:25-26). Of course, John suffered martyrdom more than two decades before this time, so many doubt if he had directly baptized these men.

Had the men recently arrived at Ephesus or were they natives? Were they Jews or Gentiles? Did the men lead a celibate, austere life like John apparently had or did they have families? Did they become the Ephesian elders Paul addressed at Miletus (Acts 20:17), as commentators occasionally conjecture? Firm answers to such questions remain elusive.

"Almost but lost" *or* converted but needing fullness?

A more major issue concerns whether the twelve Ephesians had experienced the new birth before meeting Paul. Although many heavyweight commentators assert that they had, some scholars stoutly dissent on doctrinal grounds. The major reason given for affirming that the twelve had found no new birth centers in the idea that every true Christian already has the Holy Spirit.

Hence such writers unfortunately fail to see this experience mentioned in Acts 19:2, 6 as an infilling with the Spirit after regeneration. One example of such thinking follows. "There is . . . no record in . . . the New Testament of a first, partial infilling of the

Holy Spirit completed, perfected, or filled later by a second personal reception of the Spirit."[331] By contrast, Walvoord, chancellor of Dallas Theological Seminary, observes the need for fullness in those already indwelt by the Holy Spirit.

> While in this age it is impossible to be filled with the Holy Spirit unless permanently indwelt, it is a sad reflection on the spiritual state of many Christians that though their bodies are the temple of the Holy Spirit they are not yielded to Him and know nothing of the great blessings which His unhindered ministry would bring.[332]

Combating Pentecostalism, Bruner cites the Ephesians' lack of the Spirit and of Christian baptism as proof that they were not yet regenerate.[333] Dunn concurs. "The twelve Ephesians . . . were not far short of Christianity, but were not yet Christians because they lacked the vital factor—the Holy Spirit."[334]

Ervin counters that "implicit in the Pentecostal position" one should understand an important idea. "If they were Christians, then they had experienced the regenerating work of the Holy Spirit through repentance and faith but had not been baptized in the Spirit for power-in-mission."[335]

Likewise Barnes, a Presbyterian, writes on Acts 19:2, "Have ye received the extraordinary and miraculous influences of the Holy Ghost? Paul would not doubt that, if they had 'believed,' they had received the ordinary converting influences of the Holy Spirit. . . ."[336] Other Pentecostals, Charismatics, Wesleyans, Keswickians, and considerable numbers of other Christians would agree with Ervin's essential thrust.

It is one thing to receive the Spirit in the sense of his saving ministry in becoming a Christian. It is a different issue for a Christian to receive his sanctifying and empowering ministry.

Since he is a personality, we do not receive a segment of him at a time. Since he is a personality, though, we can know and experience him more fully at various times and needs. He indwells *all* believers. Scripture, however, appears to use the phrase "receive the Holy Spirit" as one of many terms for his sanctifying and empowering ministry.

Scripture introduces the dozen men as "some disciples" (Acts 19:1). People have occasionally conjectured that "disciples" simply means learners, not converts. In every use in Acts, however, the word "disciples" identifies people as believers. Even Bruner admits that it is "the normal description in Acts for Christians," citing over twenty references.[337]

Dunn objects, though, that Acts 19:1 uniquely mentions "some believers" rather than "the believers,"—the phrase in other Acts passages. He sees "the believers" elsewhere in Acts as identifying "the whole Christian community of the city or area" identified.[338] Such a community existed in other places. Luke mentions "the disciples" in Jerusalem, in Damascus, in Joppa, and in other cities.

Nevertheless, Ervin convincingly responds that—aside from the dozen—Scripture lacks evidence that any Christian community existed in Ephesus before Paul's three-month synagogue preaching. Only after persecution broke out, does the Acts record designate a core group that Paul could separate from the resistant Jews (Acts 19:8-9). Scripture calls the former group "the disciples."[339]

Ervin notes that the Acts record also uses an indefinite pronoun with the word "disciple" of Tabitha, Timothy, and Ananias (Acts 9:10, 36; 16:1).[340] Though Luke calls each one "a certain disciple," no one questions the validity of their Christian faith as Dunn seeks to "dechristianize" the Ephesian twelve.

Of course, Paul had left Aquila and Priscilla, individual disciples, there at his earlier visit. Otherwise, however, before Paul's Acts 19:1 visit, we know of no Christian community with whom the twelve could have identified.

Some influential commentators see "disciples" in Acts 19:1 as identifying the men as Christians. Bruce reasons: "But that these men were Christians is certainly to be inferred from . . . disciples."[341] Earle agrees, also citing Meyer as well as Lake and Cadbury as supporting the same view.[342] Both Calvin and Lechler similarly agree.[343]

Asking a couple diagnostic questions, Paul sought to assess the spiritual condition of these disciples (Acts 19:2-3). His first question assumed that they had come to saving faith at some time in the past.[344] He asked about their relation to the Holy Spirit when or since they believed. As earlier noticed, Acts thus uses the word "believed" without an object more than twenty times. It consistently identifies a point of conversion. The disciples never deny that a conversion had occurred.

Ironside writes, "*thereafter* no mention is ever made of an interval between conversion and the reception of the Spirit" (emphasis mine). In so speaking, however, Ironside implies an Acts 19 interval. He also implies the Ephesians' conversion before Paul met them, since the interval is between their initial experience and this recorded upgrade. Since Ironside wrote this book to refute second-blessing holiness teaching, he is grateful to see the supposedly transitional era ending. Thus he rejoices that the Ephesians "are added to the body, and the transitional state had come to an end."[345]

Instead, however, of locking the issue forever in a chest sunken in the bottom of the Pacific, his comments allow problems to linger. (1) Conversion could and did precede the Spirit's coming during an alleged transitional period, as Ironside's words admit. (2) No Scripture indicates that a transitional state had ended in Acts 19—much less that one existed.

(3) Aside from ultradispensationalists, evangelicals usually agree that events in Acts 2:4 through Acts 19 occur within the present age. Aside from any clear contrary scriptural evidence, surely the events in this segment accurately represent Christians' need in the present age to receive Spirit fullness.

(4) To say that Scripture mentions no interval thereafter sounds like an argument from silence easily toppled. Does Acts 19:8—28:31 ever mention an initial incoming of the Holy Spirit in fullness *without* an interval? Since both Apollos and twelve Ephesians knew only John's baptism, does Scripture state that no other such individuals or groups existed anywhere? It does not.

Ignorance about the Holy Spirit

The men's response to Paul surprises us: "We have not even heard whether there is a Holy Spirit." Can a person enjoy regeneration because the Holy Spirit indwells him or her without even knowing that the Spirit exists? Comparing a similar construction in John 7:39, translators see the possibility of rendering Acts 19:2 differently. "We have not even heard whether the Holy Spirit has been given" [on the day of Pentecost]. (NASB margin; cp. ASV text). Bruce thus suggests the possibility that readers should understand "Holy Spirit" in Acts 19:2 "in a special sense." He is "the Holy Spirit as sent at Pentecost with outward manifestation."[346]

Many questions must remain unanswered. Did the twelve know their Old Testaments well? God's Spirit acts in various Old Testament passages. Writers identified him with the exact name, "Holy Spirit," however, in only three verses there (Psa. 51:11; Isa. 63:10-11).

Had the twelve found Christ through Apollos' ministry before Priscilla and Aquila had led him into deeper truths and perhaps into the fullness of the Spirit?[347] Swete, the famous Anglican biblical and patristic scholar and Cambridge professor, discusses this issue. He believes that before meeting this couple, "Apollos . . . though a fervent believer had not received the baptism of the Spirit."[348]

Had their conversion occurred through believing John the Baptist's own preaching or preaching by one of his disciples before Pentecost? Had the twelve remained segregated from all Christians for many years, thus understanding little of Christ's death, resurrection, and sending the Spirit?

Message of John the Baptist

A study of John's message unveils the fact that his preaching prepared for and presented many foundational Christian teachings. He proclaimed the kingdom of heaven and the need to prepare for it (Matt. 3:2). In fact, Scripture states that he preached the gospel (Luke 3:18).

What did John the Baptist preach about Jesus Christ? He repeatedly preached the greatness, superiority and Messiahship of Jesus (Mark 1:7; Luke 3:16; John 1:15, 26-27, 30-33; John 3:30-31). John proclaimed Jesus' Deity (John 1:34), Jesus' heavenly origin (John 3:31), and Jesus' ownership of all (John 3:35).

He taught that God had filled Jesus with the Spirit without limit (John 1:32-33; 3:34). John announced Jesus' provision of redemption as the Lamb of God (John 1:29).

John the Baptist taught much about the way to become right with God, including repentance (Matt. 3:2) and confession of sins (Matt. 3:6). Moreover, he instructed people about salvation by the forgiveness of sins (Luke 1:77; 3:3) and eternal life through faith in Christ (John 1:7; 3:36).

He preached and practiced water baptism (Mark 1:5; Luke 3:16) and urged converts to exhibit transformed behavior (Luke 3:8, 10-14). In addition, he taught the coming baptism with the Holy Spirit that Jesus would administer (Luke 3:16).

John faithfully warned that God's wrath and eternal judgment await those who reject Jesus Christ (Luke 3:7, 9, 17; John 3:36). Thus, if the twelve who received John's baptism accurately understood his message, they knew an immense amount about God's saving revelation.

Since Paul deemed it necessary to give Christian baptism to the twelve, he no doubt provided any instruction they lacked. Despite their rich heritage of faith, or their possible rich heritage, Paul sensed their spiritual lack. He apparently needed to fill in for them an understanding of some basic events that occurred after John's martyrdom.

Jesus proved himself the Lamb of God as John had acclaimed him. In other words, Jesus exhibited spotlessness, having lived a sinless life. Dying on the cross, Jesus became the perfect sacrifice in the sinner's place. He arose from the grave and ascended into heaven. As John had explained, Jesus then could baptize with the Holy Spirit. He began to do so on the day of Pentecost.

Unique Rebaptism

The twelve gladly submitted to Christian baptism because it represented a full identification with Jesus Christ in his death and resurrection. After this, Paul laid his hands upon them and the Holy Spirit came *upon* them, probably emphasizing his empowering for service.

At any rate, Paul must have believed that their ignorance about the Holy Spirit must not continue. He saw the Spirit's fullness indispensable for successful Christian living. As the great apostle to the Gentiles, Paul saw the Spirit's empowering essential for their undertaking the worldwide witness. The power Jesus had sent necessarily prepared his followers to concentrate their energies on fulfilling the commission he had left them.

To the best of our knowledge, Jesus himself received water baptism only once—at the hands of *John the Baptist*, as did some or all
of Jesus' apostles. News reached the Pharisees that Jesus was baptizing more disciples than John (John 4:1-4).Jesus deliberately left
Judea for Galilee so that he would not seem to run competition
with John the Baptist.

Scripture lacks any account of anyone whom Jesus' disciples
ever rebaptized after an initial immersion by John or John's disciples. In fact, Scripture mentions no other case of rebaptism for any
reason.

Why does Luke mention the rebaptism of these Ephesians but
no rebaptism of Apollos, who also was "acquainted only with the
baptism of John"? (Acts 18:25). Dunn answers this question by
pointing out one contrast with the Ephesians. ". . . He differed
from them in one, *the* crucial respect: he already possessed the
Spirit (Acts 18:25), whereas they did not."[349] By contrast, Baker
thinks that

> knowing only the baptism of John . . . probably means that
> the Pentecost event was unknown to him. . . . It might be
> that Apollos had not received the Holy Spirit either,
> though Luke says nothing about this.[350]

On the verse selected, however, translators differ. Most contemporary versions understand Acts as depicting fervency in Apollos'
human spirit rather than in the Holy Spirit. They use words like
"earnestness," or "zeal." Bruce understands Apollos as "full of enthusiasm."[351] Hence, Dunn's explanation about Apollos at best remains open to question. Regarding the Apollos issue, Davids
expresses an opinion. "If the basic commitment to Jesus is already
there, even if somewhat defective, only further instruction, not
rebaptism, appears to be necessary."[352]

Clearly, not every incident in the Church's early years found a
place in the inspired record. Luke selectively records representative events to provide Theophilus and later readers a foundational
understanding. Twelve or thirteen at Ephesus missed receiving
the Holy Spirit's fullness because they had not heard of Pentecost
until years afterward.

If so, could multitudes of others have missed out, in those two
decades at the dawn of this age—or today? Apparently more than

500 male believers, likely plus women,[353] beheld the risen Christ at
one time (1 Cor. 15:6). On the other hand, perhaps only 120 tarried
until Pentecost. Those who tarried in obedience to Christ received
the Spirit's fullness. Does anyone dare to conjecture that all who
disobeyed the Master automatically received the same fullness?

Commenting on the twelve Ephesians, Baker reasons that their
experience may have been no isolated event. "During this period
of church history it was evidently possible for people who had believed in Jesus Christ to be ignorant of Pentecost and not to have
been baptized in the Spirit."[354] If some experience conversion but
neglect to discover the possibilities of a Spirit-filled life, can they
today miss any meaningful relationship with the Spirit?

"When" or "Since"?

Much ink has flowed to solve whether the King James translators or the contemporary translations provide the correct rendering of Acts 19:2. Did Paul ask, "Have ye received the Holy Ghost
since ye believed?" or "Did you receive the Holy Spirit when you
believed?"

The word in question is a Greek aorist participle, "having believed." A person believes unto salvation at a point in time. Paul refers to that point. In relation to that point, (at it or since it) he asks
whether his hearers had received the Holy Spirit. "The Greek literally says, 'Did you receive the Holy Spirit, having believed?"[355]

Ervin keenly shows that theological prejudice, instead of context, too often determines how interpreters translate passages crucial for a doctrinal position.[356] Greek grammar expects, however,
that the *context* of a passage will show what time relationship exists. Otherwise, the *context* will show whether some other adver-
bial idea dominates in the participle's relation to the main verb
rather than time.

Greek participles may express at least such relationships as time
(before, when, while, since, after), purpose (in order to), cause (because, since), result (resulting from), conditionality (if), or conces-
sion (although). In Acts 19:2, virtually all interpreters see time as
the main aspect involved in this aorist verb.

When participles express time, the *context* must show whether it
is time before, after, or during the time expressed in the main verb.

In the immediate context of Acts 19:1-7, obviously people did not receive the Spirit before they believed.

In most New Testament cases, the main verb expresses action *after* the action in the aorist participle. Since some main verbs do not, however, a closer look at smaller and larger contexts of Acts 19:2 must indicate how to translate. Again, should Acts 19:2 read, "Did you receive the Holy Spirit when you believed" or "Have you received the Holy Spirit since you believed?"

First, an observer can compare other participles in the immediate context. Brown notices that the identical grammatical construction occurs in the preceding verse. ". . . Paul took the road through the interior and arrived at Ephesus" (Acts 19:1, NIV). "Took" translates an aorist participle. Did Paul arrive at Ephesus at the identical instant he was trudging along the road through the interior, or after leaving the interior? The question is ridiculous. Definitely, he arrived at Ephesus after he had traversed the interior.[357]

A second example immediately follows: "There he found certain disciples and asked them. . ." (Acts 19:1-2, NIV). The action of the main verb, "asked" surely followed the action of the aorist participle, "found." It seems undebatable that Paul asked the question after he found them. Probably he asked after having some opportunity to converse and observe their lives. As noted above, in a majority of New Testament uses, a main verb's action happens after the action in the aorist participle.[358]

Did people in this passage receive the Holy Spirit when they believed? The twelve themselves respond, "No" (Acts 19:2, NIV). Taking the position toward which the evidence points (and which Paul's question had assumed), the twelve *had* experienced salvation before meeting Paul. Nevertheless, they had not yet received the Spirit, in the sense that Paul was using that expression.

Even if my conclusion on the time of conversion should prove incorrect, surely the twelve experienced conversion *before* they received rebaptism (Acts 19:5). The New Testament order includes renunciation of sin and faith in Christ prior to baptism. Even those who practice infant baptism understand that when a minister baptizes an adult, that adult must first repent and believe. "The recipient must have believed and must have repented, if he is an adult," writes Clark. This was New Testament practice.[359]

Following the baptism of the twelve (perhaps soon after it), "when Paul had laid his hands upon them, the Holy Spirit came on them. . ." (Acts 19:6). Thus, the immediate context shows that people receive the Holy Spirit after they believe for salvation.

This reception is in the sense of fullness, not the initial automatic indwelling of the Spirit in every regenerate person. James Orr distinguishes the two. ". . . An important distinction is to be drawn between the work of the Spirit in producing faith, *i.e.* in initial regeneration, and the bestowal of the Spirit on those who have been brought to faith."[360]

When we consider the larger context, the book of Acts, here too, this research has shown consistent answers. The Spirit came to the 120 at Pentecost after their conversion. Davids notes that "all of those in the upper room were believers in Christ and baptized."[361] Likewise, members of the early church had experienced new birth before their Acts 4:31 filling.

Similarly, Peter and John treated the Samaritans as validly converted under Philip—although Simon the sorcerer may well be an exception. If so, receiving the Spirit came after conversion.

Paul, too, received the fullness after submission to Jesus as Lord on the Damascus Road. Based on these Acts accounts, evidence points in the same direction. People customarily receive the Spirit for holiness and ministry after the point of believing in Jesus for salvation. Ockenga confirms this research. "The general pattern of . . . Acts" includes believers later passing through "a critical experience," becoming "filled with the Holy Spirit."[362]

Hence the evidence from the smaller and larger contexts agree. Because of contextual considerations, one would best translate Acts 19:2, "Have you received the Holy Spirit since you believed?"[363] The ancient church tradition confirms that in people's lives regeneration came first, then baptism, and then the receiving of the Holy Spirit. This last step eventually evolved into a ceremony of confirmation, climaxing in anointing with oil when the convert was to receive the Spirit.[364]

To his question to the Ephesian twelve,

> Paul evidently expected a definite "yes" or a definite "no" for an answer. Unless the experience were definite and of such a character that one could know whether he had re-

ceived it or not, how could these disciples answer Paul's
question![365]

Despite claims by a few recent writers that Tozer failed to teach
a deeper-life crisis, his own words prove otherwise. Stating that
"Satan opposes the doctrine of the Spirit-filled life about as bit-
terly as any doctrine, . . ." Tozer insists on a knowable point.

> . . . None of the persons in the Bible and none that I can find
> in church history or biography was ever filled with the
> Holy Ghost who didn't know when he was filled. I cannot
> find that anyone was ever filled gradually. . . . You are going
> to be filled as an act or you are not going to be filled—you
> can be sure of that![366]

In chapter 19, as in other Acts cases studied, Spirit-fullness occurred at an entry point rather than simply as a process. The same
fact appears in the lives of individuals like Paul as in groups.
Hence, these accounts provide rather strong evidence of an entry
point into dynamic sanctification.

25

The Proof of the Pudding: Contemporary Fullness Testimonies

I saw the Lord . . . on a throne . . . exalted (Isa. 6:1).

When instant pudding burst upon the market in the early 1950s, some Houghton College girls wondered how any uncooked pudding could be worth eating. They tried strawberry flavor, which became a favorite.

Finding that it provided a quick, easy inexpensive evening treat, a group gathered nightly to enjoy fellowship and refreshment at pink-pudding parties. The proof of the pudding was in the eating, as a common maxim states. Its ease and good taste sold the college girls. It worked.

If this doctrine of dynamic sanctification appears to be biblical truth that meets a definite need, has it been working for anyone? Have any believers found their Christian lives transformed because of entering into dynamic sanctification?

Whereas the next chapter notes some dynamic sanctification experiences in various periods of the Church, this chapter concerns contemporary people. In other words, it relates accounts of people alive today or alive within the past hundred years or so.

Physician, Performer, and Poet

Walter L. Wilson

"What is the Holy Spirit to you?" ventured a white-haired missionary visiting in the Wilson home from France. Answering conventionally that he is the third Person of the Trinity, Wilson heard his inquirer object, "But still you have not answered my question, what is He to you?"

Wilson, a physician and businessman, shocked himself by his own honest reply, "He is nothing to me." Understanding that he had been relegating the Spirit to an empty, inferior role, he sensed that a personal relationship was missing. Perhaps this had made his own eager witnessing so futile ever since his conversion seventeen years before.

"If you will seek to know personally the Holy Spirit," his friend was explaining, "He will transform your life." Some months later, James M. Gray, a Reformed Episcopal minister, later president of Moody Bible Institute, preached on Romans 12:1 in Kansas City. Conviction gripped Wilson as the sermon penetrated his defenses.

> Have you noticed that this verse does not tell us to whom [sic][367] we should give our bodies? It is not the Lord Jesus Who asks for it. He has his [sic] own body. It is not the Father Who asks for it. He remains upon His throne. Another has come to earth without a body. God could have made a body for Him as He did for Jesus, but He did not do so. God gives you . . . the indescribable honor of presenting your bodies to the Holy Spirit, to be His dwelling place on earth. If you have been washed in the blood of the Lamb, then yours is a holy body, washed whiter than snow, and will be accepted by the Spirit when you give it. Will you do so now?

Retreating directly to his study afterward, Wilson lay on the carpet sorrowing over his fruitless life. As he gave his body to the Holy Spirit, however, hope filled his heart that all would now be different. He admitted mistreating the Spirit his whole Christian life. When he needed help, he had considered God's Spirit as a servant whom he could order around. He determined to do so no longer.

He continued,

> Just now I give You this body of mine; from my head to my feet, I give it to You. I give you my hands, my limbs, my eyes and lips, my brain, all that I am within and without, I hand over to You for You to live in it the life that You please.

He gave the Spirit permission to send his body to a foreign land or even to afflict it. "It is your body from this moment on. Help yourself to it. . . . I believe you have accepted it. . . . Thank you again, my Lord, for taking me. . . ."

This surrender of his body and appropriation of Spirit-fullness resulted in immediate and continual fruit. The next morning when two salesladies came again, he realized that his lips were the Holy Spirit's. For the first time, he spoke to them of Christ. Both received the Savior then and there.

When he gave the Holy Spirit his body, in Wilson's words, the transformation "was greater, much greater than the change which took place when I was saved. . . ." He has ministered as a pastor, conference speaker, and broadcaster. I have heard him preach in Nyack, NY, and Winona Lake, IN. I recall a witnessing opportunity he related from the platform forty years ago.

His clever, informative books and addresses on evangelistic "fishing" challenge many. Perceiving the need for prepared Christian workers, he founded and served as president of a Bible college, that after merging survives as Calvary Bible College.[368]

Richard C. Halverson

Traveling at age ten as one of the vaudeville group, "Winnipeg Kiddies," Richard C. Halverson would one day fill very different roles. He would minister as a Presbyterian pastor, mobilize laymen in International Christian Leadership, and keep in constant contact with his nation's lawmakers. He is best known for having served as chaplain of the United States Senate.

Successes in dramatics and singing led him to Hollywood at age 19. Disappointed when movie contracts eluded him, he visited a Presbyterian church and found Christ as Savior. When he attended a Bible conference six months later, Halverson felt uncomfortable. He asked if he could go home. His pastor answered affirmatively provided he would try one more day.

That night he sensed clearly a need to yield all to Christ. Feeling that surrender would cost him his aspirations of climbing to stardom in the movies, he left the meeting in agony. In a cabin prayer time, though, he yielded all.

Later, Halverson commented, "This experience of utter yieldedness to the Savior and the consequent joy that filled my life was far more cataclysmic than my conversion." Although he had lacked teaching on the Spirit and knew not what to expect, his friends noted a marked change. Thereafter, he saw the Spirit's reigning presence as most desirable and relevant to daily needs.

Graduating from Wheaton College and Princeton Theological Seminary, Halverson found the Holy Spirit leading him into pastorates. The Spirit also directed him to places of leadership in significant Christian organizations. During a nine-year pastoral-staff position in California, he influenced hundreds of youth to total commitment to Christ.

When I heard him speak in Washington, DC, at a national meeting of the Evangelical Theological Society, his informal talk impressed me. His constant access to his nation's top political leadership opens many doors. This revered, Spirit-filled gentleman regularly speaks and jots words of challenge, encouragement, and truth to lawmakers who shape America's destiny. What if he had never surrendered his total life to the Holy Spirit?[369]

Frances Ridley Havergal

The vivacious, intelligent youngest child of an English minister and composer, Frances Ridley Havergal, wrote lengthy letters in rhyme at age nine. Convicted at six, she prayed repeatedly for pardon but failed to receive salvation since she failed to trust the Lord for it.

Miss Cooke, later to become her stepmother, once challenged her to believe. "Why cannot you trust yourself to your Savior at once?" This question brought Frances a burst of hope that made her breathless. She responded, "I *could* surely." Running upstairs to think it through, she fell to her knees and committed her soul to Christ. She reports, *"I did trust the Lord Jesus."* She found assurance.

Studying in England and Germany, her excellent education included proficiency in Latin, Greek, Hebrew, French, and German. By age twenty-two she had memorized all of the Gospels, Epistles, Revelation, Psalms, and Isaiah. She also memorized the Minor Prophets later. She asked the Lord to supply every word in her writings, including the rhymes.

She prayed regularly three times daily. Each morning she prayed to receive the Holy Spirit's fullness. Longing for it, she wrote, "Why cannot I trust Him fully?" Later she diagnosed herself. ". . . The great root of all my trouble and alienation is that I do not now make an unconditional surrender of myself to God. . . ." She continued, "Until this is done I shall know no peace. I am sure of it."

When she received a little booklet, *All for Jesus,* in a friend's letter, she perused its contents intently. Her letter to its author expressed appreciation—and her yearning. Her correspondent showed her that Christ's blood remains present and powerful. Finding in the Greek New Testament that the verb "cleanseth" is in the present tense (1 John 1:7), implying continuous action, Frances appropriated. Joyously she responded, *"I see it all, and I have the blessing."* Later, she requested that this verse appear on her tombstone.

After this, she lived full of power—for obedient living and for her many ministries. She sang, gave public Bible readings, wrote impressive poetry, promoted temperance, penned books, and visited house-to-house to evangelize. Often she conducted consecration services. Writing to her sister during the second year after her dynamic sanctification, she confided, "It is far more distinct than my conversion. . . ."

She once visited for five days in a home where ten people lived, with various spiritual needs. After she had prayed, "Lord, give me *all* in this house," God literally granted her request. So overjoyed her last night that sleep fled, she wrote her consecration hymn, "Take my life, and let it be consecrated. . . ."

In her final illness, when friends sought to cheer her, she showed joyous submission. "Never mind!" she whispered, "It's home the faster! God's will is *delicious*; He makes no mistakes."[370]

Missions Promoter, Counselor, Educators

A.B. Simpson

Transferring to a new location, a pastor sometimes sees his task loom immensely. When A. B. Simpson left a successful eight-year Canadian Presbyterian pastorate in Hamilton, Ontario, he moved to a Louisville Presbyterian parsonage.

He sensed the great city's deepest needs unmet due to strife between churches. The U. S. Civil War had left deeply divided loyalties in Kentucky, a border state. Scrapping churches resulted. How could Simpson show, by example and word, the love and holiness God requires? He preached his inaugural sermon on "Jesus Only" (Matt. 17:8).

Simpson pondered whether he himself lived a holy enough life. He sensed the Holy Spirit's conviction. Recalling how his spirituality had dulled when his college roommate enjoyed coarse entertainment in their room, Simpson now sensed his own carnality. "Very thoroughly, patiently and inexorably, God had taught him his own nothingness. When seeking counsel from an old experienced friend, he was told: 'All you need . . . is to be annihilated.'"[371]

He longed for a divine cure. "In a word," he explained, "my heart was unsanctified, and I had not yet learned the secret of the indwelling Christ."[372] The Lord led him to an old book, *The Higher Christian Life* by W. E. Boardman. Here he grasped the secret to cure his hunger. Pouring over the volume, he discovered that his Justifier was waiting to sanctify him, substituting his own holiness for Simpson's helplessness.

He was in his early thirties. Describing the night of difficult but joyful transition, Simpson recalls it "with unutterable gratitude." "Mistaken in many things and imperfect in all, . . . my heart's first full consecration was made, and with unreserved surrender I could say, 'Jesus, I my cross have taken. . . .'" "If God has been pleased to make my life in any measure a little temple . . . and if He ever shall . . . use me in any fuller measure, it has been because of that hour. . . ."[373] Far-reaching results followed.

God used him soon to mobilize the Louisville pastors for a city-wide evangelistic crusade despite the previous strife. He later engaged in much intercultural ministry, launched an organization for world evangelization, and founded North America's first surviving Bible college.[374]

Charles R. Solomon

Solomon spent his preschool years in a family of six in a cramped Tennessee farmhouse without any electricity, running water, insulation, or heating stove. On the bright side, his parents were Christians who loved him.

Short in stature and poor in athletics, he developed a severe inferiority complex that colored most of his life. When he went forward in revival meetings on three occasions, people prayed but did not deal with him about his need. As a result, he had never received Christ as Savior. At about seventeen, one evening he determined to pray in bed until he knew the Lord had saved him. God answered his petitions. No one discipled him, so growth faltered.

In college he married, but the couple understood each other very poorly. While he constantly believed he would lose his employment for incompetency, he worked diligently. Soon he was supervising twenty-five men.

Distraught, anxious, depressed, and lacking meaningful relationships with people, he sought to yield himself unreservedly to the Lord in his bedroom. As in his conversion, he lacked guidance in how to enter a deeper life.

Providentially he moved to Denver, discovered an evangelical church, and began Navigators' Scripture memorization. The Bible taught him both about divine acceptance and the Holy Spirit, though the enemy still derided him. Suffering physical and emotional pain, he sought to unearth any lurking sin or unyielded areas.

When a friend lent him *Victorious Christian Living* by Alan Redpath, God was showing him truth he needed as he read daily. It reminded him of Watchman Nee's *The Normal Christian Life* that he had read several times in the past couple years or so without seeing himself in it. Now he decided he had learned more than he had realized.

After a difficult day, he retreated to Scripture and Redpath. Galatians 2:20 struck him in a new way. "I am crucified with Christ: [literally: have been] nevertheless I live; yet not I, but Christ liveth in me. . . ." He explains,

As I read this verse the reality of it was driven home by the Holy Spirit and I fell to my knees in the presence of God. In fact, it was so real that I even opened my eyes to see if He were visible. It was as though I was filled with the Spirit from head to foot; I literally tingled as the thrill of deliverance for which I had waited in unbelief was finally realized. . . . I revelled in the joy of being freed from depression, anxiety, despair, loneliness, insecurity, feelings of inferiority. . . .

He describes this as "my release from the self-life with all its shackles." He received the fullness of the Spirit eighteen years after his conversion.

Despite facing and overcoming Satanic counterattacks through spiritual warfare, life had radically changed for the better. He eagerly read Scripture and between fifty and a hundred books on Christian growth the first year after his sanctifying encounter.

Soon God led him to establish Grace Fellowship International to lead others from emotional and spiritual bondage to freedom. In the preparation process he was to earn a master's and a doctoral degree to enhance his counseling skills. His counseling method maintains a thoroughly Christian approach that he dubs Spiritual therapy. He has written several readable books and developed an international ministry.[375]

R.A. Torrey

Imagine a non-swimmer reading a book on how to swim and then plunging into the water in front of his siblings. After all, he had to try out what he had read. His "swimming" landed him on the bottom discouraged. The incident illustrates Reuben Archie Torrey's venturesomeness even as a child. He seemed to delight in narrow escapes—like taming the wildest horses.

Reading about becoming a Presbyterian, he agreed with most conditions. He balked, however, at the statement that a Christian must do precisely what God wants. Slamming the book shut, he reasoned within himself. "If I say 'yes' to that, God will just as likely call me to preach the Gospel. . . . I have determined to be a lawyer. I will not become a Christian."

At least young Torrey had realized what many professing Christians today have missed—the importance of doing God's will. As Grenz expresses it, ". . . Integral to knowing God are being and acting in conformity with God's will."[376]

When he attended Yale at fifteen, worldly habits held a strong attraction. Although he attended church, prayed daily, and read the Bible, Reuben hated these activities.

One night he jumped out of bed in a dreadful despondency, heading for his razor to commit suicide. Fumbling, he sensed God's dealings. When he fell to his knees, he prayed, "God, if you will take away this awful burden, I will preach." Peace came immediately. Soon it dawned on him that he had become a Christian. Making a public confession in his senior year, he joined the college church. He entered Yale's divinity school instead of its law school.

Struggling with doubts because he had been absorbing negativism from some famous philosophers, Torrey now sought biblical answers. He found help as he studied in completing his Yale divinity degree and in further graduate work at two major universities in Germany. He had plunged into ministries, accepting ordination from the Congregational denomination.

After several years of ministry, his study of Acts convinced him of what he must experience for effective service. Every minister must receive the baptism with the Spirit. Confiding in a businessman, he determined that he seek until he found this endowment. He would never preach again until the Lord either baptized him with the Spirit or showed him he must preach without this assurance.

Continually praying that God would supply this power from on high, he sequestered himself in his study in Minneapolis. He received what he requested within that week. If he had understood Scripture more fully (1 John 5:14-15), he explains, he could have received this baptism the day he began asking. He recalls,

> It was . . . one of the most quiet moments I ever knew; indeed, I think one reason I had to wait so long was because it took that long before my soul could get quiet before God. Then God simply said to me, not in any audible voice, but in my heart, "It's yours. Now go and preach." . . . I have been a new minister from that day to this.[376]

For Torrey, the baptism with the Holy Spirit did *not* properly describe one's new birth. Nor did it denote a subsequent experience when a person should expect to speak in tongues. Instead, it

identified the initial filling with the Spirit to empower a believer
for effective service. The Christian needs to believe God to receive
this fullness.

Torrey accurately understood several terms as describing "one
and the same experience in the New Testament." He listed "filled
with the Spirit, gift of the Spirit, poured out, receiving the Holy
Spirit, the promise of the Father." He included "baptism with the
Holy Spirit," his favorite term. Moreover, ". . . baptism with the
Holy Spirit is a definite experience of which one may and ought to
know whether he has received it or not."[377]

As an outcome of his Spirit baptism, God gave Torrey a worldwide evangelistic ministry with hundreds of thousands born again
as a result. D. L. Moody used to urge him to preach on the baptism
with the Holy Spirit.

He superintended the Minneapolis City Mission Society and
pastored Chicago's Moody Memorial Church. He served as chief
executive officer of Moody Bible Institute and later as Dean of
Biola University (then called the Bible Institute of Los Angeles).[378]
Forty books came from his pen.

Perhaps it is no coincidence that this flaming evangelist so emphasized the baptism with the Spirit. Citing Acts 1:8, Murphree notes as
"two indispensable ingredients of successful evangelism, spiritual
power and human effort." That very human effort, however, demands our acceptance of both God's agenda and his energizing.

> Evangelism is His ministry, not ours. More than invoking
> His help for our work, we are aligning our lives with His
> cause. When we enter into His purposes, He enters our
> programs and projects, empowering our efforts with His
> resources.

Calling God's Spirit the divine Energizer, Murphree explains,
"We need the Holy Spirit. For our task in evangelism, we need
high octane energy."[379]

Henry C. Thiessen

Born of German immigrant parents in rural Nebraska, Henry
Clarence Thiessen grew up in a conservative Mennonite home.
His deep, thorough-going conversion at seventeen set his life on a

positive track. After educational studies, he taught in public schools.

Because he received teaching at conversion from a devout grandmother about the Spirit, Thiessen understood the source of the Christian's power. Several years later, he perceived his need and made a fuller surrender to the Holy Spirit. Elwell explains Thiessen's belief about the willingness prerequisite to receiving "the person of the Holy Spirit." This includes willingness "to allow him into our life, to put to death the practices of the body, and to walk according to his direction."

Answering God's call to the ministry, he attended Fort Wayne Bible College (now merged with Taylor University). After graduation, the Missionary Church credentialed him, and he pastored for seven years. Next, he returned to his alma mater for seven years, first as a professor and later as principal.

Realizing the need for additional education to improve his teaching credentials, Thiessen earned a degree from Northwestern University before three others. He completed two degrees at Northern Baptist Theological Seminary and his Ph. D. from Southern Baptist Theological Seminary.

Since his own deeper Christian experience resulted in "a life of greater blessing and usefulness," he chose to study further about the Spirit. His doctoral dissertation, therefore, concerned "The Holy Spirit in the Epistle to the Romans." Another influence had aroused his interest, viz., some questionable views encountered during his pastoral and early teaching years.

He saw the Spirit's work as "ennobling and assuring." Although scarcely dogmatic, Thiessen concludes that "it is not clear that Paul teaches that the more miraculous *charismata* would continue" throughout this age.

He remained a strong evangelical champion through a lifetime in higher education. After his work at Fort Wayne Bible College, he taught at Northern Baptist Theological Seminary. He administered as dean of Evangel University College of Theology in New Jersey. For four years he taught as professor of New Testament literature and exegesis at Dallas Theological Seminary (then Evangelical Theological College).

For over ten years he instructed as a professor at Wheaton College, accepting the directorship of the Graduate School from its in-ception. For a short time he headed the Theology Department at Los Angeles Baptist Theological Seminary. Two major books he authored are *Introduction to the New Testament* and *Lectures in Systematic Theology.* Readers find both books understandable and well-organized. Elwell accurately categorizes Thiessen's theological stance as "essentially eclectic . . . moderately Reformed,[380] moderately dispensational, Baptistic evangelicalism of a practical, pastoral sort."

Thiessen's life shows that the Holy Spirit can fill a believer for the defense of the faith through lucid scholarship. Not every Spirit-filled Christian exhibits a powerful gift of evangelism. Teachers and writers need the dynamic of the Spirit as do other servants of Christ.[381]

Their own testimonies provide clear evidence that Wilson, Halverson, Simpson, Havergal, Solomon, Torrey, and Thiessen entered dynamic sanctification at a point of time. Their accomplishments afterward in victorious living, evangelism, and varied ministries confirm their testimonies. Observers confirm their testimonies as well.

Their dynamic sanctification experience did not make these seven faultless or infallible. They did not stop growing because they had entered in.

They did not all prefer the same terminology to explain their experience. They represent a variety of denominations. None of them represent either the traditional Wesleyan Arminian[382] or the Pentecostal/charismatic positions. Of course, one could muster a host of witnesses from the latter movements as well.

In every case, however, *the transformation of these seven can be traced to a moment of surrender and faith after their conversion.* Several of them claim that the change produced exceeded the amount of change at their conversion.

26

Look before You Leap— But Leap! Careful Study, Then Action

Then I heard the voice of the Lord, saying, . . . "Go" (Isa. 6:8, 9).

Experiences within Postbiblical Christendom

Rehearsing stories of St. Teresa of Avila and of John Woolman, Taylor makes the following statement. "It is surprising how often the personal pilgrimage of the saints has involved a profound crisis and change at some point after first believing on Christ."[383]

Earlier chapters scrutinized biblical accounts of people who entered dynamic sanctification. The last chapter has focused on the contemporary period. Besides biblical and contemporary examples, records survive of testimonies in the intervening centuries.

Although this chapter will not detail those eras, it will relate two ancient testimonies and mention some sources of deeper-life biographical sketches for further exploration. Next, it will briefly revisit the ground that Part Five has investigated before appealing for a logical approach. Last, it will urge action.

Ancient period

Ignatius. Ignatius (c. 35-c. 114), who spent some 40 years as one of Antioch's earliest bishops, had allegedly studied under the Apostle John. At his martyrdom by wild beasts in Rome's amphitheater (Epistle of Ignatius to the Ephesians 1:4), he spoke this prayer as his last words.[384] "I thank Thee, Lord, that thou hast vouchsafed to honor me with a perfect love toward Thee."[385] This man, however, did not claim absolute perfection: ". . . not as if I were somebody extraordinary . . . I am not yet perfect in Christ Jesus" (Ignatius to Eph. 1:10). This paradoxical contrast reminds us of Paul's similar contrast on perfection (Phil. 3:12, 15). A believer can by grace become complete in love although his behavior may yet have much need to mature more fully.

In writing to the Ephesians, Ignatius often mentions and encourages holy living:

> They that are of the flesh cannot do the works of the Spirit; neither they that are of the Spirit the works of the flesh . . . (2:9). Ye are therefore . . . full of God; his spiritual temples, full of Christ, full of holiness. . . (2:12). That no herb of the devil may be found in you: but ye may remain in all holiness and sobriety . . . (3:4). No man professing a true faith sinneth; neither does he who has charity, hate any . . . (3:15). He that possesses the word of Jesus, is truly able to hear his very silence, that he may be perfect. . . (3:21).

Furthermore Ignatius urges the Ephesians to entire sanctification. "It is therefore fitting that you should by all means glorify Jesus Christ. . . . And that . . . ye may be wholly and thoroughly sanctified" (1:8-9).

Justin Martyr. After meeting a humble, gentle old Christian at the seashore, a philosopher born to heathen parents in Samaria became a Christian. We call him Justin Martyr (c. 100-165). Settled in his philosophical smugness, Justin found the old Christian's distrust of human wisdom disarming.

As a Christian, Justin spread the faith as an itinerant lay evangelist and defended it as an apologist. He was beheaded in Rome along with six other believers.[386]

In his Dialog with Trypho, Justin had written:

> And we, who have approached God through Him (Christ),
> have received not carnal, but spiritual circumcision . . . .
> What need, then, have I of circumcision, who have been
> witnessed to by God? What need have I of that other bap-
> tism, who have been baptised [sic] with the Holy Ghost?[387]

The reader will remember the identification of dynamic sanctification with spiritual circumcision treated in Chapter 19. In addition, passages like Romans 6 employ water baptism to illustrate
sanctification through the believer's identification with Christ in
his death and resurrection as we noted near the end of Chapter 10.

Sources

H. Orton Wiley's *Christian Theology*, includes a "Historical Approach to the Subject," preserving quotations and explanations on
dynamic sanctification throughout the church age. He asserts that
the doctrine "has come down to us from apostolic days as a sacred
and uninterrupted tradition through all the Christian centuries."[388]

George Allen Turner includes a chapter on "The Christian
Ideal through the Centuries" in his book, *The Vision Which Transforms: Is Christian Perfection Scriptural?*[389] Turner's volume, *Witnesses of the Way*, narrates deeper life turning points of a hundred
noted Christians.[390] Often preserving their own words, he includes
believers from the late first through the twentieth centuries. W. E.
Boardman discusses the doctrine in the Reformation period in *The
Higher Christian Life.*[391]

Even as Wiley and Turner fix on the Christian perfection slant,
Harold D. Hunter's interest centers in baptism in the Holy Spirit
terminology and experience from a Pentecostal stance. Not limited to contemporary Pentecostal writers, his *Spirit-Baptism: A
Pentecostal Alternative* aids anyone exploring dynamic sanctification from ancient through contemporary times.[392]

Wesleyan minister Clara McLeister, penned an inspiring
542-page volume, *Men and Women of Deep Piety*, containing fifty-six
sketches of godly people. These span the ages from church fathers
to the contemporary period. The objective seems not limited to

discussing people with a specific testimony of a dynamic sanctification entry-point. Of course a number of the accounts do report such a point.[393]

After treatment of Old and New Testament experiences, J. Gilchrist Lawson's *Deeper Experiences of Famous Christians* describes briefly "early saints and sages." The latter lived during the church's first millennium. The rest of the book considers in more detail twenty men and women's experiences from Pre-Reformation times to the contemporary period. Lawson ends with eleven much briefer accounts—also from the modern and contemporary periods.[394]

In *Pioneer Experiences: Or, the Gift of Power Received by Faith*, Phoebe Palmer, nineteenth-century reviser-promoter of Wesleyanism, recounts experiences. She compiles and edits dynamic sanctification testimonies of eighty then-living ministers of six diverse mainline denominations in this good-sized volume.[395]

Virtually everyone in history with a powerful ministry in winning people to Christ had received Spirit-fullness, John R. Rice claims. Not all agree with each other on terminology or interpretation. Within *The Power of Pentecost: Or, the Fullness of the Spirit*, independent Baptist evangelist Rice reports on seven nineteenth- and twentieth-century soul-winners. He adds briefer accounts of others.[396]

V. Raymond Edman, long-time president of Wheaton College, prepared *They Found the Secret*. This volume provides sketches of twenty lives from the modern and contemporary periods, beside his own testimony.[397] Nine of the accounts of famous contemporary Christians appear with slight editing in Edman's *Crisis Experiences in the Lives of Noted Christians*.[398]

Although she did not actually interview "respondents," Leona Frances Choy used their writings to form replies to her questions. Her book bears the title, *Powerlines: What Great Evangelicals Believed about the Holy Spirit—1850-1930*. While eliciting major emphases and doctrinal differences, she includes some information on the deeper life experiences of the two dozen evangelical notables. Many of them have participated in Keswick conferences.[399]

Survey

The author has conversed with various believers who without doubt experienced a significant turning point after conversion. Although the Spirit revolutionized their lives at this full surrender, their flawed theology prevents their naming their experience a dynamic sanctification crisis. Dr. Peter Wiseman, long-time professor at Asbury Theological Seminary and later at Nyack College, accurately noted that theology and life sometimes fail to match. He used to remark that some people's theology is better than their lives. In the case of others, he would continue, their lives are better than their theology.

Evidence abounds that many experience a post-conversion entry into dynamic sanctification despite their doctrinal stance that no such experience exists. Others struggle, languish, and wish—assuming that no victorious life exists this side of heaven.

J. Robertson McQuilkin, professor and later president of Columbia International University in South Carolina, made a noteworthy study. Providing a questionnaire, he polled 5,000 students. His respondents attended Bob Jones University, Biola University, Columbia International University, Prairie Bible College, Providence Bible College, and Wheaton College. Thus, McQuilkin, a Keswick advocate, selected institutions outside of both Pentecostalism and Wesleyanism's Christian Holiness Association tradition.

The questionnaire investigated a student's conversion, service call, and deeper life experience.

> . . . Out of the total number, 90 per cent stated that they had received a second crisis experience, which they variously called "surrender," a life of "victory," "the second work of grace," "the second blessing," or "the baptism with the Spirit."[400]

This overwhelming response confirms that God provides dynamic sanctification at a turning point after regeneration.

Conclusion

Summary

In Part Five, considerable evidence has appeared in various categories on the entry point into dynamic sanctification. The need for dynamic sanctification at a point of time surfaces in the deadly nature of carnality in human experience. God opposes the activities of the twisted nature that so tenaciously devastates human lives. Gradualism proves inadequate to stomp out the enemy's strongholds within Christian experience.

The very terms which Scripture employs to depict the deeper life experience imply an entry point. These include identification with Christ's crucifixion and resurrection, baptism, "filled," receiving something promised as a gift, and putting a garment off and another on. All these actions suggest a locatable event at a point instead of a lifelong procedure.

The biblical writers' use of Greek tenses supports rather than contradicts the possibility of a crisis of dynamic sanctification. The aorist tense, in particular, does not emphasize an idea of durative action.

Similarly, certain illustrative and typological Old Testament items tend to support the idea of entering dynamic sanctification at a point in time. Such items include rites like circumcision and the cleansing of a leper. They include as well events like Jacob's wrestling at Peniel and Israel's crossing Jordan into Canaan. An item that points forward to New Testament times is the promise of involvement in a New Covenant with God.

The dynamic sanctification of people in Scripture happened in a moment. Job saw a revelation of his need and God's greatness after his sufferings. Isaiah experienced divine cleansing before answering God's calling. John the Baptist's parents became filled with the Holy Spirit on different days but each in a moment.

Similarly, the 120, the early church prayer meeting crowd, the Samaritans, Paul, and the Ephesian disciples became filled instantaneously. Since things transpired this way in the Bible, why should believers expect a different pattern today? Surely we live in the same dispensation as the Samaritans and Ephesian disciples. Examples from all parts of the church age confirm the possibility of a crisis of sanctification. This chapter and the previous one have probed personal experiences in ancient and contemporary times with notice that researchers who wish can surely find additional testimonies in the intervening centuries.

Logical resolution

Is the point of sanctification at death or at resurrection? Realizing that unholy humans must become holy to dwell with a holy God, some Reformed theologians, nonetheless, see no impressive relief on earth. Such people have clung to the notion that a truly liberating holiness remains impossible in this life. The viewpoint claims that within believers "there abide still some remnants of corruption in every part: whence ariseth a continual and irreconcilable war. . . ."[401] They have traditionally supposed that only our physical death (or the resurrection) can somehow make an adequate sanctification possible.

They infer that from death onward humans will have no carnal nature, no sinful bodily and mental cravings, and no susceptibility to Satan. Thus physical death, in this view, serves as a sanctifier. Some would argue that the resurrection will provide sanctification.

Thus, some theologians have argued that the only sanctification available beyond conversion itself comes progressively but incompletely throughout life or at physical death. Others have argued for the believers' bodily resurrection, instead of death, as the time of complete sanctification. Logically, however, *even if one such evaluation were true, sanctification still involves a crisis.* The moment of physical death comes in an instant.

Scripture shows, likewise, that "in a moment, in the twinkling of an eye, at the last trumpet" the resurrection of believers will occur. At that point, "the dead will be raised imperishable, and we shall be changed" (1 Cor. 15:52). The resurrection will happen at a point in time on "the last day." Hence, if the resurrection were the sanctifier, sanctification is a crisis.

This Part, however, has examined a considerable weight of evidence favoring a turning point of dynamic sanctification as normative *within* the Christian life. If so, this turning point is not after the Christian life. Scripture urges people to receive the fullness of the

Spirit now, not in the hereafter. The Word insists on holy victorious living in the present life.

Is the point of sanctification at the start of a process? Unfortunately, many Christians deny that one should ever expect a turning point of dynamic sanctification to dethrone self and receive the Holy Spirit's empowering. They admit that conversion included a positional sanctification. Anticipating about as many setbacks as victories, they believe that for a Christian, the only sanctification this side of eternity is a growth process. This growth process, called progressive sanctification, began at conversion.

Even if an interpreter still clings to an idea of sanctification as totally a process, scriptural commands *for immediate action bring the interpretation into question.* Two examples will suffice.

(1) Urging victorious living, God commands mental action. "Likewise reckon ye also yourselves to be dead indeed unto sin, but alive unto God through Jesus Christ our Lord" (Rom. 6:11, KJV). When a believer reads such a verse, often the Holy Spirit brings conviction. He reminds the Christian, "You keep suffering defeats because you are not counting your self-life dead unto sin. When will you begin this reckoning process?"

(2) Similarly, God's familiar, but often neglected, command directs Christians, "Be filled with the Spirit" (Eph. 5:18). The Holy Spirit reminds a saved person, "You are not living a Spirit-filled life, are you? I live within you, but you have never allowed me to fill every area of your life. When will you allow me to provide the level of control you so much need?"

In both examples above, believers often overlook, misinterpret, or ignore Scripture's commands directed to Christians. *When a believer sees the need in his or her own life, grasps the possibility of obedience, and then begins such processes, there is necessarily a starting point.*

Some will object that this start of obedience involves appropriation of something inherent in the Christian regeneration rights rather than a separate "experience." Indeed, the "conversion package" purchased at Calvary potentially contains all that a believer will ever need until glorification. Surely God has much more concern that his children live a holy life than that his children adopt a second-work-of-grace theory.

This book does not argue for a prerequisite of emotional thrill in dynamic sanctification.[402] For many, dynamic sanctification amounts to a logical transaction—a "transfer of title" to one's life. This book does argue that most people find themselves ill-prepared to use the entire "conversion package" at once. Cattell observes that although dynamic sanctification could come in connection with conversion, "in actual practice it seems for nearly everyone to happen later."[403] I do argue that appropriation is essential to enjoying the benefits of dynamic sanctification.

Dynamic sanctification centers in a point of total commitment. That total commitment, however, *must* lead to progressive sanctification. Yes, the point of dynamic sanctification is at the start of a process. Wesleyans, like other advocates of an entry point, eschew a point that leads nowhere. Purkiser affirms: "Wesleyan theologians have never thought of the crisis of entire sanctification . . . as . . . a static and unimprovable state, . . . an end or a terminus, but as a starting point."[404] Non-Wesleyans heartily concur. A total commitment without a continuing growth process will not lead to a satisfactory Christian life.

Action

"Look before you leap," a common expression, means that wisdom requires careful consideration before venturing. To act without prior investigation can prove most foolhardy. Since dynamic sanctification involves signing your life away for all time to the control of another, the decision demands care. One should search Scripture and inward motives.

This book has shown the believer's deep need for inward holiness and for power to serve the Lord effectively. It has sought to examine the Scriptures with care and honesty. It has sought to lead a believer to study the issues to understand the truth. Having seen Christ's provision and having counted the cost of *not* making a full dedication to the Lord, however, one who grasps dynamic sanctification's reality should surrender and trust without delay. Graham writes: "More and more I am coming to see that this *surrender* is a definite and conscious act on our part in obedience to the Word of God."[405]

Although one should look before leaping, one must not look instead of leaping. Once we comprehend our need and Christ's will for our dynamic sanctification, prompt action is a "must." Leap!

(1) *Surrender* to the Lord everything you are and have (Rom. 6:13; 12:1). Hold nothing back. Give him your body with all its members. Give him your mind. Yield to him the management of your emotions. Give him your affections. Surrender to him your spirit. Do not omit your future—and your past, including your hurts, your regrets, your proud achievements. Put your family fully at his disposal. Present to him all your possessions. Give up freely to him that one problem area that you believe he is especially requesting. Surrender all you know and what you do not know. Give all.

(2) *Count* yourself truly dead unto sin but alive unto God (Rom. 6:11). This involves deliberately separating from the self-life's control (Rom. 12:2). As John Stott reminds us, ". . . 'reckoning' is not make-believe."[406] Instead, it counts as true the provisional <u>fact</u> of our identification with Christ. It identifies us with Christ at Calvary, where *we* died *to* sin. The believer considers himself or herself crucified with Christ to sin as a principle. The believer is alive to the power and victory inherent in our Sanctifier's resurrection.

(3) *Ask* the Lord to fulfill his promise to sanctify you (Luke 11:9-13). Judging from Bonar's comment, he anticipated that in prayer for sanctification one should expect immediate results. "Lord, I ask at this moment to be filled with the Holy Spirit, who will be in me always, showing the things of Christ, and raising intercession for others, and who will be to me 'eye-salve.'"[407]

(4) *Trust* fully that he accepts your offering of yourself, that he now cleanses you through and through, that he now fills you with his Spirit (1 Thess. 5:23-24; Eph. 5:18), that he wants to begin using you in a new way. Leap!

Part 6

On to Maturity:
The Process of Sanctification

Lord, how long? (Isa. 6:11).

How many breathtaking basketball games remain exciting until the final seconds decide the winner! Races are frequently not decided until a runner reaches the finish line. Even if the saying is true that a good beginning is half the race, still the other half can provide a rigorous challenge.

Although Joshua's warriors decisively crossed the Jordan to enter the promised land, yet they needed to rout many Canaanites before full occupation occurred. Likewise, despite the pivotal importance of a sincere dedication, a Christian pilgrim must push beyond that moment of entrance and prove victorious through years of later conquests.

"Lord, make me pure—but not yet," cried Augustine, who later did experience God's grace to overcome his sinfulness. Today, however, procrastinating people similarly wish for holiness while lacking determination or understanding. "Lord, how long will it be before they are ready to listen" (Isa. 6:11, TLB)? How long will it be till God's child reaches maturity?

Many have assumed from an inadequate theology that sanctification involves only a process, never an entry point in a believer's life. Some fear a turning point—as though it will strap them with unbearable demands. Some long for a turning point, assuming it will cure all ills once and for all.

Other believers overemphasize the crisis, hoping for a big enough experience to last a lifetime free of further trouble. They fail to realize that *no turning point substitutes for continuous Christian growth.* Part Five has investigated many lines of evidence that favor a dynamic sanctification entry point. A turning point lasts a moment; progressive sanctification needs to last the rest of your life.

Part Six will concentrate on holy living as an ongoing process. Seeking an accurate answer to the question, "Do I Need More Sanctification?" Chapter 27 will investigate why growth is essential before launching into the rate of growth. Chapter 28 will explore the results of growth before Chapter 29 surveys resources for growth and Chapter 30 closes with requirements.

27

A Line on God's Kitchen Wall: Reasons for and Rate of Growth

Keep on. . . .
Keep on. . . .
(Isa. 6:9).

Reasons for Growth

Important to God

"**I** knew you when you were this high," middle-agers and old-sters keep repeating with a gesture. The ex-toddling adolescent abhors the reminder. In many kitchens, adults measure the children by placing a yard-stick on each tousled head. Next an adult draws a little line on an inconspic-uous spot on or near a kitchen door. Sometimes the date and child's initial appear there as well. Parents are keep-ing track of each child's growth rate.

Similarly, God keeps account of his child's spiritual growth rate. Even as increasing height delights a parent, so the Heavenly Father longs to see con-sistent spiritual growth in his family members. Shall we disappoint him by remaining unchanged—or even by de-clining?

Meaningful to believers

The process of sanctification refers to God's progressive work of maintain-ing, enriching, and enlarging that holi-ness imputed at conversion but imparted in a Christian's deeper life

271

crisis. The process applies the new life's purity and power to daily behavior and service, promoting growth in Christlikeness. Even saintliest believers stand in constant need of additional grace to overcome Satanic assaults of temptation and to keep spiritually fit. Thus they increase in holiness and love, persevere in helpful deeds and effective service, and maintain a strong offensive against evil.

As a person walks along a beach, sand stretches as far as the eye can see. Still one observes more, more, more. Although theoretically only a finite number of grains of sand can occupy the earth's coastlines, yet the growth possibilities within the Christian exceed all imaginable limits. Why does the believer never reach completeness in the present life? Only the triune God is infinite. He cannot improve because he is flawlessly perfect. Thus, the degree of our growth in knowledge and Christlikeness never reaches his absolute perfection.

Required in God's plan

Can the believer logically decide whether or not to grow? Even as no infant can decide not to grow, a believer must not decide against spiritual growth. God intends growth as the Christian's only option.

Despite its revolutionary effect, no experience of dynamic sanctification can substitute for growth. Despite the depth of one's commitment, he or she can never safely attain a place of zero growth.

Hebrews shows the essentiality of growth (5:11-6:3) to deter tragic failure (Heb. 6:4-9). Growth preserves one's heavenly inheritance, for the person who produces the works of the flesh instead of walking by the Spirit (Gal. 5:16,19-21) receives solemn warning. He or she will not inherit God's kingdom (Gal. 5:21) despite any ecstatic emotions or personal commitments. As the Greek tense shows, Christians must continue to pursue "the sanctification without which no one will see the Lord" (Heb. 12:14).

Centers in Jesus Christ

God commands growth. To avoid falling from our own steadfastness through "being carried away by the error of unprincipled men," one must grow. A person must heed God's direction to "grow in the grace and knowledge of our Lord and Savior Jesus Christ" (2 Pet. 3:17-18).

The Scriptures contain more wealth than anyone can mine in a lifetime. Successful living requires that a searcher keep learning more about Jesus Christ to know him more fully. The Word remains the prime essential for growth in knowledge.

Growth in the grace of Christ involves allowing him to transfigure us into his own likeness. A. B. Simpson coined the word "Christness" to depict such a noble objective. To grow in the grace of Christ is to produce the graces or virtues found in the life of Jesus the Sanctifier. Another name for these graces is the fruit of the Spirit (Gal. 5:22-23). They form the spiritual harvest that the Holy Spirit keeps producing in the daily behavior of a yielded Christian. Progressive sanctification requires one to keep receiving Christ's available resources for abundant fruit production. Finney writes that "entire sanctification is nothing else than the reign of Jesus in the soul." That reign necessarily assumes an abdication and coronation (the point of dynamic sanctification). If so, Christ's reign logically must continue through life, since a reign concerns a span, not simply a beginning.[408]

Regarded as essential by dissimilar theologies

Nearly all doctrinal positions admit the need for such an ongoing sanctification as we noted earlier. Sometimes Wesleyan holiness theologians place so much emphasis on a crisis that they minimize the necessity of growth. Wilcox admits, "We have talked so much about a crisis that people have thought we meant that the crisis itself was the goal—whereas it is only a gate."[409]

Some refuse to refer to growth after the sanctification crisis as progressive sanctification,[410] claiming that entire sanctification provides a clean heart full of perfect love, which is therefore unimprovable. Drury, himself an advocate of the Wesleyan holiness position, nonetheless warns against such traps as "Now-ism." He explains that the belief that the choice is "holiness or hell" hurries some to claim dynamic sanctification without fulfilling conditions and therefore without true experience. He alerts readers to "Two-Tripism," the idea that a second trip to the altar will cure a person for life.[411]

On the other hand, Wesleyan writers often distinguish purity (the crisis) from maturity (the progressive growth aspect afterward).[412] They see both as essential. Therefore, the apparent conflict may largely center in just a question of words. Should the necessary growth bear the title of sanctification or not?

Wesley admitted that "there is a gradual work of God in the soul ... both before and after that moment" of dynamic sanctification. He comments of perfect love: "It is improvable. It is so far from ... being incapable of increase, that one perfected in love may grow in grace far swifter than he did before."[413]

Traditionalist Reformed and Lutheran scholars, by contrast, often overemphasize process to the exclusion of any point of commitment.[414] They view sanctification as nothing but a gradual growth from conversion onward.

Although Charismatic and Pentecostal writers see the baptism in the Spirit as a necessary turning point, they often completely dissociate sanctification from that baptism. Following Reformed doctrinal traditions, the largest Pentecostal denomination and some Charismatics and Third Wave advocates understand sanctification exclusively as a process.[415] Thus very different theologies agree that progressive sanctification is vital. Christians must grow.

In practical living, tragedy results when any believer rests in his or her conversion, deeper life crisis, or any past triumph point. Instead, whatever one's theological persuasion, he or she must press ahead. At Sinai, the mount of divine encounter and revelation, God ordered Israel to go forward: "You have stayed long enough at this mountain" (Deut. 1:6).

Rate of Growth

Gardeners know well that two plants do not necessarily grow at the same rate. Soil composition, availability of moisture, competition from weeds, and amount of sunlight comprise a few variables that underlie the success of one plant and the failure of another. In the same way, while some new believers thrive, others suffer spiritual retardation.

Missing before regeneration

Obviously life must begin before it can grow. Before one's spiritual growth can occur, God must beget a child. Spiritual leaders puzzle over the lack of growth in church members. Sometimes the riddle's solution lies in the fact that regeneration has never occurred. Before the sanctification process can originate, a person dead in trespasses and sins must experience the impartation of divine life (Eph. 2:1,5; John 5:24-25).

Only when God has implanted divine life into a human spirit, can new Christians heed his instruction. God urges, "Like newborn babes, long for the pure milk of the word, that by it you may grow in respect to salvation" (1 Pet. 2:2). God's Word is the milk newer Christians need.

Minimal in infant Christians

When a mother enters a store carrying a newborn infant, eyes sparkle and smiles form. Everyone loves an infant. Yet all pity a 25-year-old infant—a person with health defects that have prevented growth. Although God loves newborn Christians, he expresses grief over spiritual retardation. Paul shamed Corinthian immaturity:

> And I, brethren, could not speak to you as to spiritual men, but as to men of flesh, as to babes in Christ. I gave you milk to drink, not solid food; for you were not yet able to receive it. Indeed, even now you are not yet able, for you are still fleshly.

Their bickering and jealousy showed their carnal, infantile state (1 Cor. 3:1-3). Similarly, the writer to the Hebrews charged that his readers remained too inept to profit aright from instruction that more mature readers could have grasped (Heb. 5:11-14).

Rudimentary doctrines. Since unsaved people need to awaken to life's most vital issue, a minister must never tire of preaching evangelistic sermons. Yet his assignment involves providing food for giraffes as well as rabbits. A minister must tenderly feed the infants but also provide a balanced diet for spiritual adults.

Evangelicals justly shudder when liberal churches neglect instruction about regeneration. Alas, many congregations of evangelical believers never hear anything more advanced than the way to receive salvation. The whole counsel of God (Acts 20:27) includes salvation. The whole counsel of God includes a mountain of other truth as well.

A sweet believer from my boyhood church, who had loved Christ for years, once expressed his wish for simpler preaching. Surely he would identify with the hymn writer's plea: "Tell me the story simply, for I forget so soon." At his spiritual age, should he have begged for simpler preaching or for deeper understanding? As a believer hears deeper truth and walks in its light, he or she grows. If one refuses further light or fails to obey God, arrested development results.

The writer to the Hebrews listed six rudimentary doctrines, which he considered foundational (Heb. 6:1-2). All believers, he supposed, should understand repentance, faith, baptism, the laying on of hands, the resurrection, and eternal judgment. He urged leaving these elementary teachings as we press on to maturity.

Although an unsaved person and a newly saved person alike need simple instruction, yet years later must they still listen to nothing but rudimentary instruction? A pastor who never gets beyond the ABC's of the gospel fails the test. That minister has erred as surely as the insensitive one who fails to communicate because of incomprehensible preaching.

Retarded development. The believer with retarded spiritual development experiences (1) difficulty in receiving instruction and (2) deafness to spiritual truth. Although the writer to the Hebrews wished to convey much about Melchizedek, he found his ideas "hard to explain" because of his original readers' low perception level. Rather than qualifying as teachers, they suffered (3) dullness in retention. They themselves needed a repetition of elementary principles—they could not remember. God considers this a moral fault, not a mental deficiency. He illustrates this immaturity as the need for a (4) diet of milk—not solid food (Heb. 5:11-13).

I heard a speaker explain to his congregation that a physician had once prescribed for him a diet of nothing but milk for many weeks! This period, however, included only his opening weeks on earth. Afterward solid food became appropriate fare. Christians must aim to surpass the childish state. By using discretion in selecting from their spiritual menu and by obeying God's instructions for mature living, progressive sanctification should occur.

Moderate in many believers

Even as growth appears sadly minimal in many Christians, in other cases it seems moderate. Perhaps one could so describe the original recipients of James' letter. Maintaining faith amid severe trials, they yet experienced trouble in proving their faith with consistent speech and conduct. Their attitude betrayed presumption about the future. They neither tottered on the verge of returning to Judaism nor shocked the writer with unrestrained religious emotionalism. We read no specific charge of infantile behavior. Although they seemed guilty of no severe heresy, they lacked a right attitude toward wealth, wisdom, the world, and works.

Quarrels abounded. James calls their instability double-mindedness. He condemns their failures more often than commending their virtues. Yet he does not call them incapable of perceiving his penetrating message. Perhaps one can describe their growth as moderate. Similarly, many contemporary Christians have grown a bit, but harbor many inconsistencies that hamper spiritual maturity.

Marvelous in some believers

If one considers the brevity of time since their regeneration, the Thessalonian church provides an example of phenomenal spiritual growth. The first epistle to these Christians probably arrived within the first year of their conversion to Jesus Christ. Nevertheless, they had progressed so rapidly that Paul heartily praised their exemplary lifestyle and evangelistic fervor (1 Thess. 1:6-8). The process of sanctification mightily worked in their lives.

News of their perseverance highly encouraged him (1 Thess. 3:6). Despite some things still lacking in their faith, they themselves made up his anticipated crown of exultation (1 Thess. 3:10,

2:19). Their consistent early growth made possible further growth, so that they could excel still more (1 Thess. 4:1,10). When new converts today manifest rapid early growth, Christian workers' hearts thrill. In contrast with the faults of immature believers detailed in Hebrews 5:11-6:3, a reader can infer how God characterizes mature believers.

Progress. Direction seems more crucial than speed. A football player may set an enviable record for speed, but if he is running toward the wrong goal, his exertion proves self-defeating and foolish. If a basketball player accidentally hurls the ball into his opponent's basket, no teammate applauds his skill. Even as "an athlete . . . does not win the prize unless he competes according to the rules" (2 Tim. 2:5), so the believer must move in the direction required in God's blueprint. Do you face the correct goal unflinchingly, or do you still keep casting wistful, furtive glances toward Sodom?

A new Christian, with areas of severe problems, may maintain an urgent determination to obey God implicitly. If so, he or she stands on much firmer ground than the seasoned Christian who has learned to coast, tolerating personal faults. A believer with a tender conscience, a deep love and respect for the Lord, and a determination to grow should progress well. That person will outdistance a long-saved stagnant Christian who never shows concern about growth.

Are you marching forward or slipping backward? God commands: "Forward!" Since the spiritual battlefield invariably lies uphill, the person who thinks he or she is standing still is losing ground. Whereas the choice to finish dawdling with first grade teachings is decisive, the Hebrews 6:1 command to press on demands continuing action. The Charles B. Williams translation expresses the contrast. "So then let us once for all quit the elementary teaching about Christ and continue progressing toward maturity. . . ."

Posture tells the story. As a Christian, are you posed for attention or poised for action? Can you afford to let down your guard while the enemy is advancing? Do you long to sit in idleness, or are you purposefully moving forward?

Perfection. The ideal believer in Hebrews 6:1 and 5:14 has a clear goal. He presses on toward becoming mature—a full grown person. This "holiness is not Edenic, angelic, or absolute perfection."[416] Only God has absolute perfection. Edenic perfection characterized only Adam and Eve before the fall.

As most contemporary translations show, the believer's perfection in such Scriptures as this Hebrews passage involves maturity rather than an absolutely spotless life. Yet, if belief in total sinless perfection in present experience is a grave error, then carnal satisfaction with imperfection is a greater error. "Let us press on to maturity."

Prudence. Even as adults can digest solid food, so the spiritually mature have developed prudence. Because of practice, their spiritual senses have developed a discernment of good and evil. The trickery of false teachers no longer fascinates them. Since they are no longer children, winds and waves cannot sweep them from their steadfastness (Eph. 4:14). Neither ecstatic thrills nor floods of gloom can divert them from holy committed behavior.

Proclamation. The author of Hebrews told his readers, "By this time you ought to be teachers." Apparently spiritual adulthood requires spiritual reproductive responsibilities. A taught person must teach others. In turn, a willingness to instruct others will promote our own growth. Studying carefully, a diligent teacher learns more than his or her pupils do.

Maintained growth: The Master's master plan

Commencement: At the new birth. Never in the present life should Christian growth cease. The divine master plan includes persistent growth in Christian experience from the new birth onward. A new spiritual life needs to be protected, nurtured, fed, and exercised even as an infant's physical life does. Having launched upon a life stream of holiness, as Figure 3 shows,[417] the new Christian's initial sanctification coincides with the moment of regeneration and justification. Calling such a person a saint, Scripture prods him or her to live up to such a name (1 Cor. 1:2).

Climb: At the crisis of the deeper life—and beyond. Once a believer has trusted God for cleansing from bondage to a corrupt old nature and the Spirit's concurrent infilling, a growth spurt occurs. The energizing power of the indwelling Christ enables more consistent growth. The believer has just made a conscious surrender of the entire personality with all its parts to the Lord. Consequently, with one big yes said to God, the smaller yeses of daily obedience should come more easily. In theological language, progressive sanctification should grow out of and naturally follow the turning point of dynamic sanctification. Hence a life stream of holiness also follows dynamic sanctification.[418]

Climax: At glorification. Many infer from Scripture that sanctification reaches a golden climax at the point of our glorification. When Christ returns to receive believers to himself, a bodily transformation will follow. Whether we have died or will survive unto the time of the Christ's coming, the believer will receive a deathless glorified body (1 Cor. 15:51-53; Phil. 3:20-21; 1 Thess. 4:15-17).

Does Scripture also seem to imply a connection of this time of glorification with a final sanctification? Speaking of "the city of the living God, the heavenly Jerusalem," the writer of Hebrews mentions "the spirits of righteous men made perfect" (12:22-23). Paul speaks of Christ's sanctifying his bride, resulting in holiness and blamelessness, so that in the future "He might present to Himself the church in all her glory, having no spot or wrinkle . . ." (Eph. 5:25-27).

Jude's benediction states that God is able to cause believers to "stand in the presence of His glory blameless" (Jude 24). In 1 Thessalonians 5:23, Paul prays that God will preserve believers blameless until Christ's return. In 3:12-13, he had petitioned that the Lord would cause them "to increase and abound in love," with hearts established "unblamable in holiness." This action also anticipates "the coming of our Lord Jesus with all His saints." One could cite some additional references.

It appears, however, that Scripture never shows unmistakably whether a final sanctification happens at glorification. Does it happen at that future point? Do the verses above, instead, refer exclusively to sanctification in this life? If the latter, present

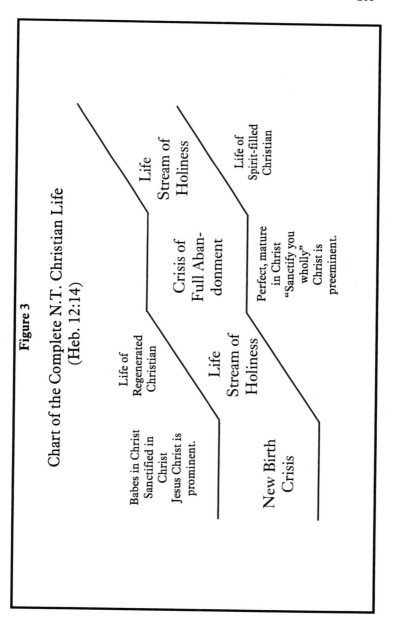

Figure 3

Chart of the Complete N.T. Christian Life
(Heb. 12:14)

Life of
Regenerated
Christian

Life
Stream of
Holiness

Life
Stream of
Holiness

Life of
Spirit-filled
Christian

Babes in Christ
Sanctified in
Christ
Jesus Christ is
prominent.

Crisis of
Full Aban-
donment

Perfect, mature
in Christ
"Sanctify you
wholly"
Christ is
preeminent.

New Birth
Crisis

sanctification becomes the vital preparation for living without spot or wrinkle in heaven among blameless perfected righteous ones. Does 1 John 3:2-3 describe our physical transformation? Or may it refer additionally or even exclusively to a spiritual transformation when Christ appears and "we shall be like him"? In either case, the transformation occurs after believers have experienced purification in anticipation of Christ's arrival.

Continuation: Forever. Even in the next life, we will never become infinitely perfect like God is. God will have confirmed us in holiness. He will choose to charge us with no blame and to hold against us no fault, yet he alone will be absolutely perfect. Here several contemporary cults like Mormons, Spiritualists, and the original doctrine of Herbert W. Armstrong's Worldwide Church of God err. They prove mistaken by teaching that frail mortals will ultimately become gods or God in their infinite upward evolution.

Instead, Scripture envisions one God himself as all in all throughout eternity. He will not share his absolute perfection with another. Only God is infinite in holiness; if any creature were infinite, that being would be God. Logically only one infinite, absolute, eternal being can exist in the universe. He is the source of other entities that exist.

If believers will not be absolutely holy even in eternity, this leads to the question of whether our holiness will increase in eternity. Christian growth must never cease in the present life while we walk by faith rather than by sight. If this is so, why should it cease when we stand more directly and consciously in God's presence?

Some think that once believers arrive in heaven, their sanctification will be constant and as complete as it will ever be. Erickson, for example, holds that "we will not grow in heaven." He reasons that it is "an extrapolation from life as now constituted" to say that heaven would be unsatisfying if we have no possibility of growth.[419]

Finney, on the other hand, supposed that "saints will continue to grow in grace to all eternity, and in the knowledge of God." He assumed, though, that all who enter heaven are "entirely holy."[420]

Similarly, Wesley believed that the sanctified can grow in grace "not only while they are in the body, but to all eternity."[421]

Granted that heaven will differ vastly from the present order, yet if eternal life were a static cessation of growth, would our existence not seem stagnant? Would not a God of infinite wisdom and perfect planning intend for his creatures to keep becoming more like himself? Since he alone is infinite, his regenerate creatures will never arrive at his absolute holiness. Since on earth, however, they may become more and more holy, will heaven provide less challenge toward growth than earth does?

Scripture seldom unveils much about the eternal heavenly state. Revelation's final chapter contains a verse that may help our quest for information about holiness in heaven. "He that is unjust, let him be unjust still: and he which is filthy, let him be filthy still: and he that is righteous, let him be righteous still: and he that is holy, let him be holy still" (Rev. 22:11, KJV).

Might this verse refer to the present period before our glorification—since the major vision of the New Jerusalem had already ended in verse 5? No, this could hardly be the correct interpretation because if it were, God himself would be advising the wicked to continue their foul practices and not to repent.

We know from 2 Peter 3:9 that God does not wish "for any to perish but for all to come to repentance." Revelation 22:17 shows that in the present age, "the Spirit and the bride say, 'Come.' . . . And let the one who is thirsty come; let the one who wishes take the water of life without cost." Grace still seeks the sinner.

When Christ arrives, however,—the topic of the immediate context of Revelation 22:11—opportunity for a drastic reversal of lifestyle shall have ended (Rev. 22:10, 12). Then the unrighteous will remain unrighteous and the righteous will remain righteous. Verses 14 and 15 resume mention of those who will have access to the eternal city and those against whom the gates must forever be shut. Hence, one should conclude that Revelation 22:11 describes the fact that those who enter heaven holy will never become unholy.

Does this verse contain any hint about whether or not sanctified people will continue to grow in holiness in eternity? The Greek word translated "still" four times in the verse also can mean "yet more." If the Holy Spirit intended such an idea here, the Berkeley

Version conveys accurately the last half of the verse. "Let the righteous too keep practicing righteousness and let the saint grow ever more holy." The verb translated above "be holy" or "grow holy" is 'αγιαζω, *hagiadzo*, the ordinary Greek verb meaning "to sanctify." Therefore, one may understand the sentence with its passive verb as "Let the saint become ever more sanctified"—an endless progressive sanctification.

The Living Bible lacks precision in rendering the verb's imperative mood. This paraphrase, however, vividly supports the concept of the believer's continuing growth in holiness. "Do not seal up what you have written, for the time of fulfillment is near. And when that time comes, all doing wrong will do it more and more; the vile will become more vile; good men will be better; those who are holy will continue on in greater holiness" (verses 10-11).

In summary, it has become apparent that God's plan for his people includes constant progress. A committed Christian can never safely choose to remain stationary on some fixed plateau instead of pursuing progressive sanctification. Fulfilling the very commands of God's Word, one finds that growth deters spiritual failure. It assures the genuineness of the Christian behavior necessarily absent before regeneration. Even infant Christians show at least minimal growth. Arrested development at this stage proves tragic. While some grow moderately, others achieve an outstanding growth pattern. God's design involves growth that commences at the new birth, surges at the deeper life crisis, climaxes at glorification, but perhaps never ceases—even in eternity.

28

How Will I Know I'm Grown Up?—Results of Growth

I saw the Lord sitting on a throne, lofty and exalted. Full of His glory (Isa. 6:1, 3).

As a child poorly grasps the marks of maturity, so a baby Christian little comprehends spiritual adulthood. The Word shows traits of spiritual maturity. Advanced believers resemble Jesus because they have exalted the Sanctifier to their hearts' throne. There Jesus will relive his life, employing the identical virtues that distinguished his from ordinary lives around.

On that solemn eve before the cross, Jesus told the twelve, "If you love me, you will keep my commandments" (John 14:15). A sincere Christian, carefully obeying, should supremely desire to please the Master. Obedience results in godly living. The maturing believer "full of His glory" lives to glorify the Lord. This chapter will introduce you to results that should show up in a mature believer's experience.

Guiding a Godly Lifestyle

Provides true freedom

Relation to values. Contemporary people insist on freedom. Crying for freedom on many levels, they demand freedom from parental authority, from the need for excellence, from traditional sexual mores, from fiscal responsibility, from self-discipline. The freedom sought, however, incurs its own bitter slavery. Running toward these freedoms, people dart into traps. Slavery fastens an iron grip on their unsuspecting lives—slavery to peer pressure, to mediocrity, to unbiblical perversions, to crushing debt, to an unbridled lifestyle.

Instead of bucking the tide of selfism and nowism, Christians also demand instant release from wisdom's restraints. Instead of maintaining Israelite separation, they adopt the ways of the surrounding nations. Evangelicals often fail to communicate God's standards to that upcoming generation that easily detects their elders' hypocrisy. The fallen world system dictates standards.

Outmoded values include obedience, excellence, purity, economy, and discipline. Why should I obey anyone or anything when I can do what I want? Why must I do my best when I can manage with less? Why should I adopt holier sexual standards than I can get by with when impure living feels so good? Why should I live within my income if I can get away with deficit spending? Why should anyone dictate my lifestyle when I prefer to let the whim of the moment decide what I do? Why live a disciplined life when many do not?

Relation to dynamic sanctification. An entrance point into dynamic sanctification must not focus on itself. To listen to many promoters of the crisis, one would suppose that it forms an end in itself. Instead, it prepares, equips, and initiates the Christian into living on the spiritual level God intends.

The objective and intention of that point center in a life of holiness amid the pressures and difficulties of this wicked world. Cattell explains: "Sanctification is a crisis experience in that one arrives at a moment of all-inclusive surrender, and it is a process in that it involves carrying the validity of that surrender into every succeeding moment of the eternal *now,* applying it to additional areas of un-Christlike living within us as they are revealed by the abiding Christ who is the Holy Spirit."[422]

Without a holy life, what unmistakable proof has a person of regeneration? Far from comprising an option, then, a godly lifestyle stands as an utter necessity.

Relation to elemental law. Arguing for more freedom, contemporaries often remain unaware of the freedom available in the sanctification process. Yet here alone lies the foundation for a happy life. Built into the universe itself by its Creator, a godly lifestyle promotes true freedom. Theologians refer to this principle as elemental law. Not only did God provide positive enactment—specific written laws like the Ten Commandments, but he also formed the universe so that it contains his laws.

Consequently, obedience to God brings automatic rewards. Disobedience bestows automatic loss—physically, mentally, emotionally, and morally. Even as stepping from a high cliff brings physical injury, so harboring hatred and jealousy brings, because of elemental law, emotional, spiritual, and even physical injury. Human beings can obey God to their benefit or disobey to their hurt. The person who behaves in an ungodly fashion is living at cross purposes to his or her own best interests. For such a person, life becomes an exercise in futility like petting the cat the wrong way or cutting cloth on the bias.

Providing one of Scripture's clearest treatises on a godly lifestyle, Galatians 5 warns believers sternly. "For you were called to freedom, brethren; only do not turn your freedom into an opportunity for the flesh. . ." (Gal. 5:13). In an impressive hymn, George Matheson captured the paradox that true liberty requires a life of total surrender:

> Make me a captive Lord,
>   And then I shall be free;
> Force me to render up my sword,
>   And I shall conqueror be.
> I sink in life's alarms
>   When by myself I stand;
> Imprison me within Thine arms,
>   And strong shall be my hand.[423]

Promotes integrated Christlike living

To survive as a balanced whole person, a believer must make godly living a supreme priority. Since holiness involves wholeness, the growing Christian can manifest spiritual balance instead of roller-coaster, fragmented living. Progressive sanctification leads to freedom from the slavery that once incarcerated God's child in carnal chains.

As one of Scripture's simplest figures of speech, the walk stands for daily behavior. Paul reasoned, "If we live by the Spirit, let us also walk by the Spirit. . . . But I say, walk by the Spirit, and you will not carry out the desire of the flesh" (Gal. 5:25, 16). If divine life from the Spirit has flooded in in the new birth, God intends to continue his work. The Word shows that the same Spirit longs to supply day-by-day power for a successful Christian life. Such power releases from bondage to the bent nature's enslaving wrong desires.

Without question, a walk illustrates a prolonged process—not a turning point. This practice of walking by the Spirit's power in the present life involves a never-ending process. Ideally it leads to a closer, sweeter relationship. Although a baby's initial steps often falter, yet soon the little one is walking with ease without thinking about the process.

Walking with or by the Spirit suggests fellowship, harmony, energizing, dependence, and guidance. God's Word shows that the Spirit liberates. He frees from a sense of the frown of God by enabling us to please him. He sets free from spiritual weakness by supplying an inward dynamic. God's Spirit frees from a rebellious self-centered independence with the effect that we can rest on God's doing instead of on our own feverish activity. By leading us to the right route, God's guiding Spirit releases us from confusion and bewilderment.

Because of our communion with him, we begin to sense God's glory—not as an observer but as a seeker. Beholding God's glory evokes spiritual hunger to become ever more like the Lord Jesus, to reflect his glorious beauty to others. The resulting transformation moves steadily upward and forward: ". . . Where the Spirit of the Lord is, there is liberty. But we all, with unveiled face beholding as in a mirror the glory of the Lord, are being transformed into the same image from glory to glory, just as from the Lord, the Spirit" (2 Cor. 3:17,18). The Holy Spirit, our Lord—not the servant who must come at our whim—inspires and promotes this life of spiritual progress and ever-increasing glory. Here stands one of a salient feature of progressive sanctification—a growth in Christlikeness.

Pacifies interpersonal relationships

How do you get along with others? When a stumbling Christian interacts with others, selfishness blossoms embarrassingly. Preferring that others glimpse my halo, their eyes catch instead my cat-that-swallowed-the-canary blush. Paul vividly exposes the quarreling at Corinth (1 Cor. 3:1-4). With a bold stroke, Paul dealt with a touchy Galatian situation where nasty disputes occurred. "But if you bite and devour one another, take care lest you be consumed by one another."

In his old-fashioned poem, "The Duel," Eugene Field humorously related a tale of woe about two stuffed animals. "The gingham dog and the calico cat side by side on the table sat," before having a terrible spat in which "the gingham and calico flew!" Field sketches the result in part of the final stanza:

Next morning where the two had sat
They found no trace of dog or cat;
And some folks think unto this day
That burglars stole that pair away!
But the truth about the cat and pup
Is this: they ate each other up![424]

When I display a nasty disposition, I mar a friendly relationship with acquaintances and loved ones. Such action also proves self-destructive. Giving someone a piece of my mind results in giving away my peace of mind. E. Stanley Jones claims that an angry rattlesnake, when cornered, may literally bite itself.[425] This illustrates the need to allow the Holy Spirit to keep governing our temperament and bridling our tongue.

Thus, Paul exhorts, "Let us not become boastful, challenging one another, envying one another" (Gal. 5:26). Living the crucified life enables God's child to live in harmony with difficult people despite compelling temptations to ruffle the tranquility. Christ wants to reign as sovereign over emotional interaction, also over our conversations.

Protects through continual watchfulness and cleansing

In biblical accounts, yeast regularly symbolized either wickedness or false doctrine. When Paul warned the Galatians that "a little leaven leavens the whole lump of dough," he intended them to understand the importance of disallowing sin within the congregation because tolerated sin spreads contagion (Gal. 5:9). Even as yeast permeates an entire batch of dough, so evil penetrates a Christian community.

In individual lives as well, a bit of harbored evil defiles the character. Even as we would refuse to drink otherwise pure water containing one or two drops of sewage, so God rejects the life that deliberately harbors sin. "For whoever keeps the whole law and yet stumbles in one *point*, he has become guilty of all" (James 2:10). The issue centers in our own attitude of commitment—not in the impossibility of pleasing God without a life of absolute perfection. Never will we behave as perfectly as God does, yet never may we safely cherish even a single transgression. Instead of pampering evil or hiding it, the growing Christian must purge out the old yeast.

Whenever the Spirit points to a need, our only safe response is repentance. The psalmists could ask God "Why?" but submitted to his superior wisdom. To its own shame a self-willed society has produced Christians who perilously dare to scream at God their rebellion: "Why God? Why can't I behave as I please? Why did you allow such circumstances? How can you treat me in this way?"

Such foolish talk ventilates bitter feelings but can stunt Christian growth and grieve an all-wise God. Such talk betrays that the speaker thinks himself god rather than God's love slave. Karl Barth rightly insisted, "Let God be God." To shout to God a list of reasons why he ought to allow one to continue in a certain sin constitutes a sad exercise in futility. Not only does God give immutable laws, but he remains the unchanging moral standard for his universe. Harbored leaven destroys sanctified living.

Today too many careless teachers have influenced believers to treat their sins flippantly. If no one guards national freedom, freedom stands in peril. Similarly, guarded living protects our spiritual liberty. "Follow on watchfully and resolutely. Seek the daily renewing of the Holy Spirit. . . ."[426]

Paul cautioned against a casual attitude regarding sin: "For you were called to freedom, brethren; only do not turn your freedom into an opportunity for the flesh. . ." (Gal. 5:13). Christian liberty must not pamper the bent nature by allowing it to seize its chance to allow ungodly behavior. Instead, the freed child of God should dwell permanently in the safety of 1 John 1:7, continually living in the light, enjoying unbroken fellowship, and experiencing continual cleansing.

Progressive sanctification involves such an ongoing experience as implied in the present tense verbs in this familiar verse. As you maintain a sincere, open, pure life, progressive sanctification means that Christ's blood provides the source of unceasing purification. Cleansing us from every act of sin, God also cleanses from all sin—from the power of the old nature as well as from transgressions. Beyond an initial moment of cleansing from carnal impulses, progressive sanctification basks in the privilege of further moment-by-moment cleansing from the old pollution.

Produces the fruit of the Spirit

God's wishes to produce greater amounts of finer quality fruit, even as Jesus implied to his disciples shortly before facing Gethsemane. "Every branch that bears fruit, He prunes it, that it may bear more fruit. . . . By this is My Father glorified, that you bear much fruit, and so prove to be My disciples." His purpose also involves bearing fruit that remains (John 15:2, 8, 16). Bishop Ryle wrote about the Christian:

> More pardoned and more justified than he is when he first believes, he cannot be, though he may feel it more. More sanctified he certainly may be, because every grace in his new character may be strengthened, enlarged, and deepened.[427]

Love. Jesus asserted that love toward God and neighbor fulfills the law. Noting that the Galatians 5:22-23 list begins with the statement, "But the fruit of the Spirit is love," expositors frequently suggest that love somehow embodies the entire list. Thus, A.B. Simpson wrote:

> We have not a great many things to do, but just one, and that one thing is to love; for all these manifestations of the fruit are but various forms of love. Joy is love exulting; peace is love reposing; long-suffering is love enduring; gentleness is love refined; meekness is love with bowed head; goodness is love in action; temperance is true self-love, and faith is love confiding, so that the whole sum of Christian living is just loving. . . . We only have to be filled with the Spirit, and then the love will flow as a fountain, spontaneously, from the life within.[428]

Although a Christian remembers that God has already shed abroad his love in our hearts through the Holy Spirit (Rom. 5:5), yet God wants the believer to overflow with more and more love. Although Paul had witnessed the labor motivated by the Thessalonians' love (1 Thess. 1:3), and Timothy had brought him good news of their love (1 Thess. 3:6), yet he prayed: "May the Lord cause you to increase and abound in love for one another, and for all men" (1 Thess. 3:12).

After God perfects love in his sanctifying refinement of attitudes (1 John 4:12, 17, 18), the Spirit-filled believer can still grow more love. Quality does not ensure quantity. The love God bestows surely would be perfect, but we need to keep sharing it with additional people and applying it to different situations. We need to love God and people more and show our love more fully.

Peace and joy. Though he as God ultimately possessed all things, Jesus had no fortune for his disciples to inherit at his death. Instead, following his last supper with them, he bequeathed to them his peace and his joy: "Peace I leave with you; My peace I give to you. . . . These things I have spoken to you, that *my* joy may be in you. . . ." He also explained how they could live in his very love (John 14:27; 15:9-11). During the hours of his ultimate mistreatment, he exhibited no hatred, no vindictiveness. On the evening when we would have most needed someone else to cheer us, he had such an abundance of peace and joy. Thus, he told his disciples that he was giving them his own peace and joy.

Yesterday a call from a Christian acquaintance interrupted my writing. The voice on the phone said that bitterness toward God had begun to vex his spirit. For three years, he admitted, he had blamed God for not answering his prayers for employment in the way he wished. Christians frequently chafe under injustice, pain, and extreme hardship, but Jesus possessed an inward source of abundant peace and joy.

Believers these days complain miserably when they fail to feel exuberant; often they blame the lack on external circumstances. Though his sufferings far exceeded ours, Jesus' emotional triumph in facing the cross demonstrates that the problem lies not with the severity of our trials but with our reactions. On the night of Gethsemane, the eve of Calvary, Jesus chose to triumph over the unrest and depression that an observer might expect to find. Not by our human striving but by Christ's gift, we, too, can choose to gaze at our divine supplier, not at our personal tragedies.

How can we produce peace and joy as fruit? Paul's prayer for his readers divulges an important secret. "Now may the God of hope fill you with all joy and peace in believing, that you may abound in hope by the power of the Holy Spirit" (Rom. 16:13). The simple condition requires us to trust.

If we focus on our emotions, we miss the point. Even if we cry to God often for peace and joy, we may continue to be disappointed—until we begin a life of committed trust. As we rest our confidence solely in the Lord, a measure of joy and peace arrives as a by-product. As we continue to live by faith, coming to trust the Lord more fully, joy and peace can abound. Abounding joy and peace depend on the Holy Spirit's power.

The God of hope, who fills people with these graces, purposes to flood believers with abounding hope. Increasing sanctification should involve the fuller use of all the virtues the Spirit gives, including hope—a never-ending grace (1 Cor. 13:13).

Today depression abounds—not hope. In an age of despair, God wants his people to trust him so fully that they anticipate good things from God's provision both here and hereafter. How often the psalmist, who freely confessed his miseries, discovered that he could yet hope in God, his source of help! Such Psalms can speak loudly to today's needs (Ps. 42:5, 11; 43:11).

In cases when depression arises from spiritual causes, the cure involves allowing God's power to rid the victim of bad habitual reactions. Often these are emotional and mental habits, etched deeply on the personality through years of bad practice. Scripture never instructs God's people to despair but often urges them to hope. Grace can restore hope, even abounding hope, as people awaken to the possibilities.

If one finds hopelessness deeply ingrained from months or decades of unscriptural attitudes, he or she may need to seek God's forgiveness. God wants to forgive the despairing for refusal to hope through those years. One may need to renounce satanic holds that otherwise would prevent a full cure. Abounding hope allies itself with joy and peace.

Patience, kindness, and gentleness. In an age of mad activity, some view impatience as a virtue. Activists refuse to sit idly by waiting for right circumstances. Manipulators of people discount kindness and gentleness as weakness.

Bearing with his disciples' spiritual dullness, Jesus continued to model graces of patience, kindness, and gentleness. Jesus had shown patience in waiting quietly in Nazareth for many years until his Father's timing for the start of his public ministry.[429]

How gently he dealt with Herod Antipas and Pilate, his judges! What kindness and gentleness he manifested toward his betrayer, bestowing on him the honored guest's sop at the Passover. Did Jesus try to awaken any lingering thread of penitence in his dark soul? What patience, kindness, and gentleness Jesus showed the sinful woman anointing his feet and the woman caught in adultery! In his patience, kindness, and gentleness, he refused to break off a battered reed or quench a smoldering wick (Matt. 12:20).

Although today's Christians long for joy and peace so they can feel good, they lack concern for developing patience, kindness, and gentleness, so others can feel good. Such shortsightedness confirms the strength of the self-life even in believers. When Spirit-filled Christians allow Christ to reign, such sweet virtues as graced Jesus' earthly sojourn will abide and abound in them.

Goodness. As God's goodness consists in his benevolent good will and right actions toward his creatures, so he designs that his dedicated children should be fountains of good toward people around them. When a lady cuts into a honeycomb, she finds a vastly different tasting substance than when she cuts into a lemon. If people ruthlessly cut into us, does sweetness or sourness overwhelm them? We show the world whatever resides on the inside.

Only divine grace can enable consistent reactions of goodness when others seek to offend and injure us.[430] If some mighty computer would require you to read a transcript of every remark spoken for a week, how many would be negative? Many Christians would experience great surprise at discovering how negatively they speak. Sometimes actions also display rancor. To impact the world for good, should not God's representatives allow Christ to live his good life through our yielded bodies?

Faith/faithfulness. The Bible's supreme love chapter mentions faith as an imperishable Christian virtue along with love and hope (1 Cor. 13:13). Your title, "believer," identifies you as one who has believed and continues to believe in Christ for salvation.

Although every true believer exercised faith at the point of regeneration, it does not follow that each consistently keeps on living by faith. Using faith as a principle for the moment-by-moment action of trusting God forms one of the Christian life's most indispensable lessons.

If one can trust God for valid reservations in the heavenly city, can he or she not trust Him for every need in the present life? Though God does *not* promise to increase the amount of faith a Christian possesses, he urges us to use more consistently the faith we have. Unused faith tends to evaporate. Regularly used faith becomes strong faith that helps believers to dare to live up to their name. As a car lot advertised, "Everybody drives a used car," so, all faith that abides is used faith.

The Greek word in Galatians 5:22 is no different from the one normally translated "faith" throughout the New Testament. Most translators and commentators, however, understand the fruit called "faith" in the King James Version as faithfulness, fidelity, trustfulness—perhaps like "good faith." This major view commands respect, harmonizing with the other virtues in the list and likely affording the correct idea. We can trust God. Does he find us trustworthy?

An essential virtue in a Christian's life, faithfulness links our past decisions with the fruition of our future hope. Faithfulness guarantees the sincerity and validity of our initial act of faith. Among other things, faithfulness includes loyalty to God, to spiritual commitments, to the body of Christ, and to our promises. God can supply the stamina to keep his people faithful despite sore trials. Christian growth must include growth in faithfulness.

Self-control. The final virtue in Gal. 5:23, self-control, implies the need for a disciplined lifestyle. Perhaps contemporary Christians most despise the quality they most desperately need—discipline. A rebellious generation refuses anyone's word on what to do or when or where to do it. Wearing the evangelical label, some postmoderns cast off all moral restrictions, insisting that the gospel provides them an antinomian freedom from all law.

The Bible soundly repudiates such libertarian notions (Rom. 6:15-16). Demanding unbridled behavior, people refuse restraints—even self-imposed ones. They wish to do whatever the moment dictates without reason, budgets, or schedules.

Lauding the value of spontaneity, they suffer spiritual malnutrition from avoiding regular private and family devotions. Some even claim a structured public worship service to be unspiritual. Does the omniscient Holy Spirit—who supposedly guides our emotional moods—find it impossible to decide beforehand the time for the offering? Can he reveal beforehand what song to sing before the sermon?

God wants disciplined warriors. Paul ordered, "Suffer hardship with me, as a good soldier of Christ Jesus" (2 Tim. 2:3). Jesus said, "If you love Me, you will keep My commandments" (John 14:15). Although he shared the very essence of Deity and ruled as Lord of all creation, Jesus lived on earth under discipline. He subordinated himself to the Father's orders, He guided his days by principle—not by whim.

When Christ lives his life unhindered through the saint, he again lives with prudent restraint. Growth in holiness involves growth in self-discipline under the control of the Holy Spirit.

Checking the checklist. When he or she sees no spiritual fruit developing and improving, the Spirit-filled Christian must not rest complacently. God keeps looking for fruit, more fruit, much fruit, abiding fruit (John 15:2, 5, 16). As the disciple keeps his or her life centered in Christ, shunning hindrances, fruit should grow. Entire clusters should ideally grow at once, since the singular word "fruit" precedes the list in Galatians 5:22-23.

If all the fruit does not develop in abundance, the Christian can profitably examine the John 15:1-16 check list, seeking divine direction. Am I abiding in Christ—centering my life in him? Am I allowing the Heavenly Father to prune hindrances from me? Am I depending on Christ for fruitful living? Am I living as though Christ is making his home within me? Am I allowing Christ's very words to abide in me, or do I ignore the Word? Am I regularly expressing my desires for fruitfulness to God in prayer? Am I abiding in Christ's love? Do I show love to others? Am I willing to have Christ's joy living in me—or do I prefer to live morosely, basking in my bitterness? Am I obeying what Christ commands me? Am I living as Christ's friend or am I ignoring him?

If I lack abounding fruit, I should also allow the Spirit to examine me in the light of the checklist in Galatians 5:9-26. Am I allowing the leaven of some evil to remain? Am I abusing freedom by allowing the flesh to take advantage of my liberty in Christ? Do I allow bitterness, conceit, rivalry, or envy to injure fellow-believers? Am I walking by the Spirit? Am I led by the Spirit? Am I tolerating the forbidden works of the flesh? Am I living the crucified life? As often as the Spirit specifies need for correction, I must submit. Then I can expect an abundant harvest.

Ignoring biblical principles, Christians sometimes attempt to produce spiritual fruit by personal striving. In his Sermon on the Mount, Jesus called attention to God's provision for vegetation. "Observe how the lilies of the field grow; they do not toil nor do they spin, yet I say to you that even Solomon in all his glory did not clothe himself like one of these" (Matt. 6:28-29). If lilies allow God to provide their clothing, ought not God's children to depend on God to produce fruit in them? After all, Paul in Galatians calls it the Spirit's fruit—fruit the Spirit produces.

Generating effective service

A Christian worker needs the Holy Spirit's infilling before seriously launching into Christian service. Anyone continuing to
serve Christ continues to need the Spirit's empowering. "Through
love keep on continually serving one another" (Gal. 5:13, expanded to show the force of the Greek present tense).

As Jericho challenged invading Israelis when the conquest of
Canaan began, new situations, new demands, and new ministries
challenge Spirit-filled workers today. Such challenges call for renewed anointings. The Christian must never face backward to rest
on a past moment of dynamic enduement, however transforming
or spectacular that may have seemed.

The endued warrior keeps looking up in continual dependence
on the Commander as he marches into service. Fresh abundant
supplies of divine insight, wisdom, and strength, can make effective one's witness for Christ. This divine assistance can power
one's current service whatever its nature. Ministry may involve a
private conversation or a public sermon to multitudes of sinners
overseas. God will empower a believer to write a letter to a trou-
bled Christian or teach a Sunday School lesson to a little class. He
can enable one to produce an article for publication or to mirror
Christ behaviorally to a lost skeptic. The anointing can increase as
dependence on the Spirit increases and one determines to keep self
out of God's way.

Glorifying God

God initially created humanity to glorify himself. In no way do
we add an iota to the distinctive, unique gloriousness of his essence. Although we make him no more splendid than he is in himself, the merciful salvation of rebels does add additional reasons for
praise. Similarly, the gracious sanctification of believers adds reasons for praise by the redeemed of earth and the heavenly throng
of saints and angels. To glorify God includes calling attention to
his supreme worth.

We can serve as a mirror to reflect his majesty, thus showing
others a few rays of his glory. Also, we apparently both honor him
and add to his own delight. Our transformation into his image pro-

gresses from one degree of splendor to another (2 Cor. 3:18). The human being's highest aspiration remains the glorification of God forever.

Why should a Spirit-filled believer desire to maintain and enrich his or her sanctification? The fullest answer supersedes direct personal advantages and advantages to surrounding people. Beside deepening one's spiritual life and enlarging one's ministry, progressive sanctification also reflects the glory of God. It honors God and brings praise to him.

The Father chose us in Christ "before the foundation of the world that we should be holy and blameless before him . . . to the praise of the glory of his grace" (Eph. 1:4, 6). Paul offered a noteworthy prayer in Ephesians 3, requesting his readers' sanctification—empowering by the Spirit, the unhindered indwelling by Christ, and the filling unto all of God the Father's fullness. He closed with a benediction ascribing to God "the glory in the church and in Christ Jesus to all generations forever and ever" (Eph. 3:21). The sanctification of God's people glorifies him.

Summary

Since God urges believers to pursue "the sanctification without which no one will see the Lord," he considers progressive holiness no peripheral option. Instead, it is an absolute essential.[431] Sought by sincere Christians of all doctrinal persuasions, growth in Christlikeness deters spiritual declension.

Even as some trees outstrip others in growth rate, some Christians grow more rapidly than others. Although valid growth proves missing before regeneration, the spiritual newborn should begin growing. What more disheartening spectacle can a pastor find than infantile Christians who long have shown no progress? Despite the value of simple truth for the spiritual baby, the writer of Hebrews urges readers to surpass rudimentary doctrines and avoid retarded development (Heb. 5:11-6:2). Whereas growth seems minimal in the Hebrews, it appears moderate in the recipients of James' letter in contrast with the marvelous growth at Thessalonica. Growth should move us toward prudent living and the sharing of God's Word with others. Making maturity one's ultimate personal goal, a believer should examine his direction even more than his speed. Let us ask, "Am I moving forward?"

Christ's plan for his own people includes maintained growth. Commencing at the new birth, spiritual growth surges at the deeper life crisis but ideally never ceases. Although advancement reaches a grand climax at glorification, perhaps the sanctified continue throughout all eternity their growth in holiness.

Christian growth features the ever-increasing freedom of godliness, progress in individual Christlikeness, an advancing harmony in working with others, watchful behavior that maintains a sensitivity against sin's approach and that enjoys continuous cleansing, and more abundant crops of spiritual fruit.

Centering on unselfish love, a life of increasing sanctification extends deeper and deeper love toward people and toward God. Although the maturing believer does not crave good feelings as his security blanket, he lives a life overflowing with God's Spirit. Such a lifestyle should enjoy a measure of peace, joy, and hope as by-products of commitment. In dealing with others, the Christ-filled life exhibits patience, kindness, and gentleness. Extending goodness to people as well as faithfulness toward God and duty, the woman or man who is growing in holiness should show discipline within. A lack of fruit calls for scriptural self-examination.

Besides producing spiritual fruit, progressive sanctification supplies sufficient power for effective service. Above benefits to oneself and to others, the supreme advantage of progressive sanctification lies in its glorification of God. Ultimately, to him belongs all the glory for all goodness in his universe. We glorify him more by a life that increases in holiness.

29

Inexhaustible Wealth: Resources for Growth

Lest they see with their eyes,
Hear with their ears,
Understand with their hearts,
And repent and be healed (Isa. 6:10).

Treasures Presented

Everyone loves a newborn baby. If that baby's body is to grow, it requires such necessities as nutritional food, shelter, care, and exercise. Chapters 29 and 30 will consider the factors that must claim priority if a Spirit-filled Christian grows. Chapter 29 will concern *resources* for growth—the provisions of a loving, able, and trustworthy God for our growth. Chapter 30 will investigate *requirements* for growth, namely, what actions a Spirit-filled believer must take to ensure essential growth.

In Isaiah's day, Jews had eyes, ears, and hearts—personal resources God had provided for seeing, hearing, and trusting the truth. In this way they could receive spiritual healing. Their own rejection, however, kept the Jews obstinate despite Isaiah's preaching. God had forewarned Isaiah of his discouraging task. Aside from our own eyes, ears, and hearts, what divine resources has God now made available to enable his redeemed children to receive his healing influences for spiritual progress? All of God's treasures come to us as his presents—gifts through grace.

On at least two occasions, I have heard well-intentioned ministers make a similar unscriptural assertion. They said that though you receive salvation by grace without works, you need to do a lot of works to keep saved. Scripture does not speak thus, however. Instead, it shows that God maintains the Christian life by grace as fully as a person had entered by grace.

Even as regeneration results from divine grace rather than human works, so God graciously provides for our progressive sanctification. Although a sanctified person will perform appropriate works, yet works comprise the fruit of the plant—not the seed. Wiggins warns, "The risen Christ does not cheerlead our efforts at self-perfection. . . . Paul took by faith what Christ provided."[432]

Triune Provisions

Paul's aforementioned rich prayer in Ephesians 3:14-21 divulges the triune God's provisions for the readers' sanctification. Although Scripture shows that Jews prayed in many postures, they commonly stood. Paul bowed his knees to pray, suggesting urgency, seriousness, and humility.

I remember standing in a hospital room with a distraught husband when his wife had just been wheeled to surgery. When I offered to pray again for his wife, this usually self-sufficient businessman surprised me by dropping suddenly to his knees in tears. He sensed deep urgency. Paul viewed the divine sanctifying of his readers as no trivial request. His prayer indicates that each member of the Godhead participates in this intimate spiritual ministry (cf. John 14:17-18, 23, 26).

Even as a married couple moves into a house not just to move in but to reside there, so does God. The Trinity's sanctifying ministry commences at a given point only to inhabit and go on filling our poor lives with God's rich presence. He will continue to supply necessary strength to us.

Induement from the strengthening Spirit

The Apostle Paul besought the Father "according to the riches of his glory" to strengthen these Asian believers "with power through His Spirit in the inner man" (Eph. 3:16). The Holy Spirit supplies the dynamic power of God. Although we must actively do the tasks God assigns, the Holy Spirit wants to supply all the power. The gleaming jumbo jet stands inert and helpless to soar into the heavens carrying its eager passengers. Without a constant fuel supply, it can undertake and complete no journey. Similarly, the Holy Spirit provides moment-by-moment energy for the Christian's daily service even as fuel continues to flow to a jet.

The inward person, or in other words, the spiritual nature receives this strengthening fuel—not the physical body about which the materialist shows so much concern. God's strengthening us does not impoverish him, for he supplies this strength out of the superabundance of his wealth.

Wuest correctly asserts that "Paul is here speaking of the fulness of the Holy Spirit."[433] How does fullness relate to progressive sanctification?

Renewal. Once a person has become filled, he or she will likely in the future need renewal after failure. When our disobedience blocks the Holy Spirit's work or we turn back to self-centered ways, we need to seek renewal. When we find that we have grasped the reins of our life's government away from our Master, we must confess our wrong. Then we can find anew the infilling that God longs to bestow.

Refurbishing. A Spirit-filled person will likely require some spiritual refurbishing just before special opportunities for service. Peter certainly had become Spirit-filled at Pentecost (Acts 2:4, 14-18). Yet when he later addressed the Sanhedrin, God's Word recounts: "Then Peter, filled with the Holy Spirit, said. . ." (Acts 4:8). The word "filled" here is an aorist participle in the original language. A person may translate a Greek participle in several different ways.

Understanding the word as showing why Peter could speak with such power, Charles B. Williams translates, "because he was filled with the Holy Spirit." This makes excellent grammatical sense. The margin of the New American Standard Bible reads, "having just been filled." Before encountering a special service opportunity or temptation, believers often beseech God for some additional filling. Perhaps this identifies Peter's experience as he found opportunity to uplift a living miracle-working Jesus Christ as the savior whom council members needed.

In either case, the passage shows that Peter was depending on the Spirit's fullness for insight needed for this remarkable service opportunity. In the same way, Paul depended on the fullness at the start of his missionary career when denouncing a magician (Acts 13:9; cf. Acts 9:17). Beyond initial filling, we too need fresh spiritual vigor to meet upsetting emergencies and special service opportunities. God promises to supply all our need.

Retention. In addition, the fullness relates to progressive sanctification in the sense of a retention throughout life. When Paul directed his readers to "be filled with the Spirit" in Ephesians 5:18, he used the present tense, which carries the thought of continuation. Hence, believers should not only become filled but should keep filled. Many writers consider this as a continuous impartation, ongoing (continuous) rather than simply episodic (at stated intervals). Whether we understand the translation as "keep filled" or "keep on being filled," in either case the verse urges constant life dependence. One must keep claiming the Spirit's energizing for daily success in Christian walk and witness.

To attain my goal of driving to Houston, it is important that I once fill the tank before leaving home. Unfortunately my car has not learned to function without gasoline. While I am passing through Alabama on the interstate, however, it may seem much more important to know whether I have *kept* the tank sufficiently filled. If so I do not need to trudge back to the nearest filling station. Thus, a Christian's current dependence on the Holy Spirit's power allows him or her to triumph in the tight plight. The recollection of a vital experience two years or thirty years ago proves foundational but requires current application.

Indwelling by Christ

Perplexity. When we find that it centers in the indwelling of Jesus, sanctification becomes a more winsome, less ominous word. Paul continued praying, "so that Christ may dwell in your hearts through faith. . ." (Eph. 3:17).

Explaining his intention of *indwelling* his disciples, Jesus must have mystified them. His expressions in the upper room include "I will come to you," and "I in you." Another expression there is "My Father will love him, and We will come to him, and make Our abode with him" (John 14:18, 20, 23). Similarly, Paul expressed to the Colossians the stunning mystery as "Christ in you, the hope of glory" (Col. 1:27).

Possibility. Despite Christ's perpetuity, he can indwell believers. When theologians speak of the doctrine of perpetuity, they mean that Jesus Christ will always retain the fully human body that he obtained when he came into the world. How can Jesus Christ live within a surrendered believer now since he ascended into heaven in a glorified human body? The question puzzles thinkers.

Since Jesus is Deity, he, of course, shares all of the divine attributes, including omnipresence. In this sense Jesus could be described as in heaven even while he lived on earth for a few decades. One can find a passage possibly supporting the latter idea in John 3:13, King James Version, based on some later manuscripts. Just before *leaving* the disciples at the ascension, Jesus promised, "Lo, I am with you always, even to the end of the age" (Matt. 28:20). Perhaps the best answer to the riddle involves the fact that Jesus and the Holy Spirit remain one essence. The Holy Spirit has come into the world in a special sense of ministry in the present age. Therefore, where the Holy Spirit lives, Jesus lives. In a similar sense Jesus had told Thomas, "He who has seen Me has seen the Father" (John 14:9). Jesus and the Father were one in essence, also.

Purity. The fact of the indwelling Christ should inspire holier living. The indwelling Christ also enables holier living. The former idea—inspiring—means that the presence of Jesus should bring out our very best behavior. If we could behold Jesus sitting at our dining table, surely we would show care in conversation and demeanor.

The latter concept—enabling—means that the Christian should give Jesus Christ ongoing free access to relive his holy life through his or her yielded body. Only after we have made our surrender complete, can he logically inhabit us in this degree. He should live there as Lord of all, for he is Lord; thus, he must preside as well as reside. To this end the believer must keep yielding the right of way to him, for he would rather inspire our daily submissiveness than force it.

Permanence. In Ephesians 3:17, Kenneth S. Wuest's Expanded Translation says: "that the Christ might finally settle down and feel completely at home in your hearts through your faith."[434] Obviously this wording suggests a point when Christ moves in to live an unhindered life within readers who are already believers. Also the translation suggests an intimate, comfortable relationship. Even as we invite a guest to make herself at home at our house, how much more should we desire Christ to be at home.

A major element in the term, however, is permanence. The incoming of Christ as sanctifier, constitutes only the beginning of a lifelong relationship suggested in that original word "dwell."

Christ does not come as a tourist to leave soon for another home but as a true resident who makes our mailing address his. As Munger's famous message expresses it, Jesus longs to share every room including the rooms for resting, studying, eating, playing games, and all other activities.[435]

Is it wrong to speak of Christ's coming into a person's heart at conversion? No, he comes then as Savior (John 1:12). The sanctified life simply allows him to occupy and supervise every room and closet. He arrives not as an overnight visitor but as the new owner who now holds the title deed to the home into which he has permanently moved.

Principle. By faith, the believer allows Christ to come to reside. Even as trust determines the pivotal moments of decision, so also for this divine indwelling to continue hourly, one continues to trust.

Purposes. While the Scripture shows faith as the principle of the indwelling, its purpose centers in love. Paul prays that "you, being rooted and grounded in love, may be able to comprehend with all the saints what is the breadth and length and height and depth, and to know the love of Christ which surpasses knowledge. . ." (Eph. 3:17-19). The passage lists a threefold purpose for the indwelling:

(1) Because Christ inhabits the believer, he or she should live firmly established in love. Two metaphors illustrate this anchoring—one agricultural and one architectural. Paul likens the believer's firm grounding in divine love to a plant's deep roots and a building's foundation. When God's child has received an implanting of the loving Christ, love begins to control his or her motivations so that all of life becomes founded on an unshakable love. Richard Erickson sees the "rooted" figure as including nourishment from Christ's love.[436]

(2) Because Christ dwells within the believer, then, he or she should learn to grasp the immensity of love's dimensions. As the primary fruit of the Spirit, love underlies, guides, and motivates the production and use of other fruit. Christ's love informs the Christian's view of himself or herself, the interpersonal relationships, and the grasp of God's purposes in severe trials. Radiating love amid difficult relationships of daily experience, the rooted and grounded life inspires the believer to size up how love relates to each problem. Paul's prayer shows that one does not sense all the dimensions in isolation as an anti-church loner, but along with the body of Christ. "With all saints" a believer finds strength to comprehend love's dimensions.

Christ's supreme new commandment requires his followers to love, love, love. We must love because he loves, as he loves, and with his love. Love to God and our fellow creatures fulfills the demands of Old Testament law. We must see love as a choice that impels right conduct rather than as a warm feeling. As Paul urged the Thessalonians, our love must keep increasing, advancing, abounding, overflowing (1 Thess. 3:12; 4:11).

(3) Because Christ lives within the believer, he or she should come to a highly experiential knowledge of Christ's love, that surpasses knowledge. How does one know the unknowable? Like an infinite ocean with no shorelines and no bottom, Christ's love measures so deep that no one can fathom it. God's immeasurable grace, however, makes it possible for wretched rebels to know in experience that boundless love which no love-starved human being could ever exhaust. We can know it but not its consummation.

Infilling with God

God's people may experience not only the Holy Spirit's strengthening and Christ's indwelling but also the fullness of the Father. In fact, Paul prays that his readers "may be filled up to all the fulness of God" (Eph. 3:19). This filling relates strongly to progressive sanctification. Carter notes that the word "unto" [or, up to] in Ephesians 4:13 "indicates not a static state of fullness, but rather a progressive filling which looks toward the goal of Christ's perfection."[438]

God does not fill with a fraction of himself, but with all of himself. He fills to our utmost capacity, provided we have emptied our vessel for his exclusive use.

He does not, however, raise people to an equality with himself. He does not make his creatures into his own essence, nor does he impart his own unique omnipresence, omnipotence, or omniscience. We do not become God. Longing to share his *moral* attributes, however, God wants his people filled with them. God freely shares his goodness, love, justice, righteousness, and truth. Surely no privilege of royalty could compare with the meekest saint, who serves as a temple where God dwells.

Trustworthy Possibility

Availability of God's wealth

When companies offer sweepstakes to potential customers, they sometimes include some assurance that the money necessary to cover the awards remains deposited in a safe account. Since Paul requests such an immense treasure to share with the body of Christ, his prayer early gives passing mention of God's assets. No limitation circumscribes Paul's request except "the riches of His glory." God owns all created things and his character so fully surpasses all others as to be the supreme standard of excellence (Eph. 3:16). Some scholars interpret "glory" here as a description of God's riches and others as God's manifest excellence, the summing up of his perfect character. God has available all necessary grace to fulfill Paul's inspired prayer for every believer who will ever have lived.

Ability of God to give beyond our requests

Paul's benediction identifies God as "able [literally, powerful] to do exceeding abundantly beyond all that we ask or think" (Eph. 3:20). Paul stacks up superlatives to describe God's omnipotence—to answer prayer. Gordon Clark notes that "Paul here asserts the divine omnipotence . . . not in its relation to the wonders of astronomy, but to its exercise in us."[438]

God allows us to ask for ourselves. Occasionally in ministry, I have heard people apologize for praying for their own need. The middle voice of "ask" validates asking for ourselves (3:20). Wuest interprets it: "to ask for one's self or in one's own interest."[439]

Counseling people who have found their situation utterly intolerable and improvement impossible, I have sometimes called attention to this verse. Especially when God's children keep asking for spiritual progress and Christlikeness, they can never ask too large a request. His ability surpasses our mind's ability to think. Although the human mind has astounding capabilities, it seems meager when compared with his ability. One should literally expect incredible answers.

Assurance of God's help

Coupled with God's inherent wealth and his ability to answer daring prayers stands his assurance that he will help. Ephesians 3:20 emphasizes God's ability to work marvelously "according to the power that works within us." Help need not come from afar. Rather than a long distance call to another planet, think of a whisper to one closer than that dearest earthly loved one at our side.

Confirming to his child of his divine ability and willingness to answer prayers for growth, God continues to sanctify through his Spirit. As a divine personality he is now working within. Assurance of this truth forms a limitation as well as an encouragement, since the person without the fullness of this powerful Spirit lacks the necessary inward resource. Unlimited additional growth requires dependence on this provided power.

Summary

So magnificently do triune provisions for progressive sanctification abound because, wonder of wonders, they literally consist of God himself! The maker of heaven and earth, gives himself to inhabit his people, as Paul's inspired prayer reminds us.

In the inmost depths of the human personality, the Spirit supplies the strength needed for abundant living. Always, but especially after failure and before special service, the sanctified believer needs to keep filled to overflowing as God asks. Of course, the Spirit, who applies redemption, makes possible this love life in which the whole trinity makes his home in a believer.

As the Son became a member of the human race, we can a bit better comprehend what his reliving his holy life within us would mean. The same thing cannot be said of the Father or the Spirit within us. Appropriating by faith Jesus' continuous indwelling, we learn to size up the immeasurable dimensions of divine love. Sensing the sanctified life as overflowing love to God and our fellow humans, we sense Christ pouring his love in us to flow out in holiness and service.

The Father supplies potential for filling without any limitation. We may become filled unto the very fullness of God.

Faltering so easily and feeling so insignificant at times, no wonder we need reminders of God's resources. He makes available this divine wealth and proves his ability to give far beyond our most daring requests. God assures us of his resources to meet every need by showing again that the powerful Spirit has been at work within us.

30

Are You Taking Your Vitamins?— Requirements for Growth

*A tree cut down,
whose stump still lives
to grow . . .
(Isa. 6:13, TLB).*

Agarden may grow nothing but weeds without a gardener's due attention to the process of gardening. Even so, a Christian needs to learn how his or her life can receive God's continuous sanctifying benefits. Only God can grant sunshine and rain (Acts 14:17); we understand that he ordinarily chooses to do so by natural law. God has created soil with capabilities of housing seed, allowing germination, and fostering growth. A gardener, however, must plant the seed and maintain the plot so that growth will occur.

Having received life in a new birth, a normal Christian "lives to grow." Sometimes the crowding in of multiplied other concerns prevents a Christian from giving due attention to growth. Once seeing the necessity for much additional spiritual growth and sensing God's immense resources to enable growth, a consecrated Christian will yearn for information on how to advance. What activities promote progress in holiness?

Living with Yourself

Reinforcing your surrender

Often a test comes very soon after a believer enters the fullness of the Spirit. This even happened in the case of Jesus, whose temptation proved severe. After the Spirit descended on him (Luke 3:22), "Jesus, full of the Holy Spirit, returned from the Jordan and was led about by the Spirit in the wilderness for forty days, while tempted by the devil" (Luke 4:1-2).

Some time after an absolute surrender, temptations may influence a Christian to regain the reins of his or her life. Although this transfer of power may come consciously because of some rebellion against life's grueling circumstances, more often it occurs imperceptibly. One remains unaware of a lack of submission. Then a sermon, testimony, book, or Scripture passage may arouse the waverer to sense the need of returning to a committed life. Gently the Holy Spirit has wooed and drawn.

Scripture expects a finality in one's act of commitment that differs markedly from current evangelicalism's mood of endless reconsecrations. Why must one daily decide whether to obey the Lord? That matter should remain a closed issue. One calculated, determined, resounding "yes" should simplify daily choices on lesser problems. Apparently I am not to keep digging up the tomato seed to make sure I really planted it. Acting as if it was planted, I recall that I planted it and it remains planted. Yet today's Christian keeps on handing over the life to God as though no surrender had occurred. Apparently this happens because of a lack of clear assurance that one really completed the transaction.

Because I now belong to the Lord, to whom I did conclusively give the keys of my life, I must keep making choices that agree with my life commitment. If a student chooses to join the army, a host of daily decisions suddenly become already settled because of the meaning of serving in the armed forces. One no longer needs to decide in what state or house to reside nor how early to arise. Why should anyone view God's army differently?

Although a sanctified believer need not repeat hourly recommitments, yet every new challenge in a day requires one to reinforce the surrender by acting on the basis of it. Many situations require action in harmony with a person's basic life commitment. Difficulties include perplexing dilemmas, choices on the use of time, occupational decisions, battering temptations, and reactions to misunderstandings from colleagues and loved ones. Each moment becomes a sacred altar. The life commitment did not prove inadequate or need to be repeated. Instead, the believer who already surrendered to Christ is applying that commitment to life's events—both the momentous and the trivial.

Retaining your separation

The separation necessary for entering a deeper life involves not merely severing oneself at a point in time. Adopting a negative attitude toward evil without and within, every sanctified believer should utterly loathe sin as a detestable intrusion. As soon as a person senses that the hankering to spread a rumor springs from Adamic fallenness, he or she should consciously separate from the wish. The Spirit-filled believer, who put off the old self, must continue a stance of rejecting self's attempts to maneuver its way back.

The yielded believer must maintain that initial deliberate rejection of the world system with its desires and pride. Whether the besetting temptation involves illegal drugs, illicit sex, or a socially-acceptable love of money, sanctification requires that a believer refuse. God's saint must not love the world system arrayed against God's purposes (1 John 2:15). Every desire must submit to God's will since a decisive separation earlier set our course. Even as he or she decisively renounced allegiance to Satan, the victorious Christian must keep on firmly resisting the devil and his hosts as new temptations beset (1 Pet. 5:9).

Reckoning of self

When Christ died for our sins (Rom. 5:6), he also died unto sin (Rom. 6:10) for our sanctification. When he died, we died (Rom. 6:6). Counting this crucifixion with Christ to be true, an individual discovers an extremely vital element at the heart of progressive sanctification.

God commands that we keep on regarding this fact to be so: "You must be constantly counting upon the fact" (Rom. 6:11, Wuest). A mathematical or bookkeeping term in the original language, the word "reckon" or "count" implies that the Christian chooses. From now on, the believer considers this doctrine to become his or her own experience. One does not trick the mind into thinking the self life's threat no longer exists. Instead, the provision of Christ's death means that the new state of affairs already stands as potentially true for every born again believer. One has only to actualize it experientially by a continual process of considering it so.

Applying such an attitude day by day in situations of temptation, a believer can employ this basic reckoning principle to maintain a life freed from sin's slavery. Whether covetousness, lust, anger outbursts, or another pitfall allures the liberated Christian, the theoretical becomes practical when he or she starts reckoning. The believer declares, "I count myself to be dead to this work of the flesh." The reckoning process *must* work. God's Word cannot lie: "For sin shall not be master over you . . ." (Rom. 6:14).

How should one respond if, after going on record as counting the old self dead, the horrible bondage seems to come back? Explaining that the old self truly died, A.B. Simpson advises that we should reject any attempt at his reappearance as simply Satan's unreal trickery:

> When your old self comes back, if you listen to it, fear it, believe it, it will have the same influence upon you as if it were not dead; it will control you and destroy you. But if you will ignore it and say: "You are not I, but Satan trying to make me believe that the old self is not dead; I refuse you. . . ."; if you treat it as a wife would her divorced husband, saying: "You are nothing to me, you have no power over me, I have renounced you, in the name of Jesus I bid you hence,"—lo! the evil thing will disappear, the shadow will vanish.[440]

When the self-life seems to reappear, grave peril follows ascribing any reality or credibility to it; instead, the sanctified person should staunchly refuse to treat it as anything but a satanic ghost with no more validity than ghosts that Spiritualism conjures.

The believer finds continuing victory by firmly resisting the temptation to suppose that no transformation occurred. Continuing to reckon upon the facts, he or she must insist, "I count myself dead to you. I reject your presence." This simple formula can produce transforming results.

Living with Others

Responding to stresses

I hate trouble. Although I have heard many people pray for safety in travel, I have never heard anyone pray to experience an accident. Many people pray to get well. Does anyone ever ask to experience sickness? Many pray for funds, but who prays for poverty? I suspect that children sometimes pray to escape a whipping, but who prays to be punished? Pounding every person like a relentless hurricane, however, troubles seem inescapable.

Often trials come in bunches. Although God often spares us distresses in answer to prayer, the sad proverb complains: "When it rains, it pours." I have always had difficulty singing the stanza of "More Love to Thee," that requests:

Let sorrow do its work,
Send grief and pain;
Sweet are Thy messengers,
Sweet their refrain.

Do people in the Bible pray for more troubles—for accidents to occur, for illness to come upon themselves, or for poverty to sweep away their financial resources? Does Scripture ever encourage people to pray for more reverses? Searchers probably would delve in vain to find such passages. Normal people do not delight in troubles.

Unwelcome troubles, nevertheless, invade every life. Bearing the title, "man of sorrows," Jesus himself, the only perfect P, experienced great numbers of troubles. Jesus did not delight in shame but despised it. He apparently did not pray to become ill. In Gethsemane, he did not long for the suffering as sin-bearer but shrank from its horror—deeply grieved and distressed (Matt. 26:37-39). "Although He was a Son," even Jesus "learned obedience from the things which He suffered" (Heb. 5:8).

Apparently God knows, however, that troubles bring values obtainable in no other way. Most Christians suppose that God knows

best how much trouble to allow. They would prefer to trust his
discretion than to petition him for more reverses. Although Satan
uses troubles to overwhelm an unsuspecting sufferer, yet in God's
permissive will, troubles come for our good (Heb. 12:10).

"Yielding the peaceful fruit of righteousness" (Heb. 12:11),
God's discipline comes purposefully. Although he does not recommend our bringing troubles on ourselves, still he designs life so
that one's trials add remarkable beauty.

We should never imagine the beautification as automatic, however. Troubles make a person bitter or better. The issue does not
lie in the quantity of troubles or their severity, but in our reaction
to them. God warns that, apart from chastisement, supposed
Christians prove to be illegitimate children (Heb. 12:8).

Willingly suffering privations, perils, and punishments, Paul
had endured hardness for the sake of spreading the gospel (2 Cor.
4:7-11; 6:4-10; 11:23-27). No wonder he could exclaim, "we also
exult in our tribulation, knowing that tribulation brings about perseverance" (Rom. 5:3). He commented to the Corinthians that
"momentary, light affliction is producing for us an eternal weight
of glory far beyond all comparison" (2 Cor. 4:17).

Can joy really accompany trials in the present life? The
Thessalonians "received the word in much tribulation with the joy
of the Holy Spirit" (1 Thess. 1:6). James asserted that the wealthy
must glory in being humbled (James 1:10). Going *down* the ladder
of wealth can apparently prove to be a cause for rejoicing. James
advised all his readers to "consider it all joy" whenever they would
"encounter various trials" (1:2).

Experiencing a painful ordeal, Peter and John later rejoiced
"that they had been considered worthy to suffer shame" for
Christ's name (Acts 5:41). In his Beatitudes, Jesus advised the per-
secuted to rejoice and be exceeding glad (Matt. 5:12, KJV). Although trials in themselves do not sanctify, a person's reactions to
troubles can deepen his or her sanctification. God designs that
through troubles we should share his holiness (Heb. 12:10).

Relating to the saints

When believers live mediocre spiritual lives without a vibrant
fellowship with God, the sense of needing to form a part of a dy-

namic Christian community often grows dim. On the other hand, many who bask in communion with God long for the communion of saints. Supposing they can worship sufficiently with a once-per-week appearance in a local assembly, even many evangelicals today abandon God's house. Much of the time they absent themselves from church activities without regret and without counting their losses.

Like liberal churches a generation or two ago, now entire evangelical assemblies have canceled Sunday services, except for those in the morning. Admittedly, as times and needs change, churches should adjust, but they should adopt improved alternatives that keep God first and best meet human needs.

The contemporary mind-set bristles with selfish individualism. If people do not notice your absence from the local church and smother you with attention, why not forsake that congregation? Isolation replaces interaction with a church assembly.

If one cannot find a church to suit his or her doctrinal and behavioral views, such a person decides simply to quit. They commune with God in the woods or worship alone at home. If no existing church proves perfect, why not originate a new group or perhaps give up on people altogether? In some areas, people see no need to join with others in a local church setting. In this way, self-importance substitutes for submission to one another.

Nevertheless, Scripture proclaims that a believer begins to comprehend the dimensions of Christ's love "with all the saints" (Eph. 3:18). In company with others we develop in fellowship and teamwork.[441] By ourselves we tend to remain short-sighted. The Apostle Paul shows that in Christ's church, glory flows to God for his abundant sanctifying grace (Eph. 3:21).

A prime necessity for successful Christian living continues to be subjection to one another and accountability in a Christian assembly. We must refuse to forsake that assembly (Eph. 3:18; Heb. 10:24-25). Fellowshipping with the saints, one grows in holiness. A major environment for growth remains the body of Christ.

In community with God's people, Christians hear the preached Word. In community with fellow saints, they exhort and receive exhortation. Edification results from biblical instruction from a capable pastor. A worship meeting fortifies believers to overcome the week's temptations and climb to higher victories. Interaction with the saints can promote growth.

Ancient, medieval, and recent ascetics have sought holiness by solitude. Though every life needs periods of quiet devotion, a life that *remains* in solitude misses outreach to a bleeding world.

Seeking a deeper outpouring one New Year's Day, A.B. Simpson decided to closet himself in his study for an entire month. He waited, waited, waited—until God would overwhelm him with more holiness.

After persisting in prayer for a week, his eye fell upon a passage. God was applying this Matthew 28 section to him: "He is not here, for He has risen. . . . Go therefore and make disciples of all the nations. . . ." Neglecting pastoral duties, he had been seeking a fuller baptism, but now the thought flashed to him: "Not dreaming, but doing." He had sequestered himself away from human need. He had sought a more intimate experience of God, but the continual flow of enduement was available only if he would step out to minister.[442]

Living with God

Reading of Scripture

If the sanctified believer consistently devours the Word and digests the Word by allowing the Holy Spirit to illuminate and apply it in practical life situations, growth should occur. The process can, however, falter at any point. Since many Christians puzzle over their lack of profit from Bible reading, attention to the issue becomes necessary here.

Whenever a Christian allows other activities to crowd out devotional Scripture reading, the lack of nourishment may stunt growth. Amazingly, God's servants sometimes allow Christian work so fully to occupy time and energy that they skip spiritual meals themselves. As a farmer cannot expect a fine harvest without ever cultivating, a dedicated Christian cannot expect to succeed in spirituality without reading Scripture.

On the other hand, too often a Christian from duty does read—without absorbing much nourishment. Believers often say that they read but that they soon forget the passage and seldom experience much uplift. Two reasons for the problem include failure to concentrate and to meditate.

If one were perusing a manual that could divulge a cure for the reader's own fatal disease, thorough study would occur. If a person could earn a free vacation home, he or she would find strong incentive to study intently to understand fully. If believers perceived how practically a given biblical meal could contribute to spiritual health, they would rivet full attention on each line. No stone would lie unturned.

We claim to believe that the Bible produces growth. If we really believed spiritual growth more important than a cancer cure or a vacation home, would we not eagerly concentrate on Scripture?

Even if a Christian cannot long recall content of his or her devotional reading, that reading will normally have had a cleansing, refreshing effect. The believer must continue to read despite how little he or she could recite afterwards.

People should not, however, become satisfied with such a lack of retention. If I see myself in the Bible and choose to profit from what I see, I will remember more. I will have less trouble with retention than the person who reads merely out of habit. Much help can result from judicious inclusion of my own name in the passage. Then God keeps addressing golden promises and solemn warnings to me rather than just to pre-Christian Israel or first century Galatian believers. A seeker can find further benefit by personal journaling about the contents of Bible exploration as well as his or her own spiritual progress.

Also, meditation on today's Bible reading throughout the day can help fasten it in the memory. Ignoring the contents after reading greatly restricts the sanctifying effect God intends. If the Christian reads but fails to understand, growth will diminish. Eastern mystics practice forms of meditation that can lead to spiritual bondage. Most Christians fail to take time to ponder spiritual things because of the pressures of contemporary life. Meditation on God's Word pays dividends.

Perhaps one remains oblivious to the rules of interpretation because he or she has never sensed their importance or taken time to study them even in elementary fashion. Having recently recommended that a middle-aged college graduate enroll in a hermeneutics course, I heard her exclaim this week:

"Now I see why you advised me to take hermeneutics. Why, every Christian needs a course like this!" For those unable to enroll in a formal class, any of several understandable books could clarify the Word immensely.

We live in an age of the quick fix. We want instant truth no less than instant breakfast cereal and instant car washes. Similarly, preferring God to drop truth from heaven, today's reader wishes to avoid effort in study. Perhaps this in part explains the yen for alleged Spirit revelations, words of wisdom, and sudden impressions. Instead of laboriously searching Scripture to find an inspired answer, people prefer to look to a Christian guru to pronounce over them instruction. They unwisely look to fallible people for God's plan for their future.

Others fail to grasp Scripture's meaning due to a lack of dependence on the Holy Spirit's enlightenment. Since the Spirit inspired original authors to write the Word, surely he wants to illuminate contemporary readers. Besides employing diligence in studying, a believer should depend on the Spirit. This Christian can sense Scripture's spiritual intent and find its relevance to his or her current need.

In review, failure to read Scripture regularly, to concentrate while reading, and to meditate after reading can spell defeat. Failure to understand, to interpret, and to depend on the Spirit's illumination can all hamper Christian growth. A believer with trouble should check to see where he or she has missed a turn.

At still other times, a Christian allows Satan to snatch the seed before it takes root in the personality, as Jesus illustrated in the parable of the sower. Falling along the path, the seed proved unproductive because birds devoured it. Jesus explained that the devil removes the Word from hearts lest people receive salvation (Luke 8:5, 12).

This insight into the way the evil one works suggests that he also robs Christians of the truth that would increase holiness. If believers keep alert, however, they can successfully thwart Satan's malicious attempts to steal. God's children can ponder the preached Word they hear and read Scripture with regularity, attention, comprehension, and application. By insight into the enemy's schemes, they can avoid becoming victims (2 Cor. 2:11).

The psalmist affirmed that a motive for hiding God's Word in his heart included the avoidance of sin (Ps. 119:11) even as John stated that young people become strong when the Word abides within (1 John 2:14). When Jesus' high priestly prayer invoked God to sanctify his followers through the truth, he added that God's Word constitutes truth (John 17:17). God, its inspirer, yearns to make and keep his children more holy. Thus the Word gives directions for the Christian to progress in the sanctified walk.

Moreover, that very Word enters the life in sanctifying power. As digested food within the body somehow becomes nourishment, energy, health, renewal, and growth, so the digested manna of Scripture becomes the believer's ongoing sanctification. Therefore, Scripture both informs believers about continuing sanctification and supplies a dynamic for such abundant living.

The reading of fine Christian books can explain and reinforce what we read in Scripture. Although such reading must never substitute for the Word, yet it can supplement it. We can help to develop our spirituality by reading and studying the truth.

Regularity in supplication

Necessity. God has designed prayer as an indispensable procedure for effecting growth. Ephesians 3:14 finds Paul bowing his knees to offer a searching prayer for his readers' sanctification. After a person has assurance of the indwelling Christ, empowering Spirit, and filling Father, he or she surely has not ceased to pray. God wants his children to depend on prayer. Prayer is a way of life.

Sanctified living requires prayer for its fellowship, calmness, freshness, and supply of needs. A holy heart basks in communion with the source of all holiness. Comprising the direct telephone line for enjoying God's presence, prayer serves as a channel for worship and praise. In the words of John Gill, a scholarly eighteenth-century Baptist minister from England: "The holy actings of sanctification may be discerned in the earnest panting and eager desires of the soul after communion with God, both in private and public. . . ."[443]

When life becomes turbulent with problems and cares, prayer allows the saint to remain calm while seeking to survive trium-

phantly that stormy sea. Now God's child can begin to glimpse a
way through the trackless ocean.

When no path through a maze seems apparent, in prayer one
finds God traveling alongside—not standing back ridiculing timid
sincere attempts. For all its severe faults, process theology at least
teaches us God's presence as an ally amid human griefs—God suffers with us. In contrast, our contemporaries hurl invectives at
God—blaming him for their troubles! Prayer can aid the yielded
believer to enjoy inner calmness despite the storm outside.

When vegetation languishes because of prolonged drought, rain
restores freshness. Similarly, prayer restores vibrancy to the life
out of which all the vigor has drained through daily busyness.
Some personalities always remain burdened by a mountain of
needs. Others behold themselves and those around them as generally fulfilled. Despite various perceptions of need, needs do exist.
Needs provide one constant reason for prayer. When a Christian
senses a need, God invites prayer.

Prayer sometimes alerts us to action we should take. Sometimes
it brings us to a point of trusting God for a definite answer. At
other times it aids us to accept adverse circumstances that for the
present cannot change. In any of these possibilities, prayer should
lead to a solution. Moreover, proper prayer brings a believer to a
richer relationship with God. Our greatest need is to know God
better and to grow in holiness. Therefore, the sanctified believer
should always profit from prayer offered with a right attitude and
in accord with scriptural guidelines.

Barriers. Unfortunately, even dedicated people complain of
prayer barriers. The difficulty of finding time to pray forms one
barrier. Neglecting prayer because of pressing duties, many otherwise healthy Christians allow so little time for prayer that they live
under a continuing burden of guilt over prayerlessness. The guilt
makes God seem far away.

For some, prayer seems useless. They claim that their prayers
never rise higher than the ceiling. Why can they not believe that
God hears? Disobedience or failure to rest in the fact of divine forgiveness or failure to forgive God for allowing life's frustrating circumstances can prevent a happy prayer life. In other cases, unless
praying gives thrilling sensations, many falsely suppose it accom-

plishes nothing. Finding that merely letting the air out of the tire of one's emotions will suffice, Satan easily puts a halt to praying.

Times. Must we pray on stated occasions? Or can we pray by speaking to the Lord a bit at various moments throughout the day or night as needs arise? The best answer is both. Even as Jesus spent prime time addressing his Father on many occasions, we need regularly to focus on prayer alone. A lover wants to enjoy the total attention of her loved one. Yet if lovers, engaged in routine duties in each other's presence, never speak throughout the day, something seems amiss. Practicing God's presence affords much personal benefit and promotes increased holiness. This ennobling custom lies at the heart of spiritual formation.[444]

Consecrated believers should not substitute a daily date for moment-by-moment fellowship. On the other hand, keeping tuned in to God's channel (1 Thess. 5:17) should not prevent one's engaging in specific times of prayer at regular intervals.

Removing hindrances from the Christian life and helping the believer to take practical forward steps, prayer promotes growth in holiness. Also, regularity in Bible-guided praying itself requires growth in holiness. Why? Such praying consists of spending time in harmonious fellowship with a holy God.

One of the greatest helps to holy living involves instant appropriation of spiritual truths. Reading a passage or listening to a sermon, as soon as the Spirit shows a neglected duty or unclaimed promise, I can profit. I can shoot up an arrow of prayer for forgiveness, trust, or commitment. If the issue has become clear but I delay until later, often no transaction will occur because the vividness of the issue will have faded. When God speaks, obey. Obedience promotes spiritual deepening. Prayer claims the benefits and commits us to new obedience.

One appropriate time for prayer is during fasting. Noting that all eras of the church have practiced fasting, Taylor connects it with three objects—prayer, "mortification of bodily lusts," and repentance.[445] Fasting, going without food for spiritual purposes, most closely accompanies prayer. Although one should never view it as a work to buy divine favor, it can help show the seriousness of our desire for holiness and other prayer requests. It includes and symbolizes separation from material concerns to seek God. The fasting person will profit from avoiding the pressures of secular demands to concentrate on God and his will.

Fasting can assist spiritual development. Taylor admits that "there is no end to which fasting serves but may be obtained by other instruments." He explains that people should not regard fasting as something to be proud of or as an essential duty but as an instrument for benefit.[446]

Relying on the Sanctifier

Commitment. Reliance issues from a past surrender to the Sanctifier. True commitment should neither leak out nor fossilize. Resting on a sure foundation, a committed Christian finds that a past act of commitment to a reliable Lord leads to a habit of deepening reliance.

Faith. Including elements of knowledge, an act of trust, and continuance, faith occupies a central place in victorious living. To exercise faith one must first know God's promises. In this way we can grasp the amazing possibilities within God's will that he intends us to understand. Next we believe God to accomplish what he has agreed to do. After one has thus acted in faith, he or she must continue to rest in faith. Many people stumble over the simplicity of this middle step. They fail to exercise faith.

Even as faith opens the door to eternal life, faith opens the way into the deeper life. Many linger outside such portals for they have never mastered the simplest faith lesson. Jesus taught: ". . . Believe that you have received them, and they shall be granted you" (Mark 11:24). Trusting God to fulfill his promises delights him.

Faith, however, must never end just inside the door. Trust enables growth. In a real sense, one must think of faith as a verb. No value attaches to having a storehouse full of unused faith. When the disciples begged Jesus to increase their faith, he responded that even mustard seed-sized faith could uproot and remove trees of difficulty (Luke 17:5-6). If one has any faith at all and dares to use it, impossibilities become possibilities.

In a deeper life classic, Hannah Whitall Smith wrote:

> Your idea of faith, I suppose, has been something like this.
> You have looked upon it as in some way a sort of *thing*,—ei-

ther a religious exercise of soul, or an inward, gracious disposition of heart; something tangible, in fact, which, when you have secured it, you can look at and rejoice over, and use as a passport to God's favor, or a coin with which to purchase His gifts. . . . Now, faith, in fact, is not in the least like this. It is nothing at all tangible. It is simply believing God. . . . You might as well shut your eyes and look inside, and see whether you have sight, as to look inside to discover whether you have faith. You see something, and thus know that you have sight; you believe something, and thus know that you have faith. For as sight is only seeing, so faith is only believing.[447]

When Jesus on several occasions reproved his contemporaries as people "of little faith" (Luke 12:28), he apparently was urging them to choose boldly to believe since they were exercising none at the moment. Amid a fierce gale on Galilee, Jesus censured his disciples: "How is it that you have no faith?" (Mark 4:40).

Similarly, having and using faith today can produce astounding results. One must launch out to use faith or faith spoils like day-old manna. "Show me your faith without the works, and I will show you my faith by my works" (James 2:18). All faith is invisible. People cannot see pretended invisible faith, and of course a non-existent farce produces no works. On the other hand, true invisible faith will produce visible works.

Increasing the use of trust enlarges one's capacity for experiencing greater holiness because it unlocks all the blessings of God's storehouse. As long as Satan can keep Christians blinded to the possibilities of faith and the simplicity of using faith, he has little to fear of Christian exploits.

Once people have gone on record as believing God, we need to continue trusting until full fruition. Once our expectation has become materialization, we then continue to believe that God did accomplish what he promised and that he will keep what we have committed to him.

In addition, we continue expecting that we can keep on proving God's faithfulness by additional use of faith as a life habit. Trust has happily become a way of living. Trust opens our hearts to greater and greater receptivity. Growth possibilities seem virtually unlimited. Jesus declared, "All things are possible to him who believes." We can know God better as we insist upon eliminating every hindrance that would obscure our trust.

In this way, faith serves as a means of growth in sanctification. For example, when the committed person becomes aware of malice toward a neighbor, faith enables the Christian (1) to believe in God's provision for victory, (2) to confess and forsake the sin, (3) to believe that God has forgiven it, (4) to choose to count himself or herself dead to this old-nature activity, and (5) to trust the Holy Spirit to fill this area of the life with love instead of malice.

One does not renounce what God has accomplished in the life in the past. He or she simply believes God to apply the potential obtained in the past to solve a current problem.

Obedience. Reliance on Christ ideally results in obedience, for he who knows best shows us how to live better than we would choose unaided. Because we have often proved him trustworthy, we can gladly submit once we know what he wants. Reliance should result in obedience. Faith shows itself by its works. A sanctified person zealously desires to obey the Lord in everything.

Reliance on Christ as our continuing sanctifier means that we remain committed to him, that we are learning fuller lessons of faith, and that we obey him implicitly.

Summary

What requirements prove essential for the continuing growth of progressive sanctification? Our responsibility includes reinforcing our initial surrender and applying it in life's many new situations. Retaining our separation from all evil, we continue by choice to live as the opponent of Satan's system.

In the face of temptations, we must hourly maintain the habit of counting our self-life as crucified and resurrected with Christ. No secret of success in victorious living bears more practical fruit. When troubles surround, our stance should be yieldedness to the greater wisdom of God. He yearns to sanctify us further through the trial so that we may more fully share his holiness.

Instead of constructing a multiplicity of isolated ascetics, Christ built his church (Matt. 16:18). A person best understands and lives holiness in union with the body of Christ. Maintaining our place in the local assembly aids our spiritual progress.

Those vital personal devotional exercises, Scripture reading and prayer, we can never safely abandon. The climax of our responsibility in ongoing sanctification involves reliance on Christ as our sanctifier. Our commitment must defy compromise. Our trust comprises one of the most necessary ingredients of Spirit-filled living. We live by faith. In obeying God's commands, however, we supremely prove our love and commitment. Holy living consists of obedient living.

Appendix

Bible Versions Used
in Launch Out Academic

Unless otherwise indicated, all Bible quotations are taken from the New American Standard Bible, © 1960, 1962, 1963, 1968, 1971, 1972, 1973 by The Lockman Foundation.

Scripture labeled "Amp." is taken from the Amplified Bible: The Amplified Old Testament, (C) 1964 by Zondervan Publishing House; The Amplified New Testament, (C) 1958 by The Lockman Foundation.

Scripture labeled "Beck" is taken from Beck, William F., The New Testament in the Language of Today, (C) 1963 by Concordia Publishing House.

Scripture labeled "Berkeley" is taken from The Holy Bible: The Berkeley Version in Modern English, (C) 1945, 1959 by Zondervan Publishing House.

The Centenary Translation, translated by Helen Barrett Montgomery, (C) 1924 by The American Baptist Publication Society.

The Holy Bible: Contemporary English Version, text (C) 1995 by American Bible Society.

Scripture labeled "KJV" is taken from The Holy Bible: King James Version.

Scripture labeled "Wuest" is taken from The New Testament: An Expanded Translated, translated by Kenneth S. Wuest, (C) 1956, 1958, 1959, 1961 by Wm. B. Eerdmans Publishing Co. All rights reserved.

Endnotes

1 Although no clear evidence survives, some commentators surmise that Isaiah was Uzziah's relative. Others explain Isaiah's ready access to subsequent kings by describing him as the court preacher, a respected spiritual adviser.

2 Joseph Agar Beet, *Holiness as Understood by the Writers of the Bible: A Bible Study* (Salem, OH: Schmul Pub. Co., 1985), pp. 36-37.

3 This statement offers evidence from a line from a song. The inspired record states that Moses sang it, along with the sons of Israel (Exod. 15:1). Liberal scholars arrive, instead, at the notion that Israel's religion emerged from a lengthy evolution. Hence, Kohler writes: ". . . It was only slowly and comparatively late that the idea of holiness was transferred to God himself," and Knudson concurs that holiness as ethical perfection "was not . . . the conception that prevails throughout *most* (emphasis mine) of the Old Testament. . . . The word wherever found, is used in a religious sense." Ludwig Kohler, *Old Testament Theology*, trans. A.S. Todd (Philadelphia: Westminster Press, 1957), p. 52; Albert C. Knudson, *The Religious Teaching of the Old Testament* (New York: Abingdon-Cokesbury Press, 1918), pp. 137-38.

4 Augustus Hopkins Strong, *Systematic Theology* (Philadelphia: Judson Press, 1907), p. 296.

5 James Oliver Buswell, *A Systematic Theology of the Christian Religion* (Grand Rapids: Zondervan Publishing House, 1962), 1:64.

6 Millard J. Erickson, *Christian Theology* (Grand Rapids: Baker Book House, 1985), p. 285.

7 William Bates, *The Harmony of the Divine Attributes in the Contrivance and Accomplishment of Man's Redemption* (New York: Jonathan Leavitt, 1831), p. 218.

8 John Miley, *Systematic Theology* (New York: Eaton & Mains, 1892), 1:199.

9 H. Orton Wiley, *Christian Theology.* 3 vols. (Kansas City: Nazarene Publishing House, 1940), 1:370.

10 Norman H. Snaith, *The Distinctive Ideas of the Old Testament* (London: Epworth Press, 1944), p. 43.

11 Albert Truesdale, "Theism: The Eternal, Personal, Creative God," in *A Contemporary Wesleyan Theology: Biblical, Systematic, and Practical,* ed. Charles W. Carter (Grand Rapids: Zondervan Publishing House, 1983), 1:116-17.

12 Snaith, p. 52; cf. Knudson, pp. 143-44: " 'Holiness' and 'divinity' were almost synonymous terms. . . . But . . . holiness . . . had a distinct connotation of its own. It directed attention to the unapproachableness of God, to that aspect of his nature which awakened in men the feeling of awe." Cf. p. 152.

13 H. Ray Dunning, *Grace, Faith, and Holiness: A Wesleyan Systematic Theology* (Kansas City: Beacon Hill Press, 1988), pp. 192-93.

14 Strong, p. 271.

15 *Donald S. Metz, Studies in Biblical Holiness* (Kansas City: Beacon Hill Press, 1971), p. 51.

16 Stephen Charnock, *The Existence and Attributes of God* (N. p.: Sovereign Grace Book Club, 1969), p. 449.

17 Miley, 1:199-200.

18 Strong, p. 273.

19 Thomas Watson, *A Body of Divinity* (Grand Rapids: Sovereign Grace Publishers, n. d.), p. 60; cf. John Gill, *A Body of Divinity* (Grand Rapids: Sovereign Grace Publishers, 1971), p. 103.

20 Strong, p. 272.

21 Langdon Gilkey, *Maker of Heaven and Earth: A Study of the Christian Doctrine of Creation* (Garden City, NY: Doubleday & Co., 1965), pp. 85-88.

22 Erickson, p. 284.

23 Louis Berkhof, *Systematic Theology* (Grand Rapids: Wm. B. Eerdmans Publishing Company, 1953), p. 73.

24 Truesdale, p. 117, considers it a lamentable error, traceable to Immanuel Kant, to think "that God's holiness is primarily a moral category,

rather than a religious one." Compare Rudolph Otto's famous mystical "numinous" "Wholly Other" perception, as well as Baab, who identifies holiness with mana and taboo: "Originally holiness was exclusively a magical concept which designated persons, objects, or places to which a quasi-physical quality of nonhuman origin was attached. . . . When the pattern of the God idea emerged more distinctly . . . holiness . . . served to call attention to what was exclusively divine." Obviously Baab's view coincides with the anti-revelational liberal notion that the impression of God evolved over the centuries in Israel's thought. Rudolph Otto, *The Idea of the Holy*, trans. John W. Harvey (New York: Oxford University Press, 1958), pp. 5-7; Otto J. Baab, *The Theology of the Old Testament* (New York: Abingdon Press, 1949), pp. 33-34; cf. Knudson, pp. 140, 150, 153, who attributes to Christianity the finale of the "process of moralization" of the term, "holiness."

25 Charles Hodge, *Systematic Theology* (New York: Charles Scribner's Sons, 1895), 1:413; Strong, pp. 268-69.

26 This argument, of course, assumes that Scripture accurately affirms that God really did speak these commands to Moses, who recorded them. Liberals hold a documentary view, viz., that some unknown author first penned this section of Leviticus some eight hundred years after Moses' death.

27 Gustav Friedrich Oehler, *Theology of the Old Testament*, rev. by George E. Day, 6th ed. (New York: Funk & Wagnalls Co., 1883), p. 110.

28 John Gill, p. 104.

29 Charnock, p. 453.

30 Erickson, p. 285.

31 Richard S. Taylor, *The Theological Formulation* in *Exploring Christian Holiness* (Kansas City: Beacon Hill Press, 1985), 3:16.

32 Charnock, p. 472.

33 J. I. Packer, *Rediscovering Holiness* (Ann Arbor, MI: Servant Pubs., 1992), pp. 90-91.

34 J. Paul Taylor, *Holiness, the Finished Foundation*, unabridged ed. (Winona Lake, IN: Light and Life Press, 1963), p. 18.

35 Glenn W. Barker, "1 John," in *The Expositor's Bible Commentary*, ed. Frank E. Gaebelein, 12 vols. (Grand Rapids: Zondervan Publishing House, 1981), p. 311.

36 W. M. Clow, *The Cross in Christian Experience* (London: Hodder and Stoughton, 1913).

37 John R. W. Stott, *The Epistles of John: An Introduction and Commentary* in *The Tyndale New Testament Commentaries*, ed. R. V. G. Tasker (Grand Rapids: Wm. B. Eerdmans Pub. Co., 1964), p. 75.

38 Paul Enns, *The Moody Handbook of Theology*, with a Foreword by J. Dwight Pentecost (Chicago: Moody Press, 1989), p. 235.

39 T.G. Tappert, trans. and ed., *The Book of Concord* (Philadelphia: Muhlenberg Press, 1959), pp. 29-30, article III.

40 Leon Morris, "Hebrews," in *The Expositor's Bible Commentary*, 12 vols. (Grand Rapids: Zondervan Publishing House, 1981), 12:71.

41 Although, as usual, it presents a paraphrase, the Living Bible renders this verse so that the common reader can easily grasp its intent.

42 Kenneth S. Wuest, *Wuest's Word Studies from the Greek New Testament*, 4 vols. *Ephesians and Colossians: In the Greek New Testament* (Grand Rapids: Wm. B. Eerdmans Pub. Co., 1966), 1:132.

43 John Wesley, "Minutes of Some Late Conversations between the Rev. Mr. Wesleys and Others," *The Works of John Wesley*, 3d ed. (Peabody, MA: Hendrickson Pub., 1986), 8:285.

44 J. A. Wood, *Perfect Love: Or, Plain Things for Those Who Need Them concerning the Doctrine, Experience, Profession and Practice of Christian Holiness*, rev. ed. (Noblesville, IN: Newby Book Room, 1967), p. 53.

45 Jon Tal Murphree, *The Love Motive: A Practical Psychology of Sanctification*, with a Foreword by Robert E. Coleman (Camp Hill, PA: Christian Publications, 1990), p. 8.

46 P.B. Fitzwater, *Christian Theology: A Systematic Presentation*, 2d ed. (Grand Rapids: Wm. B. Eerdmans Pub. Co., 1956), p. 454.

47 John Wesley, *Plain Account of Christian Perfection* (Chicago: Christian Witness Co., n. d.), p. 33: ". . . the term *sanctified*, is continually applied by St. Paul, to all that were justified. . . . Consequently, it is not proper to use it in that sense [of a post-conversion crisis], without adding the word *wholly, entirely*, or the like."

48 A. W. Tozer, *Man: The Dwelling Place of God* (Harrisburg: Christian Publications, 1966), p. 104. Those who defend second blessing terminology by referring to an alternate reading of 2 Cor. 1:15 need to reread the following verse to grasp that Paul was anticipating two future visits to Corinth.

49 Andrew A. Bonar, *Heavenly Springs*, comp. Marjory Bonar (1904; reprint ed., Edinburgh: Banner of Truth Trust, 1986), p. 24.

50 W. R. Matthews, *The Search for Perfection* (London: SPCK, 1957), p. 3.

51 William Law, *Christian Perfection*, ed. Erwin Rudolph (Carol Stream, IL: Creation House, 1975), pp. 19-20.

52 . Wesley, *Plain Account*, pp. 43, 78, 103: "Therefore *sinless perfection* is a phrase I never use. . . . We do not find any general state described in Scripture, from which a man cannot draw back to sin. . . . Absolute perfection belongs not to man, nor to angels, but to God alone." Likewise Dieter writes: "Wesleyanism is not perfectionism (which implies a Pelagianism), and it certainly does not imply sinless perfection; it is probably more misrepresented at this point than at any other." Melvin E. Dieter, "Response to Hoekema," in *Five Views on Sanctification* by Melvin E. Dieter et al. (Grand Rapids: Zondervan Pub. House, 1987), p. 91.

53 Metz, p. 221.

54 Since, with John Wesley, Wesleyans define a sin as "a voluntary transgression of a known law," they teach that normally acts of sin (explained as deliberate rebellion) cease at the new birth. Though not all Arminians take so radical an approach, J. A. Wood writes in *Perfect Love*, p. 14, that "believers can not *commit* sin without forfeiting justification. . . ." Cf. Wesley, *Plain Account*, p. 43.

55 Murphree, *Love Motive*, pp. 15-16.

56 W. E. Vine, *Vine's Expository Dictionary of Old and New Testament Words*, 1981 ed., s. v. "PERFECT (Adjective and Verb)," "PERFECTLY."

57 George Allen Turner, *The Vision Which Transforms: Is Christian Perfection Scriptural?* (Kansas City, MO: Beacon Hill Press, 1964), pp. 133-34.

58 Dunning, pp. 470-71: "Daniel Steele . . . said that he had counted 26 terms used by Wesley to refer to the experience of sanctification," but the list did not include the baptism with the Holy Spirit. "Beginning with John Fletcher and Joseph Benson, Wesley's successors began to make more use of pneumatological language. While Wesley was apparently uneasy with this, he did not consider Fletcher's teaching to contradict his own."

59 Harold D. Hunter, *Spirit-Baptism: A Pentecostal Alternative* (Lanham, MD: University Press of America, 1963), p. 169.

60 Charles G. Finney, *The Promise of the Spirit*, comp. and ed. Timothy L. Smith (Minneapolis: Bethany House Pub., 1980), p. 262. John Leroy Gresham, Jr., *Charles G. Finney's Doctrine of the Baptism of the Holy Spirit* (Peabody, MA: Hendrickson Pubs., 1987), pp. 86-91. Daniel N. Berg, "The Theological Context of American Wesleyanism," *Wesleyan Theological Journal* 20 (Spring 1985): 53: "The baptism of the Holy Ghost is introduced to American Wesleyans and tied to the doctrine of sanctification by Asa Mahan and Oberlin theology." Major 20th century multi-volume American Wesleyan holiness theologies see baptism with the Holy Spirit as a valid term for entering entire sanctification: Wiley, *Christian Theology*, 2:444. Wilber T. Dayton, "Entire Sanctification: The Divine Purification and Perfection of Man," in *A Contemporary Wesleyan Theology: Biblical, Systematic, and Practical*, ed. Carter, 1:565.

61 H[annah] W. S[mith], "The Baptism of the Holy Ghost," in *The Christian's Secret of a Happy Life*, pp. 237-257, rev. ed. (Boston: Christian Witness Co., 1885) in *The Devotional Writings of Robert Pearsall Smith and Hannah Whitall Smith*, in "The Higher Christian Life," ed. Donald W. Dayton (Reprint ed., New York: Garland Pub., 1984). F. B. Meyer, *Meet for the Master's Use* (Chicago: Moody Press, 1898), pp. 11, 17, 106.

62 Charles F. Parham, "The Latter Rain: The Story of the Original Apostolic or Pentecostal Movements," in Sarah E. Parham, *The Life of Charles F. Parham, Founder of the Apostolic Faith Movement*, in "The Higher Christian Life," ed. Donald W. Dayton (Joplin, MO: Hunter Printing Co., 1930; reprint ed., New York: Garland Pub., 1985), pp. 51-55.

63 John Rea, *The Holy Spirit in the Bible* (Lake Mary, FL: Creation House, 1990), pp. 122, 141, 165-66, 203.

64 Asa Mahan, *Baptism of the Holy Ghost* (New York: Palmer & Hughes, 1870), p. 16.

65 W. E. Boardman, *The Higher Christian Life* in "The Higher Christian Life," ed. Donald W. Dayton (Boston: Henry Hoyt, 1858; reprint ed., New York: Garland Pub., 1984), pp. 94, 237, 245.

66 R. A. Torrey, *The Baptism with the Holy Spirit*, with a Foreword by Harold J. Brokke, new Dimension ed. (Minneapolis: Bethany Fellowship, 1972).

67 Gerald E. McGraw, *The Doctrine of Sanctification in the Published Writings of Albert Benjamin Simpson* (Ann Arbor, MI: UMI, 1986), p. 285: "Very high on Simpson's list of priority sanctification terms stands 'the baptism of the Holy Spirit.' . . . Simpson called this terminology very satisfactory. . . ." A. B. Simpson, *Walking in the Spirit: The Holy Spirit in Christian Experience* (Harrisburg: Christian Pubs., n.d.), p. 134. A. B. Simpson,

"The Baptism with the Holy Ghost," in *The Holy Spirit: Or, Power from on High*, with a Foreword by Walter M. Turnbull (Harrisburg: Christian Pubs., n.d.), 2:21-28: "The truth is, the Spirit Himself is the baptism. Christ baptizes, and it is with or in the Spirit that He baptizes us" (2:23).

68 Harold Lindsell, *The Holy Spirit in the Latter Days* (Nashville: Thomas Nelson Pubs., 1983), pp. 90-94.

69 Martyn Lloyd-Jones, *Joy Unspeakable: Power and Renewal in the Holy Spirit*, ed. Christopher Catherwood, with a Foreword by Peter Lewis (Wheaton, IL: Harold Shaw, Pubs., 1984), pp. 21-23, 48, 197-201, 249-65. Sermons in Westminster Chapel, 1964-65: "He believed passionately in the baptism with the Holy Spirit as a distinct, post-conversion experience.... He refused to hold . . . that any one gift was necessary as proof of baptism with the Spirit (p. 13).

70 John R. Rice, *The Power of Pentecost: Or, the Fullness of the Spirit* (Wheaton, IL: Sword of the Lord Pub., 1949), pp. 157-62.

71 Tony Campolo, *How to Be Pentecostal without Speaking in Tongues* (Dallas: Word Pub., 1991), pp. 90, 173-75.

72 Keith M. Bailey, interview at General Council of the Christian and Missionary Alliance, Pittsburgh, PA, 25 May 1995. Keith M. Bailey, "The Holiness Movement" in *Holiness Voices: A Practical Theology of Holiness*, ed. H. Robert Cowles and K. Neill Foster (Camp Hill, PA: Christian Publications, 1995), pp. 43, 48.

73 Armin R. Gesswein, Foreword to *Powerlines: What Great Evangelicals Believed about the Holy Spirit—1850-1930*, by Leona Frances Choy (Camp Hill, PA: Christian Pubs., 1990), pp. 1-5. Armin R. Gesswein, interview at General Council of the Christian and Missionary Alliance, Pittsburgh, PA, 24 May 1995. Dr. Gesswein, an ordained Missouri Synod Lutheran minister, calls "baptism with the Holy Spirit" a proper term for entry into the Spirit-filled life. He uses it cautiously to prevent discord on the current religious scene. He ministers widely in prayer and revival opportunities among various denominations. He holds credentials in The Christian and Missionary Alliance. Armin R. Gesswein, *How Can I Be Filled with the Holy Spirit? Biblical Truth and Personal Testimony* (Camp Hill, PA: Christian Publications, 1995), pp. 75-84.

74 Morris A. Inch, *The Saga of the Spirit: A Biblical, Systematic, and Historical Theology of the Holy Spirit* (Grand Rapids: Baker Book House, 1985), p. 150.

75 John F. Walvoord, "Response to Dieter," in *Five Views on Sanctification* by Melvin E. Dieter et al., p. 57.

76 Anthony A. Hoekema, *Holy Spirit Baptism* (Grand Rapids: William B. Eerdmans Pub. Co., 1972), p. 21; cf. James D. G. Dunn, *Baptism in the Holy Spirit* (Philadelphia: Westminster Press, 1979).

77 Jasper Abraham Huffman, *A Recent Inside Miracle Story relating to the Revised Standard Version of the Bible*, with a Foreword by Charles V. Fairbairn (Winona Lake, IN: Wesley Press Agency, 1959), pp. 21-34, 37, 46.

78 George R. Beasley-Murray, *John*, with a Foreword by Ralph P. Martin, in *Word Biblical Themes*, ed. David A. Hubbard (Dallas: Word Pub., 1989), pp. 78-79.

79 Comentators differ on whether this occurred on the feast's seventh or eighth day. Old Testament directions, specifying a seven-day feast, nevertheless mentioned the eighth day as a rest day like the first (Lev. 23:39). In later times, Jews celebrated an eighth day as the Apocrypha mentions (2 Macc. 10:6). Some surmise that Jesus' voice rang out on the eighth day when no water ceremony was practiced.

80 Harold M. Freligh, *Newborn*, with a Foreword by A. W. Tozer (Minneapolis: Bethany Fellowship, 1962), p. 91.

81 Karl Barth, *A Shorter Commentary on Romans*, trans. D. H. van Daalen (London: SCM Press, 1959), p. 65.

82 Thomas R. Kelly, *A Testament of Devotion*, with a Biographical Memoir by Douglas V. Steere (New York: Harper & Brothers, 1941), p. 54.

83 Campolo, p. 175.

84 Donald G. Bloesch, *Essentials of Evangelical Theology*, 2 vols. (San Francisco: Harper & Row, 1978), 2:31.

85 Buswell, 1:286.

86 For an excellent discussion, see Gill, pp. 330-37.

87 Richard S. Taylor, *Theological Formulation*, 3:74, 81.

88 Metz, p. 85.

89 Charles Hodge, *Systematic Theology*, 3 vols. (New York: Charles Scribner's Sons, 1895), 3:220.

90 Ralph Earle, *Word Meanings in the New Testament* (Grand Rapids: Baker Book House, 1986), pp. 170-71.

91 Grimm Wilke, *A Greek-English Lexicon of the New Testament*, trans. and rev. John Henry Thayer, 4th ed. (Edinburgh: T. & T. Clark, 1901), p. 571.

92 Charles R. Swindoll, *Flying Closer to the Flame* (Dallas: Word Pub., 1993), pp. 80-81.

93 Some scholars see the "body of sin" in Rom. 6:6 as representing this same warped nature, while others understand "body" in this verse to refer to the human body whose relationship to sin sanctification nullifies.

94 John Owen, *Sin and Temptation: The Challenge to Personal Godliness*, ed. by James M. Houston, with an Introduction by J. I. Packer (William H. Goold, 1850-53; reprint ed., Portland, OR: Multnomah Press, 1983), p. 21.

95 Frederick L. Godet, *Commentary on St. Paul's Epistle to the Romans*, trans. A. Cusin with revisions by Talbot W. Chambers (New York: Funk & Wagnalls, 1883), p. 244.

96 *Sin and Temptation*, p. 8.

97 A. B. Simpson, *Standing on Faith: And Talks on the Self-Life* (London: Marshall, Morgan & Scott, n.d.), p. 63.

98 Mildred Bangs Wynkoop, *A Theology of Love: The Dynamic of Wesleyanism* (Kansas City: Beacon Hill Press, 1972), p. 164.

99 Dunning, p. 484.

100 Laurence W. Wood, *Pentecostal Grace* (Wilmore, KY: Francis Asbury Publishing Company, 1980), p. 168.

101 Wilbur T. Dayton, "Romans and Galatians," *The Wesleyan Bible Commentary*, edited by Charles W. Carter, 6 vols. (Grand Rapids: William B. Eerdmans Publishing Co., 1965), 5:49.

102 Horatius Bonar, *God's Way of Holiness* (Chicago: Moody Press, n.d.), pp. 91, 90.

103 Various commentators mention some or all of these names. A contemporary Biola professor, Walt Russell, believes that people are asking the wrong question when they inquire whether Romans 7 describes the struggles of a regenerate or unregenerate person. His work is informed and largely original but unconvincing. Paul's whole thrust in Romans deals with the doctrines of sin and redemption for the entire race. All human beings are either regenerate or unregenerate. Walt Russell, "Have We Wrongly Interpreted Romans 7?" Paper presented at the 46th annual meeting of the Evangelical Theological Society, Lisle, Illinois, No-

vember 17-19, 1994, available on audio cassette (Ballwin, MO: ACTS, 1994).

104 Vine, *Expository Dictionary*, s.v. "World."

105 Owen, *Sin and Temptation*, pp. 10-11.

106 Ibid., pp. 30-31.

107 Early in the 20th century, theologian George P. Pardington, entitled a chapter "The Vision of Victory" in *The Crisis of the Deeper Life* (Camp Hill, PA: Christian Publications, 1991).

108 Torrey has shocked many readers into the reality that we as Christian workers must stop trying to do what only the Holy Spirit can do. Only he can convict the sinner (John 16:8). R. A. Torrey, *The Person and Work of the Holy Spirit* (Grand Rapids: Zondervan Pub. House, 1974), pp. 70-71.

109 "These" in vs. 21 seems vague. The context must help. My word, "evil" remains vague like the N.T. text while keeping in mind a couple major possibilities. No doubt thinking of vss. 17, 18, Way translates, "cleanse himself from these pollutions of false teaching." Likewise, Wuest thinks "Timothy is to separate himself from communion with 'these,' the vessels of dishonor spoken of in verse 20, such as are mentioned in verses 16, 17." Hence, he sees a central reference to false teachers. By contrast, the Phillips translation freely renders it, "clean from the contaminations of evil" even as REB says, "cleanses himself from all this wickedness." Arthur S. Way, trans. *The Letters of St. Paul to Seven Churches and Three Friends with the Letter to the Hebrews*, 6th ed. (London: MacMillan Co., 1926), p. 216. Wuest, *Wuest's Word Studies, The Pastoral Epistles in the Greek New Testament*, 2:139.

110 Harry L. Turner, *The Voice of the Spirit* (Harrisburg: Christian Pubs., n.d.), pp. 49-50.

111 Rice, p. 123.

112 Andrew A. Bonar, *Heavenly Springs*, pp. 34-35.

113 Finney, *Promise*, p. 107.

114 Charles F. Parham, *The Everlasting Gospel*, with a Foreword by Robert L. Parham (Baxter Springs, KS: Apostolic Faith Bible College, [1911]), pp. 55, 72, 120-21, in *The Sermons of Charles F. Parham*, a volume in "The Higher Christian Life," ed. Donald W. Dayton (Reprint ed., New York: Garland Pub., 1985). See also Gerald E. McGraw, *Tongues: Devilish Snare or Heavenly Language?* (Westminster, SC: Shamaim Ministries, 215 Shoreline LN, 1989).

115 Morris A. Inch, *The Saga of the Spirit: A Biblical, Systematic, and Historical Theology of the Holy Spirit* (Grand Rapids: Baker Book House, 1985), p. 150.

116 Inch, p. 175.

117 James D. G. Dunn, *Romans 1-8* in *Word Biblical Commentary*, ed. David A. Hubbard and Glenn W. Barker (Milton Keynes, England: Word (UK), 1991), 38A:319.

118 John Peter Lange, *Commentary on the Holy Scriptures: Critical, Doctrinal and Homiletical*, trans., ed. by Philip Schaff, *Romans* (Grand Rapids: Zondervan Publishing House, n.d.), pp. 203-4.

119 F. F. Bruce, *The Epistle of Paul to the Romans: An Introduction and Commentary*, in Tyndale New Testament Commentaries, ed. R. V. G. Tasker (Grand Rapids: Wm. B. Eerdmans Pub. Co., 1963), pp. 139, 155.

120 Ibid., p. 138.

121 H. B. Elliot, "Testimony," in *Pioneer Experiences: Or, the Gift of Power Received by Faith*, ed. Phoebe Palmer in "The Higher Christian Life": Sources for the Study of the Holiness, Pentecostal, and Keswick Movements, ed. Donald W. Dayton (New York: W. C. Palmer, 1868; reprint ed., New York: Garland Publishing, 1984), pp. 196, 201.

122 Leona Frances Choy, *Powerlines: What Great Evangelicals Believed about the Holy Spirit, 1850-1930* (Camp Hill, PA: Christian Publications, 1990), p. 55.

123 H. C. G. Moule, *The Epistle of Paul the Apostle to the Romans: With Introduction and Notes*, In The Cambridge Bible for Schools and Colleges, ed. J. J. S. Perowne (Cambridge: University Press, 1884), p. 120.

124 Vine, *Expository Dictionary*, p. 317.

125 Godet, p. 259.

126 Vine, *Expository Dictionary*, p. 109.

127 James Denney, "Romans," in *The Expositor's Greek Testament*, edited by W. Robertson Nicoll, 5 vols. (Grand Rapids: William B. Eerdmans Pub. Co., 1967), 2:633.

128 Earle, p. 168.

129 William Sanday and Arthur C. Headlam, *A Critical and Exegetical Commentary on the Epistle to the Romans*, 7th ed., in *The International Critical Commentary on the Holy Scriptures of the Old and New Testaments*, ed. Charles

Augustus Briggs, Samuel Rolles Driver, and Alfred Plummer (New York: Charles Scribner's Sons, 1902), p. 155.

130 G. Adolf Deissmann, *Bible Studies*, trans. Alexander Grieve (Edinburgh: T. & T. Clark, 1901; reprint ed., Peabody, MA: Hendrickson Pub., 1988), p. 254.

131 Sanday and Headlam, p. 155.

132 Archibald Thomas Robertson, *Word Pictures in the New Testament*, Vol. 4: *The Epistles of Paul* (New York: Harper & Brothers, 1931), p. 363.

133 Kelly, p. 34.

134 Charles G. Finney, *Principles of Union with Christ*, comp. and ed. Louis Gifford Parkhurst, Jr. (Minneapolis: Bethany House Pub., 1985), p. 141, 143.

135 Packer, p. 83.

136 Andrew Murray, *Covenants and Blessings* (N.p.: Whitaker House, 1984), p. 40.

137 A. W. Tozer, comp., *The Christian Book of Mystical Verse* (Camp Hill, PA: Christian Publications, 1963), p. 48.

138 Murray, p. 72.

139 G. Campbell Morgan, *The Spirit of God* (New York: Fleming H. Revell Co., 1900), p. 229.

140 R. Arthur Matthews, *Born for Battle: 31 Studies on Spiritual Warfare*, With a Foreword by Alan Redpath (Wheaton, IL: Harold Shaw Pub., 1993), p. 41.

141 Beet, p. 50.

142 R. J. Drummond and Leon Morris, "The Epistles of John," in *The New Bible Commentary*, ed. F. Davidson, A. M. Stibbs, and E. F. Kevan, 2d ed. (London: Inter-Varsity Fellowship, 1954), p. 1154.

143 Daniel L. Migliore, *Faith Seeking Understanding: An Introduction to Christian Theology* (Grand Rapids: William B. Eerdmans Pub. Co., 1991), p. 180.

144   Ed Murphy, *The Handbook for Spiritual Warfare* (Nashville: Thomas Nelson, 1992), pp. vi, 102.

145 Tom White, *Breaking Strongholds: How Spiritual Warfare Sets Captives Free* (Ann Arbor: Servant Pub., 1993), p. 40.

146 Freligh, *Newborn*, p. 96.

147 Kelly, p. 66.

148 Tozer, Foreword to *Newborn*, by Freligh, p. 8.

149 Torrey, *Person and Work*, p. 58.

150 Erickson, p. 539.

151 Freligh, *Newborn*, p. 98.

152 Godet, p. 425.

153 Vine, *Expository Dictionary*, s.v. "Wrath."

154 Edwin H. Palmer, *The Person and Ministry of the Holy Spirit: The Traditional Calvinistic Perspective* (Grand Rapids: Baker Book House, 1974), p. 92.

155 Murray, *Covenants and Blessings*, p. 80.

156 A. B. Simpson, *Wholly Sanctified* (New York: Christian Alliance Pub. Co., 1893), p. 37.

157 Murray, *Covenants and Blessings,* pp. 100-101.

158 Harold J. Ockenga, *The Spirit of the Living God* (New York: Fleming H. Revell Co., 1947), p. 88.

159 Freligh, *Newborn*, p. 95.

160 Tozer, *The Christian Book of Mystical Verse*, p. 65.

161 Inch, p. 174.

162 Tozer, *The Christian Book of Mystical Verse*, p. 26.

163 Inch, p. 150.

164 Morgan, *Spirit of God,* p. 227.

165 Donald Grey Barnhouse, *Life by the Son: Practical Lessons in Experimental Holiness* (Philadelphia: Revelation Publications, 1939), pp. 114-27.

166 Timothy L. Smith, "A Historical and Contemporary Appraisal of Wesleyan Theology," in Carter, *A Contemporary Wesleyan Theology*, 1:82: Hymns, tracts and sermons demonstrate John and Charles Wesley as "preeminently biblical theologians." Smith notes that for John "reason cannot produce either the faith or the hope in Christ from which love flows." Despite Outler's contemporary contention that Wesley esteemed tradition, "Wesley subjected both ancient and Anglican traditions to the test of Scripture." Smith continues, "Concerning experience, Wesley's doctrine of entire sanctification was hewn entirely out of Scripture before any of his followers began to profess that grace." Cp. Albert C. Outler,

John Wesley, Library of Protestant Thought (New York: Oxford, 1964), pp. 14-17, 135.

167 Wesley's movement sprang from Anglican roots. A contemporary Methodist theologian alludes to the threefold basis of Anglicanism: "In substance it followed the ancient traditional position, but sought to find a clearer vindication for the primary authority of Scripture than was apparent in much Roman Catholic teaching. It has been held that authority rests upon the threefold foundation of Scripture, tradition, and reason." John Lawson, *Introduction to Christian Doctrine* (Englewood Cliffs, NJ: Prentice-Hall, 1967; reprint ed., Grand Rapids: Francis Asbury Press of Zondervan Pub. House, 1986), pp. 7-8.

168 "Wesley . . . was ready, in fact, to be considered a 'Bible bigot,' insisting on more than one occasion that the Scriptures alone had been his mentor and guide." John Leland Peters, *Christian Perfection and American Methodism,* with a Foreword by Albert C. Outler (Nashville: Pierce & Washabaugh, 1956; reprint ed., Grand Rapids: Frances Asbury Press of Zondervan Pub. House, 1985), p. 15.

169 Although he has spoken in strong terms about Scripture as Wesley's theological source, Peters grants Wesleyan experience a large place as well. He seems to differ considerably with Timothy Smith's perception of it. "Hereafter, religious experience—his own and others—would be for Wesley an authoritative criterion of theology." Peters, pp. 21-22.

170 The Wesleyan Arminian theologian, Miley, refers to natural and (special) revelation as valid sources of theology, whereas creeds, tradition, and mystical experience lack authoritative status as sources. He sees Scripture as the absolutely preeminent source. Miley, 1:7-22.

171 C. W. Ruth, *Entire Sanctification: A Second Blessing* (Chicago: Christian Witness Co., 1903), p. 48.

172 Theological terms for these transactions are regeneration and justification, respectively.

173 Melvin E. Dieter, "The Wesleyan Perspective," in Dieter, et al., p. 18.

174 Murphree, *Love Motive,* pp. 60, 24.

175 Billy Graham, *The Holy Spirit: Activating God's Power in Your Life* (Waco: Word Books, 1978), p. 111.

176 D. W. Whittle, *Life, Warfare and Victory* (Chicago: Moody Press, 1884), p. 73.

177 Murphree, *Love Motive,* pp. 37, 39.

178 Floyd Hays Barackman, *Practical Christian Theology* (Old Tappan, NJ: Fleming H. Revell Co., 1984), pp. 276, 254.

179 W. T. Purkiser, *Conflicting Concepts of Holiness* (Kansas City, MO: Beacon Hill Press, 1972), p. 21.

180 Everett Lewis Cattell, *The Spirit of Holiness* (Grand Rapids: William B. Eerdmans Pub. Co., 1963), pp. 23-24.

181 Kelly, p. 31.

182 Stanley J. Grenz, *Revisioning Evangelical Theology: A Fresh Agenda for the 21st Century* (Downers Grove, IL: InterVarsity Press, 1993), p. 102: "But as messengers we must be sure that the stumbling-block in our proclamation is the 'absurdity of the cross' and not the opaqueness of the categories we employ. In its quest to speak, the church must always formulate the biblical message in thought-forms that communicate with culture. . . ."

183 Needless quibbling about trivial points rightly disgusts a generation dedicated to practicality. On the other hand, precise words sometimes convey vital distinctions that impatience hopelessly muddles. Virtually every field includes a vocabulary that enables communication. If I refuse to learn my computer's vocabulary, it stubbornly rejects mine. My physician uses some of the same words that other human beings use but with a different meaning; to communicate I must understand him. If a generation of Christians learns enough computer and medical language to communicate but refuses to master any theological language, can any solution emerge? Clergy and teachers must either keep defining their terms with every use or select less technical and therefore often less precise ones so that Christians can understand and grow. The only alternative would be to foster a generation of Christians who were as eager to communicate about God and spiritual things as they are to communicate with computers and physicians.

184 Charles Caldwell Ryrie, *The Holy Spirit,* Handbook of Christian Doctrine series (Chicago: Moody Press, 1965), p. 93.

185 Wuest, *Wuest's Word Studies, Untranslatable Riches from the Greek New Testament,* 4:104-5.

186 Quoted from Kelly, p. 52.

187 Murphree, *Love Motive,* pp. 59, 58.

188 Richard Gilbertson, *The Baptism of the Holy Spirit: The Views of A. B. Simpson and His Contemporaries* (Camp Hill, PA: Christian Publications, 1993), pp. 110-11, 207-8, 256.

189 Gesswein, Foreword to *Powerlines* by Choy, p. 3.

190 Anthony A. Hoekema, "The Reformed View," in Dieter, et al., *Five Views on Sanctification*, p. 74.

191 H. E. Dana and Julius R. Mantey, *A Manual Grammar of the Greek New Testament* (New York: Macmillan Co., 1950), p. 177.

192 D. A. Carson, *Exegetical Fallacies* (Grand Rapids: Baker Book House, 1984), p. 69.

193 Daniel Steele, *Mile-Stone Papers: Doctrinal, Ethical, and Experimental on Christian Progress* (Minneapolis: Bethany Fellowship, n.d.), pp. 51-52, 72.

194 Olive M. Winchester, *Crisis Experiences in the Greek New Testament*, ed. with a final chapter by Ross E. Price, with a Foreword by Coral E. Demaray (Kansas City: Beacon Hill Press, 1953).

195 A trail-blazing article is Frank Stagg, "The Abused Aorist," *Journal of Biblical Literature* 91 (June 1972): 222-31. Taking a bit more drastic stance is Charles R. Smith, "Errant Aorist Interpreters," *Grace Theological Journal* 2 (Fall 1980): 205-26.

196 F. F. Bruce, *The Gospel of John: Introduction, Exposition and Notes.* (Grand Rapids: William B. Eerdmans Pub. Co., 1983), p. 76: "The reconstruction of the temple in the form which it had at this time was begun by Herod the Great early in 19 BC. The main part of the work was completed and consecrated in ten years, but other parts were still being carried out; in fact, the finishing touches were not put to the whole enterprise until AD 63, only seven years before its destruction. The 'forty-six years' of verse 20 are reckoned from the beginning of the reconstruction." Bruce is not, of course, dealing with the aorist tense.

197 Stagg, "The Abused Aorist," p. 227. Words abound like "fallacious," "misrepresent," "indefensible," "aoristic trap," "misleads," "misunderstanding," "tyranny," and "overtranslates."

198 Charles R. Smith, p. 211.

199 Carson, pp. 72-73.

200 Randy Maddox, "The Use of the Aorist Tense in Holiness Exegesis," *Wesleyan Theological Journal* 16 (Fall 1981):107.

201 Stagg, p. 222.

202 A. T. Robertson, *A Grammar of the Greek New Testament in the Light of Historical Research* (Nashville: Broadman Press, 1934), p. 833.

203 Stagg, p. 231.

204 Maddox, p. 115.

205 Ibid., 112-13.

206 Stagg, p. 231.

207 John J. Davis, *Paradise to Prison: Studies in Genesis* (Grand Rapids: Baker Book House, 1975), p. 244.

208 Gordon Talbot, *A Study of the Book of Genesis* (Harrisburg: Christian Publications, 1981), p. 200.

209 C. F. Keil and Franz Delitzsch, *Biblical Commentary on the Old Testament*, 25 vols. (Edinburgh: T. & T. Clark, 1864-1901), 1:304.

210 Talbot, pp. 200-201.

211 Charles Wesley, "Wrestling Jacob," in *The Wesleyan Methodist Hymnal* (Syracuse, NY: Wesleyan Methodist Publishing Assn., 1910), p. 341:

> Come, O thou Traveler unknown,
>   Whom still I hold, but cannot see;
> My company before is gone,
>   And I am left alone with thee:
> With thee all night I mean to stay,
> And wrestle till the break of day.
>
> I need not tell thee who I am,
>   My sin and misery declare;
> Thyself hast called me by my name,
>   Look on thy hands, and read it there:
> But who, I ask thee, who art thou?
> Tell me thy name, and tell me now.
>
> In vain thou strugglest to get free;
>   I never will unloose my hold:
> Art thou the Man that died for me?
>   The secret of thy love unfold:
> Wrestling, I will not let thee go,
> Till I thy name, thy nature know.
>
> Wilt thou not yet to me reveal
>   Thy new, unutterable name?
> Tell me, I still beseech thee, tell;
>   To know it now resolved I am:
> Wrestling, I will not let thee go,
> Till I thy name, thy nature know.

What tho' my shrinking flesh complain,
  And murmur to contend so long?
I rise superior to my pain:
  When I am weak, then am I strong,
And when my all of strength shall fail,
I shall with the God-man prevail.

212 Thomas Hewitt, *The Epistle to the Hebrews: An Introduction and Commentary*, The Tyndale New Testament Commentaries, ed. R. V. G. Tasker (Grand Rapids: Wm. B. Eerdmans Pub. Co., 1960), p. 87.

213 Johannes Schneider, *The Letter to the Hebrews*, trans. William A. Mueller (Grand Rapids: Wm. B. Eerdmans Pub. Co., 1957), p. 33.

214 Hewitt, *Hebrews*, p. 89.

215 Simon J. Kistemaker, *Exposition of the Epistle to the Hebrews*, New Testament Commentary (Grand Rapids: Baker Book House, 1984), pp. 108-14.

216 Brooke Foss Westcott, *The Epistle to the Hebrews* (Reprint ed. Grand Rapids: Eerdmans Pub. Co., 1974), p. 95.

217 John F. Walvoord, *Jesus Christ Our Lord* (Chicago: Moody Press, 1969), pp. 70-71: "It is preferable to consider Canaan not as a type of heaven but as the believer's present sphere of conflict and possession in Christ. Crossing the Jordan . . . is entrance into the enjoyment of our possessions in Christ . . . by crucifixion with Christ and by the mighty power of God."

218 John Owen, *Hebrews: The Epistle of Warning* (Reprint ed., Grand Rapids: Kregel Pubs., 1953), p. 63.

219 H. Orton Wiley, *The Epistle to the Hebrews*, ed. Morris A. Weigelt (Kansas City, MO: Beacon Hill Press, 1984), pp. 137-39.

220 A. B. Simpson, *The Land of Promise*, Reprint ed. (Harrisburg: Christian Publications, 1969), pp. 59-60: "It is a definite committal of self in all its forms to the waves of death. . . . There is no dragging around of the old life or any efforts to make it better. We have got something better, even Christ Himself, our life." Robert Meredith Stevens, *Promised Land* (N.p.: Yoke Publications, 1963), pp. 91-92: "Have I plunged into the Jordan and identified myself with Him in His death and resurrection? or Do I know Jesus Christ as my Sanctifier? . . . I must (with His help) take this step in faith. . . . By an act of my will I now yield myself fully to You, and by faith I now step down in humility, down into the dark waters and up into the abundant life."

221 Wiley, *Hebrews*, pp. 111-112, 122, 126.

222 William R. Newell, *Romans: Verse by Verse* (Chicago: Moody Press, 1952), p. 69.

223 James Hastings, ed., *Dictionary of Christ and the Gospels*, 1906 ed., s.v. "Circumcision," by W. O. E. Oesterley.

224 James Hastings, ed. *A Dictionary of the Bible*, 4 vols., 1898 ed., s.v. "Circumcision," by Alexander Macalister.

225 Dunn, *Romans 1-8*, pp. 127, 124.

226 C. A. Coates, *An Outline of the Book of Leviticus* (Kingston-on-Thames, England: Stow Hill Bible and Tract Depot, n.d.), p. 157.

227 Oesterley, s.v. "Circumcision."

228 B. Carradine, *The Second Blessing in Symbol* (Noblesville, IN: Newby Book Room, 1968), p. 263. Wesley, *Plain Account*, pp. 5-7: The first writing of John Wesley that saw publication comprised his sermon, "The Circumcision of the Heart," which he preached before the university at Oxford on January 1, 1733. Exhorting, "Let every affection, and thought, and word, and action, be subordinate to this," he concluded in part, "Here is the sum of the perfect law, the circumcision of the heart. . . . Have a pure intention of heart, a steadfast regard to His glory in all our actions."

229 Robert O. Coleman, "Leviticus," *The Wycliffe Bible Commentary*, ed. Charles F. Pfeiffer and Everett F. Harrison (Chicago: Moody Press, 1962), p. 93.

230 Thomas R. Schreiner, "Luke," and J. Knox Chamblin, "Matthew," in *Evangelical Commentary on the Bible*, ed. Walter A. Elwell (Grand Rapids: Baker Book House, 1989), pp. 812, 731.

231 Elmer A. Martens, "צרעת" in *Theological Wordbook of the Old Testament*, ed. R. Laird Harris 2 vols. (Chicago: Moody Press, 1980), 2:777.

232 S. G. Browne, s. v. "Leper, Leprosy," in *Wycliffe Bible Encyclopedia*, ed. Charles F. Pfeiffer, Howard F. Vos, and John Rea, 2 vols. (Chicago: Moody Press, 1975), 2:1027.

233 Vine, *Expository Dictionary*, N. T. section, s.v. "leper," 2:330.

234 Bruce M. Metzger, ed., "Topical Index to the Bible," *NRSV Exhaustive Concordance* (Nashville: Thomas Nelson Publishers, 1991), p. 122.

235 A. A. Bonar, *An Exposition of Leviticus* (Grand Rapids: Sovereign Grace Publishers, 1971), p. 115.

236 Ibid.

237 Ibid.

238 Coates, pp. 159-60; cf. Ibid., p. 116.

239 Carradine, p. 38.

240 Vine, *Expository Dictionary*, N. T. section, s.v. "Covenant," 1:250-51. Cf. O. T. section, s.v. "Covenant," pp. 52-53.

241 Peter Toon, *Justification and Sanctification* in *Foundations for Faith* series, ed. Peter Toon (Westchester, IL: Crossway Books, 1983), p. 144.

242 Paul R. Gilchrist, "Deuteronomy," in Elwell, *Evangelical Commentary*, p. 115.

243 Hewitt, p. 137.

244 R. K. Harrison, *Jeremiah and Lamentations: An Introduction and Commentary*, Tyndale Old Testament Commentaries, D. J. Wiseman, ed. (Leicester, England: Inter-Varsity Press, 1973), pp. 137, 140.

245 Ibid., p. 140.

246 Other views exist for the instituting of the New Covenant. Carradine, e.g., holds that "this covenant began on the day of Pentecost" (Carradine, p. 90). At the Lord's Supper on the night before the crucifixion, however, Jesus called the contents of the cup "the new covenant in My blood" (Luke 22:20; 1 Cor. 11:25). Hence, the connection with Calvary seems preferable. Likewise, some trace the Old Covenant concept back to Adam or to a patriarch like Abraham, considering that the Old Testament knows of only one covenant, with various later renewals. Nevertheless, the writer to the Hebrews observed that "even the first *covenant* was not inaugurated without blood. For when every commandment had been spoken by Moses to all the people according to the Law, he took the blood of the calves and the goats, . . . saying, 'THIS IS THE BLOOD OF THE COVENANT WHICH GOD COMMANDED YOU' (Heb. 9:18-20)."

247 In arguing that Pentecost marks the point at which God established the New Covenant, Gerok writes that "the people of Israel commemorated on their day of Pentecost the *festival of the first harvest* of the year, but here [in Acts 2] in the outpouring of the Spirit, [they commemorated] the giving of the law under the new covenant; but the will of God is now written with a pen of fire, not on tables of stone, but, as a law of the

Spirit, on the hearts of men." This provides a tempting explanation, since the 120 form a group of people with whom God could establish the New Covenant as the Israelite nation at Sinai became the recipients of the Old Covenant. In addition, the New Testament links the keeping of the New Covenant with sanctification by the Spirit. Two problems with the theory, however, are that (1) no Scripture asserts that God established the New Covenant with the Church on the day of Pentecost; and (2) scholars often hold that the recognition of the feast of Pentecost as the commemoration of the giving of the Law at Sinai did not originate until later than New Testament times. Gotthard Victor Lechler, *The Acts of the Apostles*, with homiletical additions by Charles Gerok, trans. Charles F. Schaeffer, in *A Commentary on the Holy Scriptures: Critical, Doctrinal and Homiletical*, by John Peter Lange, trans. and ed. Philip Schaff from 2d German edition (Edinburgh: T. & T. Clark, 1872), p. 30.

248 Carradine, pp. 90-91.

249 Too many writers assume that God makes sanctification available only to the present age—not to those living in Old Testament times. Consequently Harry L. Turner refutes this shortsightedness (p. 100): "It is a queer logic that limits the power of the Spirit to the saints of the last two thousand years. Some would deny this power to the saints of the preceding four thousand years, who lived in the same world, in the same kind of flesh, and had to contend with the same Satan." Turner sees the major difference since Pentecost to be more intensive power to carry on the worldwide witness so essential in God's plan for this age.

250 Francis I. Andersen, *Job: An Introduction and Commentary*, The Tyndale Old Testament Commentaries, ed. D. J. Wiseman (Leicester, England: Inter-Varsity Press, n.d.), p. 79: "Job is not to be considered to be perfect or sinless. All the speakers in the book, including Job himself, are convinced that all men are sinful."

251 Harold Meredith Freligh, *Job—An Early Document of Fundamental Doctrines* (Harrisburg: Christian Publications, 1947), p. 57.

252 Ibid., pp. 59, 61.

253 G. Campbell Morgan, *The Answers of Jesus to Job*, rev. ed. (London: Marshall, Morgan & Scott, 1950), pp. 88-91, 103-4.

254 Freligh, *Job*, pp. 72-75.

255 Andersen, p. 292.

256 Gill, p. 555.

257 Morgan, *Answers of Jesus to Job*, pp. 105-6.

258 Freligh, *Job*, p. 80.

259 W. Fitch, "Isaiah," in *The New Bible Commentary*, ed. F. Davidson (London: Inter-Varsity Fellowship, 1954), p. 568. David F. Payne, "Isaiah," in *The New Layman's Bible Commentary*, ed. G. C. D. Howley (Grand Rapids: Zondervan Pub. House, 1979), p. 774.

260 Vine places Isaiah's call in 756 B.C., some sixteen years prior to the usual date given for Uzziah's death. If so, the prophet had been serving the Lord for quite a few years before his startling vision and may have been writing chapters 1-5. Vine specifically identifies events in chapter 5 as portraying sad conditions in Uzziah's reign. W. E. Vine, *Isaiah—Prophecies, Promises, Warnings*, 2d ed. (London: Oliphants, 1947), pp. 9, 29. Kilpatrick conjectures that Isaiah had come to the temple "in his official capacity as prophet" when he beheld the vision and received a commission from the Lord. G. G. D. Kilpatrick, "The Book of Isaiah: Chapters 1-39—Exposition," in *The Interpreter's Bible*, ed. George Arthur Buttrick, 12 vols. (New York: Abingdon Press, 1956), 5:204-5.

261 Two Isaiah scholars in *The New Bible Commentary* disagree on the time sequence. Assuming that the Isaiah 6 call represents the earliest biblical writing by Isaiah, Kidner believes that Uzziah "died after, not before, Isaiah's call. . . ." On the other hand, W. Fitch keeps repeating that Uzziah did not receive his vision and call until immediately after Uzziah's death: "The most outstanding and lasting influence in the life of Isaiah was undoubtedly his own personal and direct call to the ministry of the prophet's office within the temple precincts after the death of Uzziah." Derek Kidner, "Isaiah," in *The New Bible Commentary: Revised*, 3d ed., rev., edited by D. Guthrie, and J. A. Motyer (Leicester, England: Inter-Varsity Press, 1970), p. 595. Fitch, pp. 568, 556-57.

262 A. B. Simpson, *Isaiah*, Christ in the Bible Series (Harrisburg: Christian Publications, n.d.), p. 9. J. R. Dummelow, ed., *A Commentary on the Holy Bible* (London: MacMillan and Co., 1915), p. 417.

263 Kidner, p. 595. Scott thinks that Isaiah placed the account of his call in its present position so that it would precede his biographical experiences that involve his children in chapters 7 and 8: R. B. Y. Scott, "The Book of Isaiah: Chapters 1-39—Introduction and Exegesis," in *The Interpreter's Bible*, ed. George Arthur Buttrick, 12 vols. (New York: Abingdon Press, 1956), 5:158.

264 James D. Newsome, Jr., *The Hebrew Prophets* (Atlanta: John Knox Press, 1984), p. 73.

265 Simpson, *Holy Spirit*, 1:206-7.

266 James Leo Green, *God Reigns: Expository Studies in the Prophecy of Isaiah* (Nashville: Broadman Press, 1968), p. 34.

267 Willem A. Van Gemeren, "Isaiah," in *Evangelical Commentary on the Bible*, ed. Walter A. Elwell (Grand Rapids: Baker Book House, 1989), p. 480.

268 The term "reinterpreters" identifies contemporaries who see most Acts Holy Spirit passages as exceptions to the rule that he automatically enters at regeneration. Or else, they claim that Acts groups had not become truly regenerate at their initial experience. In fact, the Holy Spirit *does* come to live in every convert without exception at regeneration. In various Acts passages an infilling with the Spirit occurred *after* the moment of regeneration. In Acts, Luke uses several expressions to depict this fuller ministry of the Holy Spirit in dynamic sanctification. Jesus, similarly, had employed several expressions. By contrast with the "reinterpreters," a considerable number of previous interpreters—regardless of their views or denominational affiliation—accurately understood this distinction. Later chapters will show this.

269 Inch, p. 150.

270 A. J. Gordon, *The Ministry of the Spirit*, with an Introduction by F. B. Meyer (Philadelphia: American Baptist Pub. Society, 1896), pp. 27-29.

271 Milton S. Agnew, *Transformed Christians: New Testament Messages on Holy Living*, with a Foreword by Clarence D. Wiseman (Kansas City, MO: Beacon Hill Press, 1974), p. 59.

272 Lechler, p. 28.

273 Peter H. Davids, *More Hard Sayings of the New Testament* (Downers Grove, IL: InterVarsity Press, 1991), p. 73.

274 Swindoll, p. 79.

275 James D. G. Dunn, *Jesus and the Spirit* (Philadelphia: Westminster Press, 1975), p. 193.

276 Wayne E. Ward, *The Holy Spirit*, vol. 10 in *Layman's Library of Christian Doctrine*, 16 vols. (Nashville: Broadman Press, 1987), p. 93.

277 John F. Walvoord, *The Holy Spirit* (Grand Rapids: Zondervan Pub. House, 1991), p. 194.

278 Swindoll, p. 75.

279 G. Campbell Morgan, *Great Chapters of the Bible* (New York: Fleming H. Revell Co., 1935), pp. 224-25.

280 Henry Barclay Swete, *The Holy Spirit in the New Testament* (London: Macmillan and Co., 1910; reprint ed., Grand Rapids: Baker Book House, 1976), pp. 69-70.

281 E. M. Blaiklock, *The Acts of the Apostles: An Historical Commentary*, The Tyndale New Testament Commentaries, ed. R. V. G. Tasker (Grand Rapids: Wm. B. Eerdmans Pub. Co., 1975), p. 54.

282 Lechler, pp. 29, 31.

283 Charles W. Carter and Ralph Earle, *The Acts of the Apostles* in *The Evangelical Commentary on the Bible*, ed. George Allen Turner (Grand Rapids: Zondervan Publishing House, 1959), p. 39.

284 John Calvin, *Calvin's Commentaries*, vol. 10: *John-Acts*, (Wilmington: Associated Publishers and Authors, n.d.), p. 975.

285 Robertson, *Word Pictures*, 3:36.

286 Morgan, *Great Chapters*, p. 230.

287 Swete, p. 79.

288 Lechler, p. 82.

289 The definite article is missing in some manuscripts although it is present in many of the best ones. Some strong commentaries wish to omit the article, although there is some hesitation. Bruce M. Metzger, *A Textual Commentary on the Greek New Testament* (London: United Bible Societies, 1971), p. 355: "Since in the New Testament Samaria denotes the district, not the city of that name, the phrase . . . [including the article] means 'to the [main] city of Samaria.' But which city did Luke intend . . . Sebaste, . . . previously called Samaria, or . . . Neapolis, . . . the religious headquarters of the Samaritans? And why did he choose to refer to it without mentioning its name?"

290 James D. G. Dunn, *Baptism in the Holy Spirit: A Re-examination of the New Testament Teaching on the Gift of the Spirit in Relation to Pentecostalism Today*, Studies in Biblical Theology, 2d series, no. 15 (London: SCM Press, 1970), p. 66.

291 Ibid., pp. 55-72; Howard M. Ervin, *Conversion-Initiation and the Baptism in the Holy Spirit: A Critique of James D. G. Dunn, Baptism in the Holy Spirit* (Peabody, MA: Hendrickson Pub., 1984), pp. 25-40.

292 John Calvin, *Calvin's Commentaries*, vol. 10: *John-Acts*, (Wilmington: Associated Publishers and Authors, p. 1065.

293 Ibid.

294 Dunn, *Baptism in the Holy Spirit*, pp. 63-68.

295 Lechler, p. 143.

296 Dunn, *Baptism in the Holy Spirit*, p. 65.

297 Michael Green, *I Believe in the Holy Spirit* (London: Hodder and Stoughton, 1975; reprint ed. Grand Rapids: William B. Eerdmans Pub. Co., n.d.), p. 138.

298 Dunn, *Baptism in the Holy Spirit*, p. 65; Ervin, pp. 28-32.

299 Dunn, *Baptism in the Holy Spirit*, p. 65.

300 F. F. Bruce, *Commentary on the Book of the Acts*, in *The International Commentary on the New Testament*, ed. Ned B. Stonehouse (Grand Rapids: Wm. B. Eerdmans Pub. Co., 1956), p. 181.

301 Ibid. N. B. Stonehouse, "The Gifts of the Holy Spirit," *Westminster Theological Journal* 13 (1950-51): 10-11.

302 Swete, p. 91.

303 B. H. Streeter and A. J. Appasamy, *The Message of Sadhu Sundar Singh: A Study in Mysticism on Practical Religion* (New York: Macmillan Co., 1921), pp. 3-8; Cyril J. Davey, *The Story of Sadhu Sundar Singh: The Yellow Robe* (Chicago: Moody Press, 1963), pp. 21-44, 157-58.

304 Alexander Maclaren, *The Acts of the Apostles*, Maclaren's Bible Class Expositions (Grand Rapids: Zondervan Pub. House, 1959), p. 107.

305 Metz, p. 118. Dunn, however, objects to a conversion on the Damascus Road. Dunn, *Baptism in the Holy Spirit*, p. 73: "The view that Paul's conversion was instantaneous and that he was only later filled with the Spirit is very common, but it is one which must be sharply questioned." Although God both prepares one for conversion over a period and assists a new convert to become established afterward, yet conversion itself occurs in a moment of decision. Dunn's arguments are not convincing.

306 Harold John Ockenga, *Power through Pentecost*, Preaching for Today (Grand Rapids: Wm. B. Eerdmans Pub. Co., 1959), p. 55.

307 Blaiklock, pp. 92-93.

308 The famous New Testament scholar and Dean of Wheaton Graduate School, Merrill C. Tenney, made this keen observation in a Greek class on Acts and Epistles while I was his student.

309 J. Rawson Lumby, *The Acts of the Apostles* in *The Cambridge Bible for Schools and Colleges*, ed. J. J. S. Perowne (Cambridge: University Press,

1887), p. 111: "Saul is sensible of the Divine nature of the vision, and shews this by his address."

310 William H. Baker, "Acts," in *Evangelical Commentary on the Bible*, ed. Walter A. Elwell (Grand Rapids: Baker Book House, 1989), p. 897.

311 Gordon H. Clark, *The Holy Spirit* (Jefferson, MD: Trinity Foundation, 1993), pp. 85-86.

312 Lumby, p. 112.

313 Baker, p. 897.

314 Arthur T. Pierson, *The Acts of the Holy Spirit* (New York: Fleming H. Revell Co., 1898), pp. 76-77.

315 R. A. Torrey, *The New Topical Text Book*, rev. ed. New York: Fleming H. Revell Co., 1935), p. 198.

316 I. e., vocative case uses of this noun.

317 Dunn, *Baptism in the Holy Spirit*, p. 74.

318 Ervin, pp. 47-48.

319 Ibid.

320 Carter and Earle, p. 129.

321 F. F. Bruce, *The Acts of the Apostles: The Greek Text with Introduction and Commentary* (Grand Rapids: Wm. B. Eerdmans Pub. Co., 1951), p. 202.

322 Albert Barnes, *Notes on the New Testament: Explanatory and Practical* (London: Blackie & Son, n.d.), 3:185.

323 Dunn, *Baptism in the Holy Spirit*, pp. 74-75.

324 Calvin, p. 1083.

325 Bruce, *Acts of the Apostles: The Greek Text*, p. 202.

326 Baker, p. 897.

327 Ibid., p. 896.

328 Blaiklock, p. 87.

329 Dunning, p. 420.

330 Frederick Dale Bruner, *A Theology of the Holy Spirit: The Pentecostal Experience and the New Testament Witness* (Grand Rapids: William B. Eerdmans, 1970), p. 164. He adds: "Thus there is an internal contradiction in the creedal use of Acts 2:4 in each *Pentecostal Evangel*, the major

American Pentecostal journal: 'We believe that the Baptism of the Holy
Spirit according to Acts 2:4 is given to believers who ask for it'. . . . Apostolic laying on of hands, tongues, and prophecy, all occurred with the
coming of the Spirit here [in Acts 19]. All accompanied the gift tangen-
tially; none is taught as the Spirit's pre-condition either essentially or pe-
ripherally and none is sought by or required of the Ephesian disciples"
(pp. 164, 212).

331 Ibid., p. 214.

332 Walvoord, *Holy Spirit*, p. 192.

333 Bruner, pp. 207-13.

334 Dunn, *Baptism in the Holy Spirit*, p. 88.

335 Ervin, p. 55.

336 Barnes, 3:310-11.

337 Bruner, p. 207.

338 Dunn, *Baptism in the Holy Spirit*, pp. 83-85.

339 Ervin, pp. 55-59.

340 Ibid., pp. 58-59.

341 Bruce, *Commentary on the Book of the Acts*, p. 385.

342 Carter and Earle, p. 280.

343 Calvin, 10:1244-45; Lechler, pp. 348-50.

344 Bruce, *Commentary on the Book of Acts*, p. 385: ". . . Paul's question,
'Did ye receive the Holy Spirit when ye believed?' suggests strongly that
he regarded them as true believers in Christ."

345 H. A. Ironside, *Holiness: The False and the True* (Neptune, NJ:
Loizeaux Brothers, 1912) p. 99. Ironside constructs the book to oppose an
eradicationist perfection, that he personally had unsuccessfully sought. A
holiness author who counters Ironside is Henry E. Brockett, *Scriptural
Freedom from Sin* (Kansas City, MO: Beacon Hill Press, 1941).

346 Bruce, *Acts of the Apostles: The Greek Text*, p. 354.

347 Ockenga, *Power through Pentecost*, pp. 88-89: Ockenga surmised
that "Aquila and Priscilla . . . yearned to lead Apollos into a deeper understanding of the truth about Christ and the knowledge of the Holy Spirit."
They did so privately, possibly reminding him of John the Baptist's prediction about Jesus' baptizing people with the Holy Spirit. Perhaps they
showed Apollos what the Spirit's power could mean to his life and minis-

try, so that he desired it. If so, "God did not refuse him. He gave him the gift of the Holy Spirit."

348 Swete, pp. 106-7.

349 Dunn, *Baptism in the Holy Spirit*, p. 88.

350 Baker, p. 913.

351 Bruce, *Acts of the Apostles: The Greek Text*, p. 351.

352 Davids, p. 75.

353 Paul's 1 Corinthians 15 roster appears to list only males. From the Gospel narratives, we know that women also saw Jesus after his resurrection. Likewise, although the other three Gospels mention five thousand miraculously fed, Matthew provides a more specific picture. A tax-collector, Matthew carefully adds, "beside women and children" here as well as at the later feeding of four thousand (Matt. 14:21; 15:38). If women supplied as large a percentage of religious gatherings then as now, likely *many* more eyes than five hundred pairs saw Jesus. Similarly, *many* more than five thousand and four thousand mouths ate the miraculously multiplied loaves and fish.

354 Baker, p. 913.

355 Earle, *Word Meanings*, p. 116.

356 Ervin, pp. 61-66.

357 Charles Ewing Brown, *The Meaning of Sanctification* (Anderson, IN: Warner Press, 1945), p. 196.

358 Ibid., pp. 196-97.

359 Gordon H. Clark, *Sanctification* (Jefferson, MD: Trinity Foundation, 1992), pp. 54, 60.

360 James Orr, *Sidelights on Christian Doctrine* (New York: A. C. Armstrong & Son, 1909), p. 160.

361 Davids, p. 73.

362 Ockenga, *Power through Pentecost*, p. 56. Brown, p. 200, concurs: "That this is the meaning of the passage in Acts 19:2 is one of the most certain points in scriptural interpretation; if doubt arises as to the exact order of the time of the reception of the Holy Ghost by the disciples at Ephesus that question is to be settled by appeal to similar instances in the Book of Acts itself, and here the evidence is overwhelmingly convincing to any unbiased reader who will accept the authority of the book."

363 Very helpful information on the problems of translating this question appear in Wilbur T. Dayton, "Entire Sanctification," in Carter, *Contemporary Wesleyan Theology*, 1:550-52.

364 Brown, p. 199.

365 Torrey, *Baptism with the Holy Spirit*, p. 14.

366 A. W. Tozer, *When He Is Come: Ten Messages on the Holy Spirit*, ed. by Gerald B. Smith (Harrisburg: Christian Publications, 1968), pp. 75-76.

367 Present capitalization rules do not capitalize either relative or personal pronouns relating to Deity. Capitalization in the original source has been retained, however, throughout this quotation even though it is inconsistent with itself twice.

368 V. Raymond Edman, ed., *Crisis Experiences in the Lives of Noted Christians* (Minneapolis: Bethany Fellowship, n.d.), pp. 39-49.

369 Ibid., pp. 69-77.

370 James Gilchrist Lawson, *Deeper Experiences of Famous Christians* (Anderson, IN: Warner Press, 1911), pp. 312-26.

371 Samuel J. Stoesz, *Sanctification: An Alliance Distinctive* (Camp Hill, PA: Christian Publications, 1992), p. 22.

372 A. E. Thompson, *A. B. Simpson: His Life and Work* (Harrisburg: Christian Publications, 1960), pp. 36-37.

373 Ibid., pp. 65-66.

374 McGraw, *Doctrine of Sanctification in Simpson*, pp. 64, 67-68, 144-62. The missionary movement he founded bears the name, The Christian and Missionary Alliance, and the college he launched survives as Nyack College.

375 Charles R. Solomon, *The Ins and Outs of Rejection* (Denver: By the Author, 1991), pp. 88-107.

376 Grenz, p. 58.

377 R. A. Torrey, *The Holy Spirit: Who He Is and What He Does* (Old Tappan, NJ: Fleming H. Revell Co., 1927), pp. 198-99; Choy, pp. 291-92.

378 Roger Martin, *R. A. Torrey: Apostle of Certainty*, with an Introduction by John R. Rice (Murphreesboro, TN: Sword of the Lord Pub., 1976), pp. 23, 28, 33-43, 72-73.

379 Jon Tal Murphree, *Responsible Evangelism: Relating Theory to Practice*, with a Preface by Paul L. Alford (Toccoa Falls, GA: Toccoa Falls College Press, 1994), pp. 143, 145-46.

380 Although Thiessen taught perseverance and predestination, his views were so moderate that his Wheaton student, Ray Ludwigson, categorizes him as more Arminian than Calvinistic overall. Vernon D. Doerksen, who edited Thiessen's work as *Lectures in Systematic Theology*, has made it a more heavily dispensational volume than Thiessen had originally penned it.

381 Walter A. Elwell, "Henry C. Thiessen," in *Handbook of Evangelical Theologians*, ed. Walter A. Elwell (Grand Rapids: Baker Books, 1993), pp. 144-55.

382 The Missionary Church has often identified with the Wesleyan holiness movement. Some might point to Thiessen's work at Fort Wayne Bible College and his pastoral ministry in the Missionary Church as categorizing him within the Wesleyan holiness movement. Thiessen's main life work, however, seems decidedly outside that movement. His *Introductory Lectures in Systematic Theology*, although not exceedingly Calvinistic, is anything but Wesleyan holiness in explaining sanctification.

383 Richard S. Taylor, "Historical and Modern Significance of Wesleyan Theology," in *A Contemporary Wesleyan Theology*, ed. Charles W. Carter (Grand Rapids: Frances Asbury Press of Zondervan Pub. House, 1983), 1:66.

384 Alfred Plummer, *The Church of the Early Fathers: External History*, in *Epochs of Church History*, ed. Mandell Creighton (London: Longmans, Green and Co., 1903), pp. 27-29; Elgin S. Moyer, *Who Was Who in Church History* (New Canaan, CT: Keats Pub., 1974), p. 209; *The Book of Saints*, comp. Benedictine Monks of St. Augustine's Abbey, Ramsgate, 3d ed. (New York: Macmillan Co., 1942), p. 140; *The Apocryphal New Testament* (London: William Iione, 1820), p. 143.

385 Wiley, *Christian Theology*, 2:449.

386 Moyer, p. 227.

387 Justin Martyr, Dialogue with Trypho 43, 20, quoted here from Harold D. Hunter, *Spirit-Baptism: A Pentecostal Alternative* (Lanham, MD: University Press of America, 1983), p. 119.

388 Wiley, *Christian Theology*, 2:449-463.

389 George Allen Turner, *Vision Which Transforms*, pp. 160-188.

390 George Allen Turner, *Witnesses of the Way* (Kansas City: Beacon Hill Press, 1981).

391 "The Higher Christian Life" series, ed. Donald W. Dayton (Boston, Henry Hoyt, 1858; reprint ed., New York: Garland Pub., 1984), pp. 19-44.

392 Hunter, pp. 117-210.

393 Clara McLeister, *Men and Women of Deep Piety*, ed. E. E. Shelhamer (Cincinnati: God's Bible School and Revivalist, 1920).

394 James Gilchrist Lawson.

395 Phoebe Palmer, *Pioneer Experiences: Or, the Gift of Power Received by Faith.* "The Higher Christian Life" series, ed. Donald W. Dayton (New York: W. C. Palmer, Jr., 1868; reprint ed., New York: Garland Pub., 1984).

396 Rice, pp. 391-412.

397 V. Raymond Edman, *They Found the Secret* (Grand Rapids: Zondervan Pub. House, 1960).

398 Edman, ed., *Crisis Experiences.*

399 Choy, *Powerlines.*

400 W. T. Purkiser, ed., *Exploring Our Christian Faith* (Kansas City, MO: Beacon Hill Press, 1960), pp. 365-66. Purkiser reports that McQuilkin published the questionnaire's results in *Christian Life* magazine, March 1954.

401 Clark, *Sanctification*, p. 100.

402 Finney: *The Promise of the Spirit*, p. 76: ". . . Here is one grand mistake of the church. They have supposed that the revival consists mostly in this state of excited emotion rather than in conformity of the human will to the will of God."

403 Cattell, p. 21.

404 Purkiser, ed., *Exploring Our Christian Faith*, p. 367.

405 Graham, p. 116.

406 John R. W. Stott, *Men Made New* (London: Inter-Varsity Fellowship, 1966), pp. 49-51.

407 Andrew A. Bonar, *Heavenly Springs*, p. 42.

408 Finney, *Principles of Union with Christ*, p. 70.

409 Leslie D. Wilcox, *Beyond the Gate* (Cincinnati: Revivalist Press, 1961), p. 9.

410 Purkiser, *Conflicting Concepts of Holiness*, pp. 23-24: "The Bible never intimates anywhere that either growth or death have the least thing to do with the soul's sanctification. . . . Entire sanctification, as understood by holiness people, does not admit of degrees. It is as perfect and complete in its kind as the work of regeneration and justification is perfect and complete in its kind. This does not mean that there is no growth in grace both before and after sanctification." Cf. Beet, p. 59.

411 Keith Drury, *Holiness for Ordinary People* (Marion, IN: Wesley Press, 1983; reprint ed., Grand Rapids: Francis Asbury Press/ Zondervan Pub. House, 1987), pp. 44-45.

412 Ora D. Lovell, "Holiness: Instantaneous and Progressive" in *Further Insights into Holiness*, comp. Kenneth Geiger (Kansas City, MO: Beacon Hill Press, 1963), pp. 135-36.

413 John Wesley, *Plain Account of Christian Perfection* (Chicago: Christian Witness Co., n.d.), pp. 80, 104.

414 Donald L. Alexander, "The Riddle of Sanctification" in *Christian Spirituality: Five Views of Sanctification*, ed. Donald L. Alexander (Downers Grove, IL: InterVarsity Press, 1988), pp. 7-32; Warfield, Benjamin Breckinridge, *Perfectionism*, 2 vols. (New York: Oxford University Press, 1931), 2:463-611; Clark, *Sanctification*, p. 100.

415 Stanley M. Horton and Anthony A. Hoekema in Dieter, pp. 51, 75.

416 Z. T. Johnson, *What Is Holiness?* with an Introduction by H. C. Morrison (Louisville: Pentecostal Pub. Co., 1936), p. 219.

417 See the chart on the following page, which shows a life stream of holiness both following the new birth and following the crisis of full abandonment. The chart preserves the major features of a 2-page chart that contains additional explanations. It appears in an interesting doctoral dissertation. Claude A. Ries, "A Greek New Testament Approach to the Teaching of the Deeper Spiritual Life" (Th.D. dissertation, Northern Baptist Theological Seminary, 1945), pp. 166-66A.

418 Ibid.

419 Erickson, pp. 1232-33.

420 Finney, *Promise of the Spirit*, p. 79.

421 Wesley, *Plain Account of Christian Perfection*, p. 83.

422 Cattell, p. 18.

423 *Hymns of the Christian Life*, rev. ed. (Harrisburg: Christian Publications, 1978), p. 238.

424 Roy J. Cook, comp., *One Hundred and One Famous Poems: With a Prose Supplement*, rev. ed. (Chicago: Cable Co., 1929), pp. 56-57.

425 E. Stanley Jones, *Abundant Living* (New York: Abingdon-Cokesbury Press, 1942), p. 54.

426 C. H. Spurgeon, *Twelve Sermons on Holiness* (Swengel, PA: Reiner Pubs., 1965), p. 152.

427 [John Carles] Ryle, *Holiness* (Grand Rapids: Associated Publishers and Authors, n.d.), p. 13.

428 Simpson, *The Holy Spirit: Or, Power from on High*, 2:140.

429 R. Mabel Francis, *Filled with the Spirit: Then What?* (Camp Hill, PA: Christian Pubs., 1974), pp. 31-34.

430 Ibid., pp. 35-38.

431 Gerald E. McGraw, "Holiness: The Doctrine," and Arnold L. Cook, "Holiness: Our Calling" in *Holiness Voices: A Practical Theology of Holiness*, ed. H. Robert Cowles and K. Neill Foster (Camp Hill, PA: Christian Pubs., 1995), pp. 52-62, 35-41. Hebrews 12:14 "implies that holiness should be your chief objective, *the top priority of your life*. . . . Hebrews 12:14 uses a verb tense suggesting an ongoing effort to live this holy life. Thus the main thrust here seems to be the need to make progress" (pp. 52, 55). "Holiness is our first calling. . . . How important is holiness? Important enough that we should 'make every effort . . . to be holy' (Hebrews 12:14)" (pp. 36, 40).

432 Donald A. Wiggins, "Christo-centric Holiness" in Cowles and Foster, pp. 142-43.

433 Wuest, *Wuest's Word Studies, Ephesians and Colossians: In the Greek New Testament*, 1:88.

434 Ibid., 1:91.

435 Robert Boyd Munger, *My Heart, Christ's Home* (Pamphlet) Minneapolis: Billy Graham Evangelistic Association, n.d.; Robert Boyd Munger, *What Jesus Says* (Westwood, NJ: Fleming H. Revell Co., 1955).

436 Richard J. Erickson, "Ephesians" in *Evangelical Commentary on the Bible*, ed. Walter A. Elwell (Grand Rapids: Baker Book House, 1989), p. 1026.

437 Charles W. Carter, "The Epistle of Paul to the Ephesians," in *The Wesleyan Bible Commentary*, ed. Charles W. Carter (Grand Rapids: William B. Eerdmans Pub. Co., 1965), 5:404.

438 Gordon H. Clark, *Ephesians* (Jefferson, MD: Trinity Foundation, 1985), p. 124.

439 Wuest, *Wuest's Word Studies, Ephesians and Colossians*, 1:91.

440 A. B. Simpson, *Days of Heaven upon Earth* (New York: Christian Alliance Pub. Co., 1925), p. 293; cf. A. B. Simpson, *The Self Life and the Christ Life* (Harrisburg: Christian Publications, n.d.), p. 12.

441 Samuel J. Stoesz, *The Glory of Christ in His Church* (Camp Hill, PA: Christian Pubs., 1994), p. 51: Dr. Stoesz believes that "the primary focus" even of promises like Rom. 8:28 is "the corporate church."

442 A. B. Simpson, *The Epistle of James.* Christ in the Bible S (Harrisburg: Christian Publications, n.d.), pp. 42-43.

443 Gill, p. 554.

444 The term, spiritual formation, relates to a variety of spiritual activities designed to know God better and live a more holy and disciplined life. Although the author has not formally treated spiritual formation in this book, many sections have touched on the subject, especially in the final four chapters.

445 Jeremy Taylor, *The Rule and Exercises of Holy Living*, abridged with a preface by Anne Lamb, with a foreword by Henry Chadwick (New York: Harper & Row, 1970), p. 122.

446 Ibid., pp. 123-25.

447 Hannah Whitall Smith, p. 70.